DESIGNING AND BUILDING A DECK

L. Donald Meyers

Prentice Hall
Englewood Cliffs, New Jersey 07632

LIBRARY OF CONGRESS
Library of Congress Cataloging-in-Publication Data

Meyers, L. Donald
  Designing and building a deck / L. Donald Meyers.
    p. cm.
  Includes index.
  ISBN 0-13-201816-0
  1. Decks (Architecture, Domestic)—Design and construction.
I. Title.
TH4970.M49 1988
643'.55—dc19
                                      87-34046
                                            CIP

Editorial/production supervision: WordCrafters Editorial Services, Inc.
Cover design: 20/20 Services, Inc.
Manufacturing buyer: Marianne Gloriandi

©1988 by Prentice-Hall, Inc.
A Division of Simon & Schuster
Englewood Cliffs, New Jersey 07632

The publisher offers discounts on this book when ordered
in bulk quantities. For more information, write:

  Special Sales/College Marketing
  Prentice-Hall, Inc.
  College Technical and Reference Division
  Englewood Cliffs, NJ 07632

To my dear wife, Mary Ann,
who suffered me with this book—
among other things.

              Dutch

Printed in the United States of America
10 9 8 7 6 5 4 3 2

ISBN 0-13-201816-0 NB2I

Prentice-Hall International (UK) Limited, *London*
Prentice-Hall of Australia Pty. Limited, *Sydney*
Prentice-Hall Canada Inc., *Toronto*
Prentice-Hall Hispanoamericana, S.A., *Mexico*
Prentice-Hall of India Private Limited, *New Delhi*
Prentice-Hall of Japan, Inc., *Tokyo*
Simon & Schuster Asia Pte. Ltd., *Singapore*
Editora Prentice-Hall do Brasil, Ltda., *Rio de Janeiro*

Contents

Preface

Who is this book for?

It is easy—and a little immodest—to answer "everyone." In truth, this book is not for everyone, but it *is* for everyone who is considering building a deck. And, if that also smacks of immodesty, let us add that it was written precisely with everyone in mind.

This is a book that takes the reader from the very first hazy thoughts about wanting a deck, through the mental labors of locating, designing and planning, to the physical labors of setting posts and building the substructure, right down to sinking the nails into the railings and finishing the wood (if necessary).

Our book is specifically designed so that, no matter what the level of your skills and knowledge, it will have some pertinence. Those who have never lifted a hammer are taken through the various steps necessary to build their own deck completely, if they want to. Experienced do-it-yourselfers will also find sections on design, special techniques, wood types, finishing and structural planning which may be new even to their extensive knowledge.

Primarily, however, the book is written for any homeowner who is contemplating a deck, regardless of his skills and knowledge. A deck is a major home improvement. Most deck books plunge right into deck construction without even giving the reader a chance to know what is in store—or making sure he or she really wants a deck. Is a patio a better choice, for example? We explore that question, among many others.

What about deck location? This is a vital question, and depends on a variety of factors. We examine all of them. Before you take hammer in hand, you should give a lot of thought to size, style, and numerous other questions, too. Once the deck is built, it's there for a long time (or should be, if you build it correctly). It is essential that it look right for your house—and your tastes.

There are numerous questions that the homeowner should ask before the deck is built, in addition to those already mentioned. Should you build it yourself? Design it yourself? Perhaps a compromise is the best solution.

The answers are not easy, but most people can design and build their own deck. But do you want to? And should you? This book was written to provide the necessary information so that the reader can consider the options, and make an intelligent decision.

Another reason that we think you will like this book is that we make no dogmatic decisions for you. It is reasonably easy to find a good-looking deck plan. It is quite another matter to make it fit your house. We do have plans—lots of them—but we also tell you how to adapt them to fit your home. And we have all the basic building and design techniques so that you can start from scratch to make your own plans.

A deck is the epitome of modern living. Weather permitting, decks have become family rooms, recreation rooms, dens, and their equivalents. When properly designed and built, a deck is an extension of indoor living space, with a smooth flow between the two.

"Properly designed and built" is the key phrase here, and the function of this book. These basic elements, when carefully thought out and executed, make the difference between a deck that is used, and one that just sits there.

A deck, in other words, must be functional—in addition to looking nice. If you want your deck to serve a purpose, to add enjoyment to your life, then this is the book for you.

The first few chapters of the book are devoted to helping you analyze why you want to build a deck, what it will be used for, and how best to achieve those goals. Since good looks are just as important in deck design, we also cover such things as deck styles and types, with numerous illustrations of some lovely, prize-winning designs.

The most handsome of decks, however, won't be of much use if it falls apart in a year or so. Therefore, after the chapters devoted to function, style and planning, there are detailed chapters of construction, both basic and detailed.

We have also added chapters on various related activities such as deck covers, furniture, lighting and landscaping. This book attempts to include anything and everything our elusive "everyman" would like to know about deck design and construction. There may be some sections you may want to skip over, but to someone else, that information may be vital. So, "It's in there."

Even if you are hiring someone such as a landscape architect or a contractor, there are many things you should know yourself about design and construction before you hire such experts. After all, these same professionals are going to ask most of the same questions that we invite you to ask yourself. You'll save time and money by solving problems and resolving issues ahead of time.

Whether you are drawing up your own plans, or doing the construction yourself—or both (or neither)—we think that you will find some very valuable information and ideas in this book. Whenever possible, we have included detailed plans and materials lists, and suggestions for adapting them to your own needs. We hope you enjoy reading it as much as we enjoyed writing it.

1

Planning Principles

So you want to build a deck.

Go out and buy some lumber, a keg of nails, grab a hammer, and go to it, right? Wrong. There's a bit more to it than that. As a matter of fact, there is a *lot* more to it.

First of all, where will you put it? What type of deck—how many levels, what pattern, what shape, what size? Attached to the house or free-standing? And before you buy the lumber, what kind of wood? What sizes of lumber? How much of each? What kind of nails? What other fasteners(if any)? How will you anchor it? Support it? Keep it from blowing away or collapsing under the weight of the barbecue?

These are just a few of the questions you must ask before you even begin to think about buying the materials (and the tools). There are answers, however, most of which will be given in this book. Our task in this chapter is to help you pose the questions. If you have never before embarked on such an enterprise, you probably don't even know what to ask.

ARE YOU SURE YOU WANT A DECK?

This is a basic question, and presumably you have already answered in the affirmative—at least tentatively. Before you skip on, however, it is wise to

Figure 1-1 A deck can transform a dull backyard into an exciting, relaxing area like this one. (*Courtesy California Redwood Association*)

reexamine the question. Perhaps you would be making a mistake in building a deck.

For example, you may have assumed you wanted a deck without examining the alternatives. What are your reasons for wanting to build a deck? There are a lot of them, but we'll just examine a few of the most common, then play devil's advocate, trying to force you to determine whether an alternate plan may perhaps be better.

One main reason, for example, for wanting a deck is that you simply want to be better able to enjoy the outdoors. A deck is great for this—but so is a patio. How about a gazebo, or even a nice, green lawn? Maybe a swimming pool would better suit the urge for outdoor living. (Of course, a deck would also be nice *around* the pool.)

Figure 1-2   You can build a deck anywhere. One of the favorite places is around a pool. (*Courtesy National Swimming Pool Institute*)

Perhaps an old-fashioned porch is more suited to your family's needs. Do you have a closed-in porch or other room you don't use much? It may be possible to knock out some walls and convert it to outdoor use.

Mind now, we aren't saying that you should do any of these. Chances are that none of these alternatives are right for you, but ask and answer the questions before concluding that a deck is the only solution. Of all those questions, the most serious is whether you should choose a deck or a patio, and this is discussed at some length in the following pages.

It may be that you think a deck would just look nice. This is a valid reason, but not as compelling as simply wanting to enjoy the outdoors. For one thing, you may find out that you're wrong. The deck may look lousy. A deck with a tacked-on look, which many have, won't do much for the appearance of your home. If that's your only—or primary—reason, for building a deck, hold off building it until you finish this chapter, at least. We'll go into it at greater length, and try to help you plan a good-looking deck and determine where it will look good.

Another good reason for building a deck may be simply to expand your living space, stretching out the walking-around room. For those with small living areas, indoors and out, a deck can be an excellent way of doing this. But there are alternatives here, too. Perhaps an addition to the home would be better. Again, consider a patio. Can you rearrange the house, knock out (or add) some walls so that it works better for you? Consider little-used areas such as basements, attics, porches, and garages—maybe they can be put to use as prime living space.

This last question doesn't take a great deal of pondering. A thorough look around the house and property should be enough to give you a rough idea. For many people, there just isn't anyplace to go. Building and zoning regulations may prohibit additions, or at least make them difficult and expensive. (This can be true for decks, too, although many people ignore the usual need for a building permit.) For many of us, however, there is just no inside space left for expansion.

If it does seem that an addition may be a better idea, you should consult an architect or knowledgeable contractor. Inside renovations ordinarily can be planned by the homeowner, but if any walls are to be torn down or broken through, make sure that they are not bearing walls. If they are bearing walls, or you aren't sure, get some expert advice.

For those in warm and moderate climates, outdoor expansion is usually an excellent idea. In cold climates, though, you have to ask how often you would use this space. If expanded living area is your only reason for building a deck, it probably isn't a good idea unless you can use it at least five to six months of the year. On the other hand, if it's on the south or west sides of the house, it still may be worthwhile. (This is discussed at greater length in Chapter 2.) And that still leaves the question of deck vs. patio or some other form of outdoor expansion.

You may have many other reasons for wanting to build a deck, most of them perfectly sensible. All we ask here is that you rationally turn them over in your mind, discuss the idea with your family, and consider all the alternatives before plunging ahead. Now, for most people, the most difficult decision. . . .

DECK VS. PATIO

Decks and patios are similar in purpose. For most people, they serve as outdoor living rooms, replacing—more or less—the front porches of an earlier, simpler day. A deck or patio is the place to soak up the sun, relax on a pleasant evening,

Figure 1-3 Decks and patios, as here, have taken the place of old-time porches for taking it easy—only a little more privately. (*Courtesy Filon Division of SOHIO*)

enjoy the breezes, chat, read, or just laze around. If you have electricity available—and you should, as detailed in Chapter 11—you can watch TV or listen to the radio or records.

The main difference between a patio and a deck is that a patio is always built on the ground. A deck can be built almost anywhere, from way up in the air to directly on the ground. (A ground-level deck is, in most respects, a patio.)

The distinguishing characteristic of all decks is that they are made of wood. It may be possible to build a deck of concrete or brick, but it just wouldn't seem like a deck. And, of course, you may want to support a deck with steel posts or beams—especially if it's high off the ground. These exceptions somehow seem to make the project less a deck than one made entirely of wood, however.

In this book, we consider a deck to be a structure built entirely or primarily of wood. It may not be all wood, but at least the portion that is walked on—the "decking"—is made of wood. The word "deck" came to us from the nautical word for the floor of a ship. At one time, at least, they were all made of wood.

Sometimes it is easy to dispose of the "deck or patio" question. If you live on a steep hillside, where there is no level ground for a patio, the only real possibility is a deck. You could regrade the hillside to make a spot for a patio, but this is usually costly and difficult. Chances are that a patio built on land like that won't look very good. You'll also need a huge retaining wall and very strong railings.

At the other extreme is a long, low house with perfectly level ground. There really isn't any place to put a deck in the usual sense. There is always the ground-level deck, of course, but a ground-level deck is basically a wooden patio. (We have nothing against ground-level decks, by the way, and discuss them completely in the book. We just like to make that distinction.)

Figure 1-4   When a deck is as low as this one, it is really a wooden patio. This handsome, nicely landscaped beauty is made of Wolmanized wood.

Unless your property falls in one of the categories above, it may be a little more difficult to decide. To make the choice between deck and patio, there are several factors you must consider. The following are the most important.

Grade

As mentioned previously, the grade of your property is a principal factor in deciding on a deck or patio. In general, the steeper the grade, the more likely the

Figure 1-5   With a steep grade, there is little choice but to build a deck, usually multilevel like this one. (*Courtesy National Landscape Association*)

choice of a deck. A patio is generally constructed of concrete, brick, or stone. All of these materials require a grade that is level or nearly so. Those with a mild to moderate property gradation have a more difficult choice. Be careful about this, because grade can be deceptive. What appears to be a level terrain can be sloped a lot more than you think. If you aren't sure, your survey may show the degrees of gradation. Otherwise, use a long board with a level, or a "hose level" (Figure 1-6) to determine the grade for yourself. Record the differences in grade for future reference. The best way of doing this is a contour map (Figure 1-7). For really complicated backyard planning, you may wish to build a scale model of the property. Remember those "salt maps" you used to make in kindergarten? Do the same for your property. (The best plan of all, if you can swing it, is to hire a landscape architect.)

Long-Distance Leveling

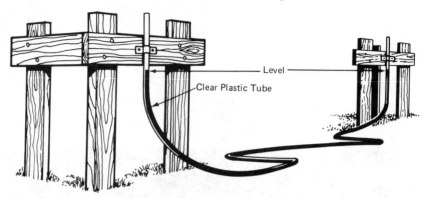

Figure 1-6 To find a level between two long distances, a clear hose filled with water is an easy method. Hold one end of the hose next to the mark and fill with liquid until it meets the mark. The other end of the fluid will be exactly level.

If you have your heart set on either a deck or patio, moderate differences in grade probably won't make much difference. If you feel that a patio is exactly what you want, and the differences in grade are not extreme, you will build a patio no matter what. If you have already determined that you want a deck and not a patio, you will have a deck.

Those who haven't quite made up their minds should realize that, on sloping land, a deck is considerably easier to build that a patio. Leveling relatively steep grades requires an extensive reshaping of the landscape. Either dirt will have to be brought in, or earth must be moved from one part of your property to another. If the latter, you may disturb a greater part of your landscape than you think. If the former, you will have huge trucks tearing up your lawn. Before you consider trucking in fill, find out from a contractor how much you will need and what it costs. People are almost always astounded by how many yards of fill it takes just to fill in a "little hole."

It is possible, though not usual, to require some fill even for a deck. For whatever reason, if you must substantially alter the landscape, you should know that this takes a lot of money and patience. There will always be more land disturbance than you think, and those big trucks can ruin your driveway. In many cases, costly retaining walls will be required. The higher these get, the uglier they are, and there will be additional landscaping costs to smooth out the eyesores.

On balance then, when your lot slopes more than a little, the choice should be a deck. The steeper the grade, the more obvious the decision.

Site and View

The site of your house and the view beyond are important factors in choosing between a deck or a patio. No matter where you live, you will want the sur-

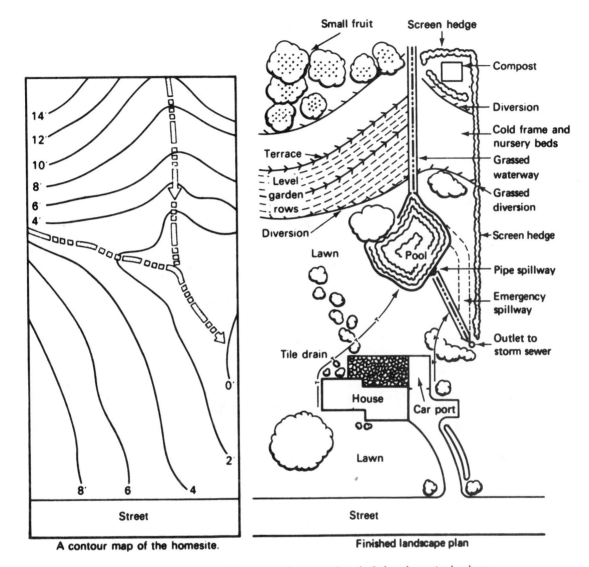

Figure 1-7 A contour map will help you plan not only a deck, but the entire landscape.

roundings to be pleasant. If the view on the other side of the fence is a garbage dump, you don't need a high deck to get a better look at it. Stick to a patio or low-level deck—and hide behind the fence. (If you don't have a fence, build one.) Also plant some showy fragrant flowers to create your own view—and smell. Better yet, build on another side of the house if possible. Or move. When the view is good, as on a hill or at the beach, a deck is probably the better choice. The higher up you are, the better the view.

If you have a choice as to which side of the house to build, it stands to reason that you should choose the best view. If there is no view to speak of, you

Figure 1-8 When you have a water view, a high deck can take best advantage of it. (*Courtesy Koppers Co.*)

should probably keep it low. Whether that will be a patio or low-level deck will depend on the other factors discussed here.

Present Landscape

The choice of patio or deck may depend partially—or even entirely—on what the landscape already looks like. You may, for example, really prefer to build a patio, but there is no convenient place to put it. The area(s) best suited for the patio may contain your favorite roses or other plantings.

Be cautioned that a deck over a favorite garden may not be feasible, either. If, for example, a patio would mean uprooting a rose garden, don't decide to put a deck overhead just to save the roses. Roses need lots of sun. If you put a deck overhead, it will block out all or most of the sun, and your roses will die anyway. A high deck will leave the present landscape intact, but will not save the plantings below unless they can tolerate shade or perhaps semishade. Most foundation plantings are shade-tolerant, for example, as are many perennials. Grasses generally do poorly in shade, so don't decide on a deck just to preserve a lawn. The lawn will not return the favor unless it is very shade-loving.

Trees take decades to grow and add immensely to the value of your home. Sometimes, a tree or two must go, regardless of whether you choose a deck or patio. In this author's opinion, it is a near-felony to cut down a tree that nature took so much time and effort nurturing to maturity. Trees provide natural shade in summer, and deciduous trees lose their leaves during the cold months, thus providing shade in hot months and allowing solar heat in the cold season. They have a lot of other virtues, too, such as just plain beauty. If at all possible, we recommend that you save them.

No matter how you feel about trees, it is inevitable that some trees must be sacrificed if they are in the way of a patio site. If you try to build around them, the roots will probably be killed anyway. Unless you choose a brick-in-sand patio, or conceive some other method of getting water to the roots, any tree surrounded by a patio will be scrawny at best.

Although it takes a lot of extra planning, you *can* devise a deck plan that will preserve any tree worth saving. Many of the photos on these pages and elsewhere in this book illustrate decks that have been built around such trees.

The type of soil is another factor to be considered. Some areas are sandy, others rocky, and there are numerous types in between. If you plan on doing any extensive regrading and are unsure of the soil conditions, test-bores may be advisable. You can't move around a lot of earth if it's all rock beneath the topsoil. Conversely, you won't want to lay a patio on top of a marsh. If you do have boggy soil, you may have difficulty laying a proper foundation for deck posts, too.

Type of House

Modern or contemporary homes ordinarily adapt well to both decks and patios. The typical deck does not blend in well with most older architecture. For example, it is difficult to imagine a typical high deck attached to a Victorian or "gingerbread" house. If you insist on adding a deck to an older home, it is wise to get some advice from an architect; otherwise you may destroy the looks of the home. For an older house, the rear of the home is probably the only place to add a deck. It will detract less from the overall beauty there. Even then, the deck may clash strongly with the lines and appearance of the house. In that event, you should consider a detached deck in some favorite corner of the yard. Furthermore, most older homes were built on narrow lots, so there is probably little extra room at the sides. It is rarely possible or advisable to add a deck to the front of an older home.

Probably a patio will be a better choice for a traditionally styled older home. If you do decide on a patio, brick or flagstone will probably look better with an older home than concrete. Those who simply *must* have a deck should

Figure 1-9   There is no need to cut down a beautiful tree it took nature decades to grow. Try to work around it, as this homeowner did. (*Courtesy California Redwood Association*)

build it low, preferably ground-level, with a formal look. Or make it free-standing, away from the house.

    Also consider the lines of the house. Squarish, boxy-type homes can often be "stretched out" and improved by the addition of a deck. When the house already h s a long, low look, it may look awkward if you add a deck to the long

Figure 1-10 The rather conventional deck in (A) blends in well at the back of a traditional home. With a contemporary home (B), you have more freedom to indulge your fancy. (*Courtesy Western Wood Products [A], Goldberg and Rodler [B]*)

dimension, stretching it out even further. Place any deck so that it adds to the short dimension, usually in back or front. A house with a high elevation on one side will usually benefit from a deck, which breaks up the higher side and gives it less of a squat appearance.

Split-level or multilevel homes usually blend in well with decks, and hillside homes almost demand a deck on the high side of the home, at the very least. Beach houses, vacation, and leisure homes are natural sites for decks. Most rural homes look fine with decks, and most city homes look awkward. In the suburbs, it depends on other factors.

It is difficult for many of us to imagine what our house will look like with a deck added, and too late to change once you've built it. The best solution is to hire an architect to locate and design your deck. He or she should be able to draw a sketch of what the end product will be. One thing we can imagine, though, is the cost of such a service.

A less expensive, but not foolproof way is to take photos of the house and draw in the deck where you think you may want it. You don't have to be an artist to get a pretty good idea as to the final result. To consider alternatives, place acetate sheets over the photo(s) and draw your various designs on the acetate, with the house showing through.

No matter what the method, take the extra time and effort to plan the deck carefully to blend in with the house. If you don't feel it's important, take a ride through the neighborhood and notice all the ugly decks around. Chances are that you will then agree that overall looks are very important.

Safety and Family Considerations

In most cases, decks and patios can be planned so that they are safe. Decks can present greater safety problems, however, especially for children or the handicapped. The higher the deck, the more cautious you should be.

A patio does not ordinarily present any safety hazards. Exceptions may be when the patio is built on sloping ground, with one or more sides higher off the ground. No matter what the type or design, there are ways to eliminate hazards. Sturdy railings, self-locking gates at tops of stairways, and other mechanisms can be devised to "take the worry out." Be especially cautious, though, about planning a high deck where there are small children. And, as you can guess, all these extra safety measures will surely add to the cost.

When there is someone who is confined to a wheelchair, or must use a cane, walker, or other navigation aids, the surface of either a deck or a patio should be relatively smooth. Widely spaced deckboards and irregular brick or flagstone should be avoided.

Space

For those with large lots and plenty of room around the home, space is not a problem. Many people, however, especially those in cities and older suburbs,

Figure 1-11 Sturdy railings and benches are mandatory for high decks. (*Courtesy Georgia-Pacific Corp.*)

live in homes that are packed in tightly on their small property. What little landscape there is may leave little or no room for a patio or low-level deck, and either one will need some sort of privacy fence.

A high deck, probably off the second story, can leave room below for a carport, play area, storage, or other practical use. You can even have your cake and eat it, too, by putting in a patio beneath. As discussed above, most plantings and grasses will not fare well, but shade-tolerant varieties can be planted below a deck. Make sure they get some water, though.

Price

Price is a factor in every decision, and deck or patio choices will be similarly affected. It is always risky to discuss prices, since they can fluctuate widely in time and region, and in such imponderables as distance from the source of materials. (See Chapter 3 for an in-depth discussion of different woods and some rough comparative prices.) Nonetheless, there are general principles to guide you in your selection. Concrete patios, for example, are generally less expensive than decks or other types of patios. As usual, there are exceptions, such as colored or exposed-aggregate concrete installed by a contractor. But the typical plain concrete patio is usually relatively inexpensive. Most reasonably handy people can build a concrete patio with the help of a rented mixer or by

Figure 1-12   You can build a low deck in a small area, but it isn't easy. This well-thought-out deck makes good use of the cramped landscape with a privacy fence. (*Courtesy Georgia-Pacific Corp.*)

ordering "ready-mix" from a concrete supplier. Consult one of the numerous books on working with concrete, if interested.

Ascending the ladder of price are patios made of brick in sand, patio block, brick on concrete, or flagstone. Generally, any deck installed by a contractor will cost more than all but the most expensive patios. Ground-level decks are close to the more expensive patios in cost. High decks are expensive because of the care required and the costly underpinnings.

Here again, though, there are some significant exceptions. For one thing, the cost of a deck is very much dependent on labor and the type of wood used. You can cut the costs of each of the factors considerably. If you do most of the work yourself, you save more on a deck, because of all the labor involved. You can also reduce the cost of a deck by using one of the less expensive woods.

As discussed in Chapter 3, we highly recommend that you use weather- and insect-repellent wood. Those that really want a deck, though, and may not be able to afford these woods, can use less expensive lumber. Although maintenance costs may be more in the long run, they are also easier to bear when spread out over the years. Again, rot- and weather-resistant woods are better, but those who don't mind frequent staining or painting may wish to consider this option. See Chapter 12 for suggestions on preserving and finishing wood.

Do It Yourself?

This factor was suggested previously, and it is an important one. Planning and building a deck (or patio) yourself saves about one-third to two-thirds of contractors' costs. Most decks or patios require more brawn than brain, with the arguable exception of high-level decks. No great skill is required to saw wood and hammer nails, and these tasks take up the major part of deck-building. The more labor-intensive a project is, the more you save by doing it yourself.

Be warned, however, that safety becomes a major factor in high decks. Ground-level decks are as safe as any patio and quite simple to construct. If you go up a few feet, you'll need railings. Go as high as a story or two, and you may have some major problems in both design and construction.

Figure 1-13   Ground-level decks, even one as large as this, are fairly easy to build. (*Courtesy Georgia-Pacific Corp.*)

Safety standards are discussed at length throughout this book, and careful attention to design and construction can overcome any safety problem. We are simply warning you here that novice carpenters are wise to ponder seriously all potential problems before attempting to tackle projects high off the ground.

Utilities

Under and around your house are a maze of pipes and other lines that may or may not be a problem. Most water lines run from the street to the front or perhaps the side of the house. If they do enter at the sides, it is usually at the front part of that side. The same is true for any underground electrical, cable, or telephone lines. One of the first things you should do while planning is to locate and map out all utilities in the deck area (Figure 1-14).

If there are public sewer lines, most of these also connect at the front of the house. The same is true of cesspools and, to some degree, septic tanks. When

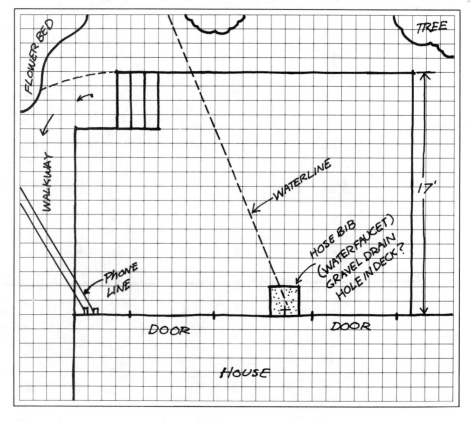

Figure 1-14 Be sure to mark the location of all existing utility lines at or near your deck site. (*Courtesy Western Wood Products Association*)

there is a leach bed required, the sewage system is probably in back of the house. But none of this is certain. If you are seriously considering a patio, be sure to check with the local utility company to make sure that you don't dig up any pipes or wires. If your home is older, there may be no record, which presents obvious problems.

There is more about this in Chapter 4. For now, let's just say that you should be careful about siting a patio where it may involve tearing up or relocating underground utilities. This is less of a problem for decks than patios, though, unless your electrical service runs right into a proposed high deck. A deck will also require underground footings, which is less of a problem. Still, it is wise to locate your utility lines in any case.

Consider other outdoor lines, too. There may be a pool, a garage, or outdoor lights in the yard. In that case, the wiring will run from the house to the light or outlet, probably in a pretty straight line. You'll have to find out if you plan on building near these wires.

On the other side of the coin, think about what utilities you will want on your deck, if any. Any desired lights or electrical outlets have to be connected to the house wiring somewhere. If you are planning an outdoor kitchen, wet bar, or anything similarly elaborate, it is wise to get some advice and estimates from the professionals. You can probably add an electric outlet or two by yourself, but whenever there are heat-producing appliances involved, a new circuit most likely will be necessary. This is discussed in Chapter 11.

Figure 1-15   In order to build this free-flowing deck between the house and the outbuilding, the electrical lines had to be located and possibly relocated. (*Courtesy Georgia-Pacific Corp.*)

The Solar Factor

This concept is tied in with location and orientation, discussed at length in the following chapter, but it is also pertinent here. Masonry, concrete in particular, absorbs a lot of solar heat. This can be a virtue, and it is used as such in passive solar construction.

The heat absorbency of masonry may make a concrete patio an excellent choice where there is a lot of cold weather. On the other hand, a patio in full sun facing South—or even West or East—can be a very hot place in Sunbelt regions, rendering it near uninhabitable. (See the next chapter for more on orientation and location.) In any event, a wood deck may well be a better choice, since it does not absorb and radiate heat like masonry.

The Final Choice

No matter what weight you give the factors discussed above, and others peculiar to your own situation, the final choice will always be what you and your family want. Personal preference is the most important factor, and you should not be deterred simply because there might be a problem.

No matter what anyone says about building a deck outside your bedroom, if that's what you want, that's what you should do. But at least consider the other factors and alternatives, and try to keep an open mind. If, after all is said and done, you still want a deck that looks onto a garbage dump, there is nothing anyone can say to change your mind. (Just be sure to include a bug-zapper.)

2

Location, Orientation, and Other Design Elements

LOCATION

You may already have the perfect spot to put your deck, and it is most probably the best one. Perhaps you used instinct or common sense, or were already aware of the factors involved in proper deck location. Even so, it is wise to further consider some of the fundamentals of location, orientation, and other elements of deck design.

Those who are planning a "wrap-around" deck to encompass the entire house don't have to ponder the best location for their deck. (Wrap-around decks are a nice idea for a vacation home, by the way.) The rest of us should at least take a look at the various options.

The primary consideration in locating a deck is to place it where you will use it most. The family should get together and discuss the reasons why they want a deck. What will you do with it once you've built it? If, for example, you want a deck primarily as a place for outdoor dining or entertaining—or both—it is quite obvious that the best location is close to the kitchen. Even if you plan on using an outdoor barbecue, and include a built-in wet bar, there will always be something that must be prepared in the kitchen. You don't want to lug a heavy casserole or a tray full of hors d'oeuvres any further than necessary. And don't forget those dirty dishes and glasses.

To take an extreme "for instance," it is foolish to build a deck designed for dining and entertainment off the second floor (unless, of course, you have a kitchen there). No one wants to climb a whole flight of stairs with the contents of a meal, or even with a couple of glasses. This doesn't mean that you should never build a deck leading off a second—or even a third—story. When your main purpose in building a deck is to create a private place for sunning and relaxing, a deck off your bedroom may be ideal.

The makeup of the family is another important consideration. As discussed above, people with disabilities or handicaps will require a deck with easy access and special safety measures. If you have—or intend to have—small children, you will want to have the deck to be within sight and hearing. That usually means a location off the kitchen or family room.

A prime location for decks, if possible, is off the family room. Many times you will already have sliding doors to the outside. In fact, wherever you already have access, preferably through sliding or swinging doors, to the outside, you probably already have natural ingress and egress to a new deck. If you don't have sliding doors, you should definitely plan to install them if at all possible. The installation of sliding doors, if you don't already have them, can be very

Figure 2-1 Decks that are designed for dining should always have good access to the kitchen. This Wolmanized deck is perfect for outdoor dinners and snacks. The gas barbecue on the upper deck and the built-in bar make it extremely usable.

Figure 2-2 One of the most popular sites for a deck is off the family room, preferably with access through a sliding door or—as here—swinging doors made of wood and reminiscent of French doors. (*Courtesy National Wood Window & Door Association*)

tricky. Unless you are adept at home construction, you will want a professional to install these. Not that the doors themselves are so difficult, but breaking into the outside walls necessarily involves removing a portion of a bearing wall. If you don't know what you're doing, you can severely weaken the entire structure of the home. The procedure for this is discussed on pp. 82–86, but it is not recommended for amateurs.

When there are no sliding doors, and you don't really want to get involved in messing around with the outside structure of the house, one good compromise is to settle for an ordinary exterior door to your patio. If there is not one already there, in most cases it is no big problem to convert a window to a door. The necessary structural headers should already be above the window.

Here again, the natural landscape must be taken into consideration. You can build around one big tree, maybe two, but you don't want to locate your deck in the middle of a forest. There are other factors, too, which should be obvious in most cases. Just in case, though, need we mention that you can't build a 20-foot deck when you only have 10 feet of clearance on that side of the house? Most municipalities have "set-back" laws that govern how close to the property line you are allowed to build. Be sure to check these if you come close to a neighbor's lot.

Figure 2-3 This entrance deck, made of western woods, was cleverly designed around several big trees that the homeowner was reluctant to destroy. In many cases, the trees will have to go, no matter how much you hate to lose them.

It may be that no location seems right for a deck leading off the house. Remember, then, that it isn't essential that the deck be attached. There may be another location, such as off the back or side of a detached garage. Many older homes have these. In fact, if one of your reasons for building a deck is to develop some private space, a secluded spot off by itself may be the best place. A free-standing deck or gazebo may be in order.

Be sure to check all zoning and building codes before getting to the final stages of your planning. Consult an attorney well versed in these matters if there is any hint of a problem.

Orientation is a concept that ties in with location, but refers to the deck's placement in regard to the elements. Mainly, this means where the deck is placed in reference to the sun. Again, the homeowner must decide what purpose(s) he or she has in mind for building the deck. The obvious example is a deck built primarily for sunbathing. If that is your main intention, your deck should face the sun as closely as possible. In almost all cases, this means locating the deck on the south side of the house.

Figure 2-4 A deck doesn't necessarily have to be attached. An excellent example is this poolside gazebo, winner of an award for Schlick Landscaping of Long Island. (*Courtesy National Landscape Association*)

Figure 2-5 This well-landscaped deck takes full advantage of the sun. (*Courtesy Goldberg and Rodler*)

There could be exceptions, though. If you are a one- or two-person family, and you work all day, what few rays remain when you get home will be from the West. In that case, you may want to locate the deck on the western side of the house. Work hours, of course, can vary. If you work an afternoon shift, the only sun you'll get will be in the morning. In that event, try the east side of the house.

In general, a deck is most useful on the south side of the house. This is especially true for those who live in the colder parts of the continent. Even when it starts to get a little nippy, natural solar warmth will allow a month or two extra each year to use the deck.

For those who envision their deck as a place to sip their morning coffee, however, an east-facing deck may be best. Those who live in the Southwest, parts of the deep South, or other areas where the problem may be too much sun, will probably find that a north-facing deck is the best choice.

Prevailing breezes are another important consideration. A west-facing location is usually best for cool breezes. It's a good idea to consult local authorities for prevailing wind patterns, but if there is no such thing, there are some general rules. If cool winds are your primary consideration, and there is no place to build a deck on the west side of the house, the next best locations are southern or northern sites. East-facing decks ordinarily catch the fewest breezes.

Figure 2-6   If one of your pleasures is morning coffee on the deck, an East-facing location may be best. (*Courtesy Western Wood Products Association*)

Mountains or other natural barriers may alter these generalities. And, if you live in a chilly area, you may wish to reverse these priorities. To avoid harsh winds, for example, a deck on the east side of the house may be the best location.

Wind flow can be redirected, if necessary, by strategic landscaping. Trees can serve as windbreaks, as shown in Figure 2-7, to direct the breezes away from—or toward—your deck. See Chapter 11 for more about landscaping.

None of this may even matter to you. Your home may be surrounded by trees, for example, and no matter where you put your deck, it'll be in shade. This may or may not be desirable, but it will spare you from worrying about orientation. (Sun-worshippers can, of course, cut down the trees and let the sunshine in, but this is—or should be—a painful decision.)

At the risk of being repetitious, let it simply be said here that there is no one ideal place to locate your deck, just as there is no ideal reason for building one. We are all individuals, and we all have our own reasons. The important thing is to examine your own wants and needs, establish your own criteria, then

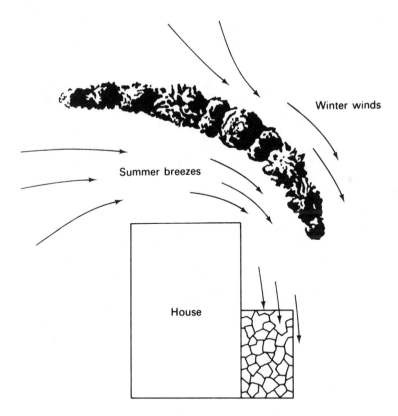

Figure 2-7 Intelligent use of plantings and windscreens can utilize sun and breezes to your advantage. The plantings shown here direct the wind away from the deck or patio in winter and toward it in summer.

evaluate the choices available. Once you've made the decision about location, there are more to come.

TYPE, SIZE, SHAPE, ETC.

You now know where you will put your deck. But there are still plenty of decisions to make. What size will it be? What type of wood? What shape? Will it be the usual square or rectangle, or maybe triangular, round, oblong—whatever.

Will you have a ground-level deck, a high deck, or something in between? Or perhaps you prefer a multilevel deck with two—or even three or more—interconnected platforms. Will the deck boards run straight across, diagonally, or some other way? These and many more questions will present themselves as you take pencil to paper and actually begin detailed plans. (And you must have a detailed plan.) In other words, the time has come to get into the basics of design and construction. Along with your brainstorming in regard to location and orientation, you surely have formed some preliminary mental picture of what the deck should look like. In most cases, the final deck will probably wind up looking pretty much like that original vision.

Before you plunge ahead, however, we think it's a good idea to at least take a look at the pictures in this book. We also urge you to take a ride through your neighborhood or other neighborhoods where you might expect to see a lot of decks—the nearest seashore, for example. See what others have done with their decks. You may find a lot of ideas worth imitating. You will surely find a lot of things to avoid.

Home builders, for example, have a generally rotten concept of what a deck is all about. Most metropolitan areas have housing developments where a deck is part of the package. It usually consists of a tacked-on rectangular platform overlooking the neighbor's self-same deck. Such a deck serves no evident purpose and is certainly monotonous, and sometimes plain ugly. This type of mindless deck doesn't usually get much use, either.

We're going to help you do better. You've already made an intelligent choice on location. Now you will decide intelligently what the deck will look like. The first thing to do—at least for the moment—is completely erase all preconceptions from your mind. That gorgeous deck you've already built in your head—forget it. (We'll come back to it, honest.) As we go through the possibilities here, try them on your house for size. Certainly, most won't fit. But perhaps some of the ideas will be adaptable. And you may wind up with a better deck, if not one that is substantially different.

Some Overall Thoughts

In an earlier, simpler time, a deck was considered simply a place for outdoor recreation. Now decks are used to give an exterior accent to many types of houses, and they are often used as airy outdoor extensions of a home's living area.

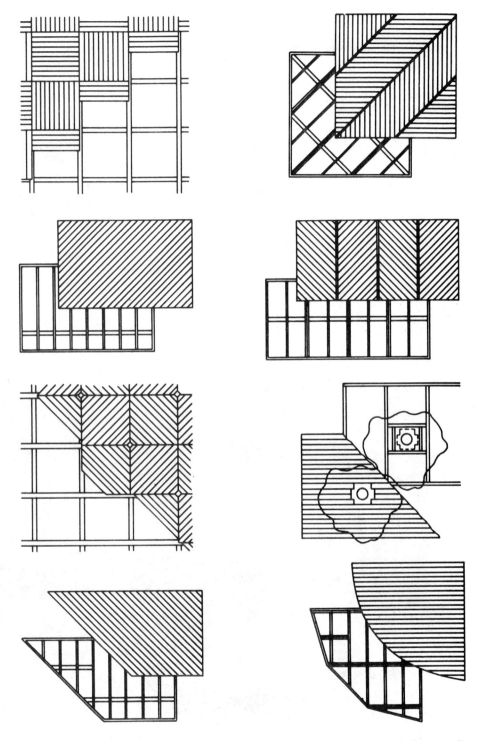

Figure 2-8 Some of the more attractive decking designs you can use. Also shown is the immediate framework beneath the deckboards. (Higher decks will need posts and other supporting members.) (*Courtesy California Redwood Association*)

Decks are now designed to blend in with, rather than obscure, the natural setting. Wood patterns can be pointed toward a pleasing nearby feature, and multiple levels make a more gradual union with the surroundings. Deckboards need not be in straight lines, but can be built in diagonals, parquet designs, and varying patterns.

Railings have been modernized and harmonized with the settings, and on low decks they have been often replaced by perimeter benches and planters. Hot tubs, planters, outdoor furniture, built-in landscaping, and other features can add interest or fun, or break up the monotony of plain bare space.

When planning, go back again to your reasons for building the deck. If warm-weather entertaining is a top priority, you'll need room for tables, seating, a service area (with built-in bar?), and probably some sort of cover to protect against a sudden rainstorm. You need to plan big, with a minimum of 300 square feet. Four hundred or more is better. When a deck is a large one, it could resemble a large platform, which can be downright ugly if not planned right. Consider several levels, or varying shapes, to give some relief to the eye.

If you have sloping land, several interconnecting levels are easier to build and more pleasant to look at than one large deck. Along the way, utilize broad steps for extra seating or any other form of livable area.

Figure 2-9 A beautifully designed landscape that won an award for Goldberg and Rodler of Huntington, New York. Note how the deck in lower right corner points toward the pool, one of the outstanding features of the yard. (*Courtesy National Landscape Association*)

Figure 2-10 With sloping land, several interconnecting levels are the best way to blend the deck into the landscape. (*Courtesy Georgia-Pacific Corp.*)

Many decks are intended mainly for private use, such as reading, relaxing, sunbathing, and similar pursuits. These don't require a lot of space. Small decks ordinarily present a clean and uncluttered look. When they are small, attached high decks should almost always be rectangular in shape.

Include railings in your deck design wherever there is a chance of injury from falling off the edge. The level of risk may vary considerably with each family or landscape—or may be set for you by the building code. Whatever the code says, your own loved ones will be the ultimate criteria. You may want to

Figure 2-11 This small ground-level, pressure-treated deck has a clean, uncluttered look. Note how it curves from a fairly standard rectangle into the concrete walk.

exceed the code (not ignore it). Generally, railings are a must whenever the edge is two feet or more off the ground. You may be able to stretch it to three feet high if the ground below is soft and hazard-free.

If you have small children, however, even two feet may be too high. Add rocks or thorny bushes underneath, and you may want railings regardless of height. In some cases, where the edge is two feet or less from the ground, perimeter benches or planters may substitute for railings.

Deck covers may be used over part or all of your deck. That depends on local climate and the expected uses of the deck. It would be overkill to roof in an entire large deck. It is wise, however, to provide some sort of cover in any dining or cooking areas. In the Pacific Northwest and similar regions where rain is prevalent, small decks may be more useful if completely covered. See Chapter 10 for suggestions on types and construction of deck covers.

You don't necessarily have to build the entire deck at one time, by the way. A deck cover, for example, can be added later. Large, multilevel decks can be built one level at a time, at your leisure, perhaps one level each year. It's a little different if you build a one-level deck and then decide to add to it later.

Adding to an existing deck—on the same level, at least—is not usually a good idea. The older section will have weathered and look considerably differ-

Figure 2-12   The family can enjoy this sturdily railinged deck with no fear of anyone getting hurt.

ent than the new part. If you must add to an existing deck, try to go to another level, or use different materials for an obvious contrast. A patio, connected by stairs, may be better. Those who think that they will be adding to the newly constructed deck in the future should keep this in mind while planning. It is best, in fact, to plan the entire landscape, including deck(s) at one time, even if you will be building in easy stages. Anyone who can afford it should consult a landscape architect, particularly when the deck area is to be large and interact with other elements of the grounds.

DECK STYLES

There is no one style of deck that will please everyone. As in everything else, style is a personal thing. Some will prefer the regularity and familiar look of a rectangular deck. Another, not inconsequential, feature of a rectangular deck is that it is easier to build and design than less common shapes.

Others may feel that the rectangular shape is just not for them, or perhaps a different style is a necessity because of an obstacle such as a tree, or an odd-shaped site. Multilevel decks are very popular and usually better-looking than single-level decks. Again, it depends on choice and personal needs. If your deck is planned as an entertainment center, with dancing and other functions requiring a large area, a single level is usually more practical.

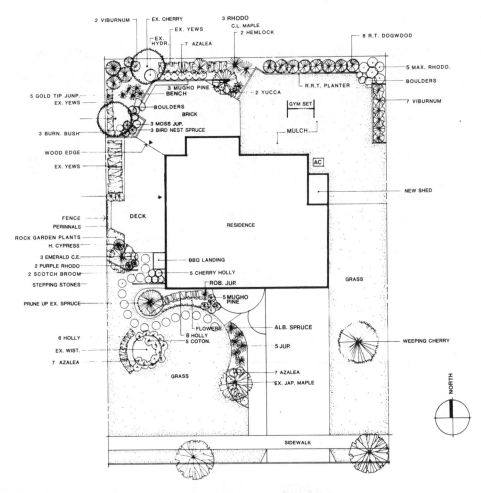

2 VIBURNUM — EX. CHERRY — 3 RHODO
EX. YEWS — C.L. MAPLE
EX. — 2 HEMLOCK
HYDR. — 7 AZALEA — 8 R.T. DOGWOOD
5 GOLD TIP JUNP. — 5 MAX. RHODO.
EX. YEWS — 3 MUGHO PINE — R.R.T. PLANTER — BOULDERS
BENCH — 2 YUCCA — 7 VIBURNUM
BOULDERS — GYM SET
3 BURN. BUSH — BRICK — MULCH
3 MOSS JUP.
3 BIRD NEST SPRUCE
WOOD EDGE
EX. YEWS — AC — NEW SHED
FENCE — DECK
PERINNALS — RESIDENCE
ROCK GARDEN PLANTS
H. CYPRESS
3 EMERALD C.E. — BBQ LANDING — GRASS
2 PURPLE RHODO — 5 CHERRY HOLLY
2 SCOTCH BROOM — ROB. JUP.
STEPPING STONES — 5 MUGHO PINE
PRUNE UP EX. SPRUCE
FLOWERS — ALB. SPRUCE
6 HOLLY — 8 HOLLY
EX. WIST. — 5 COTON. — 5 JUP. — WEEPING CHERRY
7 AZALEA — 7 AZALEA
GRASS — EX. JAP. MAPLE

NORTH

SIDEWALK

Figure 2-13 Ideally, the deck should be planned along with the rest of the landscape. A professional landscaper will draw up a plan showing existing house and plantings, location of new deck, brick patio, shrubs, etc. (*Courtesy Keely's Landscaping, Inc.*)

Fig. 2-13 *(Contd.)*

Figure 2-14 Most high decks are built in a rectangular shape. Rectangles are easier to design and build without making serious error. Note the use of steel lally poles for support.

The height of a deck pretty much depends on where you intend to locate it. If it's off a second-story room, it will automatically have at least one high level. This doesn't prevent you from having another level or two connected to the high deck. You may be able to proceed to several levels below in gradual steps. You are talking a lot of work and money, but you will have a deck to be proud of.

There is nothing inherently good or bad about shape and style. We will tell you the basics of building all the main elements of a deck and give you quite a few examples in the following chapters. None may fit your particular situation. In most cases, you will have to make some adaptations. Just remember, when adapting, that the higher the deck is, the more dangerous it can be for human traffic. Minimum sizes for spans for structural components are given in the accompanying boxes and should be strictly adhered to. But no one can guarantee safe design and construction. When you make any adaptations or alterations in the plans here, be sure to have them checked out by someone knowledgeable, such as an architect or engineer. An experienced contractor is usually all right, but some have more experience and knowledge than others.

When building at or near ground level, safety is pretty much guaranteed. Construction detail is much more forgiving. If a railing breaks on a ground-level deck, nobody is going to get much more than a cut or bruise. A broken railing can be a disaster for a second-story deck.

Figure 2-15   Sometimes deck design is dictated by location. There is really no other way to build this attractive roof-top deck than as shown. (*Courtesy Koppers Co.*)

Figure 2-16 The ideal deck will serve its function. This redwood deck is small, but well designed to enjoy the sunshine and the sea—as intended.

The most important element in good deck design is that it be functional. Keeping in mind the deck's purpose(s), try to visualize the use areas and traffic circulation patterns. Be sure to include the interior rooms that lead to the deck so that you can plan these patterns rationally.

In general, decks should be sized more or less the same way as your interior rooms. No area should be too much larger or too much smaller. If you want a large outdoor area, aim for several levels, or separate various use areas with benches, planters, or other visual aids.

If possible, make use of space pockets or "eddies," out of the way of natural traffic routes. This can be done by building in little nooks and crannies with the structure, or by using the visual aids mentioned.

As far as shapes are concerned, it is much easier to build a deck without a lot of odd shapes and angles. There is nothing wrong with shapes other than rectangles, but keep them somewhat consistent. Don't mix in a lot of curves and sharp angles just to be different. Avoid any angle less than 60,° because anything less will produce unusable dead space.

There is something that doesn't look quite right about a square deck, and elongated rectangles do not please the eye much, either. The Greek mathematician, Pythagoras, once put forth a "Golden Ratio," based on agreeable patterns he saw in nature (and later confirmed by DNA growth patterns). He put this ratio at exactly 1.618 to 1. It's tough number-crunching to apply this to decks,

A

B

C

Figure 2-17 A few ideas for setting off pockets or "eddies" for privacy, essential in designing a large deck. (*Courtesy Georgia-Pacific Corp. [A]; Western Wood Products Association [B]; and Western Red Cedar Lumber Association [C].*)

but you can use 8 to 5 as a rough guide. Decks 16 × 10, 24 × 15, and 32 × 20 all seem to have better proportions than most.

If you are using various levels, avoid having them too close to each other in height. A level just a little lower that the next one is confusing and can cause accidents. Avoid building with just a single step between levels. At least three steps are required to warn of a different level coming up. Wide steps of six feet or longer are better than shorter ones.

Attached decks are usually built over a site that slopes away from the house. If your deck will be built on land that slopes toward the house, try to build it so that there will be at least a small platform immediately next to the house. Access is difficult and awkward when you build steps up from the house to the deck.

Remember—functional, not fancy.

Figure 2-18 Multilevel decks should be separated by at least three wide steps whenever possible. (*Courtesy Western Wood Products Association*)

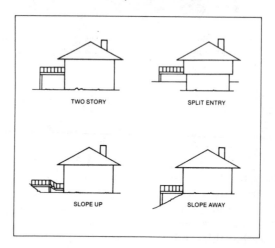

Figure 2-19 Decks can be attached on land that is level, slopes up, or slopes away from the house. When it slopes up, it is best to have a small platform adjacent to the house as shown at bottom left. (*Courtesy Koppers Co.*)

Figure 2-20 This intelligently planned deck was designed to link several back doors together in one level. Since the land slopes away, the deck leads down to a pleasant brick terrace among the oak trees. (*Courtesy Goldberg and Rodler*)

TYPE OF WOOD

One of the important elements in designing a deck is the type of wood. (We assume that your deck is to be built of wood.) It's an important question when outdoor projects are contemplated, much more so than when building indoors. It's so important, in fact, that we have devoted much of the next chapter to that discussion.

DESIGN LOADS

For on-ground and low-level decks, there is little concern about design loads; the building code may say otherwise, however, and should always be adhered to. Design loads are a major concern with high-level decks.

Design load doesn't mean much if you don't know how to use it, but for those who do, a deck should be designed for a live load of 40 pounds per square foot. The deck itself will weigh about 10 pounds per square foot (dead load). If you are designing your own substructure, be sure that all posts, beams, joists, and deckboards will support a total load, then, of 50 pounds per square foot. The tables on these pages are so engineered.

Even properly engineered decks may have a little too much spring for some people. If you want to have a perfectly steady deck, you might want to overbuild along the rough guidelines suggested below. Consult your building inspector, in any case, whenever making any type of design change.

A STRUCTURAL RULE OF THUMB

The charts on pp. 43–49 have been adapted from information given by the U.S. Department of Agriculture and the companies involved. They are the most authentic guides to maximum allowable spans for the different woods.

If you don't understand these charts, you probably should leave the structural design to a professional. On the other hand, for only a few minor structural details or modifications, it may be impractical to go through all that trouble and expense.

Where spans are concerned, a rough rule of thumb for beams or joists is to use a size (in inches) that corresponds to the length of the span in feet (e.g., a joist for a six-foot span should be 2 × 6). This can be a wasteful and expensive guideline for building an entire deck, but it is a safe one, since you will err on the side of overbuilding rather than making the structure too weak.

To give an example, where posts are four feet apart, use 4 × 4 beams. For posts six feet apart, use 4 × 6s; eight feet apart, 4 × 8s, etc. Most codes actually allow 4 × 6s up to a span of 10 feet, and 4 × 8s up to 14 feet. Use 4 × 10s for anything above that, but it isn't a good idea to have any span that exceeds 16 feet.

STRUCTURAL TABLES BY SPECIES OF WOOD (UNTREATED)

Minimum Beam Sizes and Spans

Species group	Beam sizes	4	5	6	7	8	9	10	11	12
1	4×6	up to 6-ft. spans			up to 6-ft. spans					
	3×8	up to 8-ft.		up to 7'	up to 7-ft.					
	4×8	up to 10'	up to 9'	up to 8'	up to 8-ft.		up to 6-ft. spans			
	3×10	up to 11'	up to 10'	up to 9'	up to 9-ft.		up to 7-ft.		up to 6-ft.	
	4×10	up to 12'	up to 11'	up to 10'	up to 10'		up to 8-ft.		up to 7-ft.	
	3×12		up to 12'	up to 11'		up to 9'		up to 10-ft. spans	up to 8-ft. spans	
	4×12			up to 12-ft.		up to 11'		up to 11'	up to 9-ft.	
	6×10					up to 12'	up to 11'	up to 12-ft. spans		
	6×12					up to 12'	up to 12'			
2	4×6	up to 6-ft.		up to 6-ft.		up to 6-ft.	up to 6-ft. spans		up to 6-ft.	
	3×8	up to 7-ft.		up to 7-ft.	up to 7-ft.		up to 7-ft. spans			
	4×8	up to 9'	up to 8'	up to 8'	up to 7-ft.	up to 6-ft.				
	3×10	up to 10'	up to 9'	up to 9'	up to 8-ft.		up to 7-ft. spans			
	4×10	up to 11'	up to 10'	up to 10'	up to 9'	up to 8-ft.				
	3×12	up to 12'	up to 11'	up to 11'	up to 10-ft.			up to 9-ft. spans		
	4×12		up to 12'	up to 12'		up to 11'		up to 11'		
	6×10				up to 12-ft. spans	up to 12-ft. spans				
	6×12								up to 8-ft.	up to 6-ft.

(continued on p. 44)

Minimum Beam Sizes and Spans

Species group	Beam sizes	Spacing between beams								
		4	5	6	7	8	9	10	11	12
	4×6	up to 6'								
	3×8	up to 7'	up to 6'							
	4×8	up to 8'	up to 7'	up to 6-ft.						
	3×10	up to 9'	up to 8'	up to 7'				up to 6-ft. spans		
	4×10	up to 10'	up to 9'	up to 8-ft.		up to 7-ft.		up to 6-ft. spans		
3	3×12	up to 11'	up to 10'	up to 9'	up to 8'		up to 7-ft. spans		up to 6-ft.	
	4×12	up to 12'	up to 11'	up to 10'	up to 9-ft.		up to 8-ft.		up to 7-ft.	
	6×10		up to 12'	up to 11'	up to 10'	up to 9-ft.		up to 8-ft. spans		up to 8'
	6×12			up to 12-ft.	up to 11-ft.	up to 10'				

Example: If the beams are 9'8" apart and the species in Group 2, read the 10-ft. column—3×10 up to 6-ft. spans, 4×10 or 3×12 up to 6-ft. spans, 4×12 up to 7-ft. spans, 6×10 up to 9-ft. spans, 6×12 up to 11-ft. spans

Key to species groups—1: Douglas fir, western larch, and southern pine. 2: western hemlock and white fir. 3: western pines, cedar, redwood, and spruces.

(continued from p. 43)

MINIMUM POST SIZES

Species group	Post sizes	Load area based on beam spacing × post spacing									
		36	48	60	72	84	96	108	120	132	144
1	4×4		up to 12-ft. heights							up to 8-ft. heights	
	4×6						up to 10-ft. heights				up to 10-ft. heights
	6×6						up to 12-ft. heights				up to 12-ft. heights
2	4×4	up to 12-ft.			up to 10-ft. heights		up to 8-ft. heights				
	4×6				up to 12-ft. heights		up to 10-ft. heights				
	6×6						up to 12-ft. heights				
3	4×4	up to 12- ft.	up to 10-ft.			up to 8-ft. heights		up to 6-ft. heights			
	4×6	up to 12-ft.			up to 10-ft. heights				up to 8-ft. heights		
	6×6				up to 12-ft. heights						

Example: If the beam supports are spaced 8'6" o.c. and the posts are 11'6" o.c., then the load area is 98: use next larger area 108.

45

MAXIMUM ALLOWABLE SPANS FOR SPACED DECKBOARDS

| Species group | MAXIMUM ALLOWABLE SPAN | | | | | |
| | Boards laid flat | | | | Boards laid on edge | |
	1 × 4	2 × 2	2 × 3	2 × 4	2 × 3	2 × 4
1	16	60	60	60	90	144
2	14	48	48	48	78	120
3	12	42	42	42	66	108

MAXIMUM ALLOWABLE SPANS FOR DECK JOISTS

| Species group | Joist sizes | Joist spacing | | |
		16″ o.c.	24″ o.c.	32″ o.c.
1	2 × 6	9′-9″	7′-11″	6′-2″
	2 × 8	12′-10″	10′-6″	8′-1″
	2 × 10	16′-5″	13′-4″	10′-4″
2	2 × 6	8′-7″	7′-0″	5′-8″
	2 × 8	11′-4″	9′-3″	7′-6″
	2 × 10	14′-6″	11′-10″	9′-6″
3	2 × 6	7′-9″	6′-2″	5′-0″
	2 × 8	10′-2″	8′-1″	6′-8″
	2 × 10	13′-0″	10′-4″	8′-6″

STRUCTURAL TABLES FOR
PRESSURE-TREATED WOOD

The following are recommendations by the Koppers Co., maker of Wolmanized wood and the Outdoor Wood designation:

MINIMUM BEAM SIZES

Length of span (ft.)	Spacing between beams (ft.)						
	4	5	6	7	8	9	10
6	4 × 6	4 × 6	4 × 6	4 × 8	4 × 8	4 × 8	4 × 10
7	4 × 8	4 × 8	4 × 8	4 × 8	4 × 8	4 × 10	4 × 10
8	4 × 8	4 × 8	4 × 8	4 × 10	4 × 10	4 × 10	4 × 12
9	4 × 8	4 × 8	4 × 10	4 × 10	4 × 10	4 × 12	*
10	4 × 8	4 × 10	4 × 10	4 × 12	4 × 12	*	*
11	4 × 10	4 × 10	4 × 12	4 × 12	*	*	*
12	4 × 10	4 × 12	4 × 12	4 × 12	*	*	*

*Beams larger than 4 × 12 recommended. Consult a designer for appropriate sizes.

MINIMUM POST SIZES

Height (ft.)	Load area (sq. ft.)=beam spacing × post spacing				
	48	72	96	120	144
Up to 6	4 × 4	4 × 4	6 × 6	6 × 6	6 × 6
Up to 9	6 × 6	6 × 6	6 × 6	6 × 6	6 × 6

Vertical loads figured as concentric along post axis. No lateral loads considered.

MAXIMUM ALLOWABLE SPANS FOR DECK JOISTS

Joist Size (in.)	Joist spacing (in.)		
	16	24	32
2 × 6	9'-9"	7'-11"	6'-2"
2 × 8	12'-10"	10'-6"	8'-1"
2 × 10	16'-5"	13'-4"	10'-4"

MAXIMUM ALLOWABLE SPANS FOR SPACED DECKBOARDS

Maximum allowable span (in.)		
Laid flat		Laid on edge
2 × 4	2 × 6	2 × 4
32	48	96

Though able to support greater spans, the maximum spans will result in undesirable deflection or springiness in a deck.

STRUCTURAL TABLES FOR
REDWOOD

Although redwood is included in Species 3 of the USDA tables on the previous pages, the California Redwood Association has suggested these requirements for the use of structural redwood:

SUGGESTED BEAM SPANS
For non-stress-graded redwood lumber with live load of 40 lbs. per sq. ft. and dead load of 10 lbs. per sq. ft.

Beam size and grade	Beam spacing 6'	8'	10'	12'
4 × 6	Span			
Clear all heart				
Clear	6'-6"	6'-0"	5'-0"	4'-0"
Cons't. heart				
Cons't. com.	4'-6"	4'-0"	3'-6"	3'-0"
4 × 8				
Clear all heart				
Clear	9'-0"	8'-0"	7'-0"	6'-0"
Cons't. heart				
Cons't. com.	6'-0"	5'-0"	4'-6"	4'-0"
4 × 10				
Clear all heart				
Clear	11'-6"	10'-0"	8'-6"	7'-6"
Cons't. heart				
Cons't. com.	7'-6"	6'-0"	6'-0"	5'-6"

Beam span is the distance a beam extends from one post to the next. Beam spacing is the distance between beams.

SUGGESTED DECKING SPAN
For non-stress-graded redwood lumber with live load of 40 lbs. per sq. ft.

Size	Grade	Span
2 × 4	Clear all heart and clear	24"
2 × 6	Construction heart and construction common	24"

SUGGESTED JOIST SPANS			DECKING TO COVER 100 SQUARE FEET		
For non-stress-graded redwood lumber with live load of 40 lbs. per sq. ft.					
Joist size	Clear all heart and clear	Construction heart and construction common	Materials	Standard linear ft.	Diagonal linear ft.
2 × 6			2 × 6 Decking	210	242
			2 × 4 Decking	326	375
16" o.c.	10'-0"	6'-0"			
24" o.c.	9'-0"	5'-0"	Nails		
2 × 8			2 × 6 decking, approx. 5 lbs. 16d nails		
16" o.c.	13'-0"	9'-0"	2 × 4 decking, approx. 6 lbs, 16d nails		
24" o.c.	12'-0"	7'-6"	Use stainless steel or hot-dipped, galvanized common or box nails.		
2 × 10					
16" o.c.	17'-0"	12'-0"			
24" o.c.	15'-0"	10-0"			

A FINAL WORD

Other than considering available space, safety, and personal taste, there is little that can be said to guide you in your choice of deck styles and shapes. The best we can do is to urge you again to look at the pictures here and elsewhere, and to examine every deck you can find in the neighborhood. If you are using a contractor, or just exploring the possibility, ask for any pictures, plans, or suggestions that he or she might have. After that, you're on your own.

3

Tools and Materials: Construction Basics

Every how-to book should tell readers what tools they will need to work on their new project. We will do that, but it's an easy job. If you have the ambition and confidence to build a deck, you probably have most of the tools already.

Basically, you will need tools for hammering, screwing, leveling, drilling, and digging. A great deal depends on how much of the work you will be doing yourself, and what type of deck you're putting up. You may need all or none of the following. Assuming that you will do all of the work yourself, and that the deck is not overly simple or complicated, here's what you'll need:

- Hammers—16-oz. or bigger claw hammer. You will probably also need a sledgehammer or "mash" (hand-drilling) hammer for banging heavy timbers into place.
- Wrenches—1/4 inch and up. You'll probably need two of the more common sizes, such as 3/8 inch, for carriage bolts and nuts. A decent adjustable wrench may suffice instead of a second set. A good ratchet set will save considerable time and labor.
- Portable electric drill—a good one, preferably 3/8 inch or larger. A cordless model is best if the deck is large or far from the house. You'll need a

wide range of bits, from small high-speed for predrilling to large spade-type bits for lag screws and carriage bolts.

- Saws. A simple but good crosscut saw is essential, and a circular saw with a combination blade is almost a must. You may find use for a chainsaw, too.

- Extension cord(s)—for the circular saw, at least. Get outdoor-rated, three-wire, heavy-duty cord, at least 50-feet, and preferably 100-feet, long. You may need two of them.

- Levels. A good, long carpenter's or mason's level is a must, and so is a line level (with line) for site and post work.

- Rules—both a 25-foot (or 50-foot for large decks) retractable rule and a 6-foot folding rule.

- Chisels—a range of 1/4 inch to 1 inch or wider. There will be many occasions when a piece has to be chiseled to fit.

- Squares—a large framing or T-square to ensure 90° corners and an adjustable square for marking and sawing.

- Spade. A square-end garden spade is essential for digging footings and other ground work. You will probably find use for a long-handled spade as well.

- Masonry tools. Whether you need many or none of these depends on the extent and type of footing you'll need. You should be able to get by with just a wood float. Consult a book on masonry if you plan on extensive concrete work.

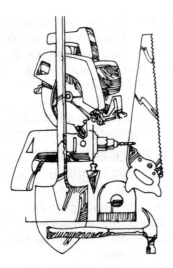

Figure 3-1

There are other tools you may or may not need, depending on the size and type of deck you're building. You'll probably need a post-hole digger, discussed on p. 76. If you do any wiring, you'll need specialized tools for that. The tools listed, however, should be all you'll need for most decks.

MATERIALS

By and large, the only material you really need is wood—lots of it—and fasteners. You will need some sort of concrete footings and piers or pedestals, unless you are building a ground-level deck directly on top of sand or gravel. You may or may not need finishing materials, or wood preservatives, as discussed in Chapter 12 and elsewhere.

Other than fasteners, there is really very little else we can think of. Perhaps some flashing material for the house ledger. The wood itself takes a lot of thought and pondering, so we will discuss this at some length.

TYPES OF WOOD

The first question relating to deck materials is what type of wood to use. Decks and other outdoor projects are subjected to all of the elements—rain, snow, wind, sleet, salt spray near beaches—whatever the weatherman brings in your area. Animals, fungi, and bugs are outdoors, too, including such nasty little things as termites and carpenter ants.

Even if you're leaving the entire job in the hands of a contractor, you will want to be very careful about the type and grade of wood used. Just one unhappy example occured in the town of Manorville, on Long Island. At a country club there, 36 people were injured when a relatively new deck collapsed. Reporters said that untreated pine was used for the supporting trusses, causing the whole structure to fall.

Most unprotected wood is helpless in the face of attacks of the elements and wood-craving creatures. Often, even before signs of deterioration are obvious, nails pull out of wood that is softened by internal rot, causing the supports to sag and even fall apart.

To prevent wood rot, you have two basic choices. You can buy regular wood and cover it with paint, exterior stain, or wood preservative; or you can begin with wood that is either naturally decay-resistant or has been chemically treated to behave that way. Of the two, the easier and better way is to build your deck of decay-resistant wood. The initial cost can be significantly higher, but a deck is a rather costly addition no matter how you build it. The last thing you want is a deck that will fall apart after a few years of use. If you believe that you will have the energy and gumption to repaint, restain, or represerve decay-prone wood year after year, you may be kidding yourself. Very few people give non-decay-resistant wood the timely attention that it needs.

Just one example—how often do you paint your house? Every few years of so, as the paint manufacturer recommends, or when it starts to peel and look unsightly? If you are the sort of person who keeps at these things and doesn't mind doing it, more power to you. You are allowed to use whatever wood you wish. But be honest with yourself. If you do have trouble getting up the ambition to perform maintenance chores, as most of us do, you should really use one of the woods discussed below.

Decay-Resistant Woods

Actually, quite a few woods are naturally resistant to weathering and insects. Most of these are "swamp" trees, such as cypress and teak, but rarely are they found in lumber yards. You can buy cypress and teak, of course, if you look hard enough and are willing to pay the price. Ordinarily, however, teak—and a wide variety of other exotic woods—is used for furniture and other finer items. Even boatbuilders find teak too pricey these days. Cypress is usually available only where it grows naturally (mainly in the Southeast) and then it is hard to find in the wide variety of lumber sizes needed for deck-building.

There are only two types of widely available woods that are naturally decay-resistant. These are redwood and red cedar.

Redwood.   Cut from the famous western titans of the same name, redwood is the premium lumber for outdoor construction. It is relatively expensive, but "garden" grades (containing knots and some other minor imperfections) are considerably less so. Garden grades are perfectly fine for most outdoor uses. Decks, however require caution.

Figure 3-2   Cypress is widely available in the Southeast, where it grows in swampy areas like this park in Wilmington, NC. Since it grows in water, cypress is extremely resistant to it.

Figure 3-3 Garden grade redwood looks good in this deck. Note the sapwood in the nonheart lumber widely used for all areas not in ground contact.

Without getting into a dissertation on wood grading, it is important to know something about the distinctions among the various grades. Garden grades include construction and merchantable grades, with the latter not recommended for most deck applications. Construction grades come in "heart" and common. Construction heart is preferred for most deckwork.

Heartwood must be used for posts, beams, and joists. "Heart" refers to the part of the tree that has been grown for years—or even centuries—and is found at the center of the tree's trunk or large branches. Most of a tree's activity or growing process takes part in the "sapwood" at the outer rings of the tree. The heartwood doesn't change much and is therefore more stable and the only part that is rot-resistant.

Redwood also comes in "architectural" grades, which are generally better looking and more expensive. There is no reason to use this type of lumber except perhaps for railings and seating, to minimize splintering and protect tender hands. When strong railings are needed for safety, and for beautiful deckboards, there is nothing like clear all-heart, but be prepared to pay a premium price (see table, p. 56).

REDWOOD GRADES AND THEIR APPLICATIONS

	Construction heart	Construction common	Merchantable heart	Merchantable	Clear all-heart	Clear	B Grade
Architectural	—	—	—	—	■	■	■
Garden	■	■	■	■	—	—	—
Knots	■	■	■	■	—	—	■
Sapwoods	—	■	—	■	—	■	■
Posts	■□	—	—	—	■	—	—
Beams	■□	—	—	—	■	—	—
Joists	■□	—	—	—	■	—	—
Decking	■	■□	—	—	■	■	■
Rails	■	■□	—	—	■	■	■
Fenceboards	■	■	■	■□	■	■	■
Benches	■	■	■	■□	■	■	■
Planters	■	—	■□		■		
Trellises	■	■	■	■□	■	■	■
Furniture	■	■	■	■□	■	■	■

■Suitable grade for use
□Most economical grade for use

Redwood is a lovely cinnamon or brownish-red color when first applied, and it weathers to a handsome silvery gray if left unfinished. Many people prefer the original reddish color, which can be retained with clear water repellents and some other finishes. Like most woods, it can be stained or painted, if desired (though most people rarely do). Be cautioned that any redwood that is not "heart" must be finished, since it may contain sapwood, which is not impervious to the elements. Sapwood is pretty easily recognized by its significantly lighter color. (See Chapter 12 for more on preserving and finishing redwood and other woods.)

Prices for both redwood and red cedar are less on the West Coasts of both the U.S. and Canada, since the trees grow there, and transportation costs are less. There are other reasons for variation, too, such as supply and demand, tariffs, and availability. For comparison's sake, though, as of this writing in the Northeast, clear all-heart vertically grained redwood was about $2.00 per foot, or $16.00 for an eight-foot 2 × 6. Construction grade all-heart was about 80 cents per foot, or $6.40 for an eight-foot 2 × 6.

Red Cedar.   This wood comes from the red cedar tree, of course, and is in the same family as the white cedar, the familiar landscaping bush "arborvitae" (*Thuya occidentalis*). If you didn't trim your arborvitaes, they'd grow into cedar trees (and some do).

Generically, red cedars are junipers (*Juniperis virginia*), which are used not only for landscaping, but are also harvested for wood. But the species grown commercially for lumber is the western red cedar (*Thuya plicata*). This tree grows big and tall in the Northwest, and has heartwood very similar to that of the redwood tree. The same chemical that gives both of these woods their red look also makes it toxic to insects and prevents them from devouring it.

Red cedar is more common than redwood and is less expensive. It is the same wood used most frequently in cedar shakes and shingles—and cedar chests and closets, which were very popular for moth prevention in earlier days. It is tough and durable wood, equal to redwood in its ability to repel insects and weathering. Its surface may not be quite as attractive as redwood, but it looks just as good for most purposes. Very often, red cedar is used in conjunction with redwood. Cedar is often used, for example, for supporting members such as posts, beams, and railings, with redwood being used for decking.

Figure 3-4   Western red cedar was used for this attractive entry deck.

Red cedar is, again, not as expensive as redwood, but it isn't exactly cheap. Clear red cedar costs about $1.25 a foot, or $11.00 for an eight-foot 2 × 6, in the Northeast as of this writing. Standard and better or "common" red cedar goes for about 65 cents a board foot or $5.20 for an eight-foot 2 × 6. (There are no "garden" grades of cedar.)

"CCA" Lumber.   "CCA" stands for chromated copper arsenate, a rather potent-sounding mixture. And it would be, if you tried to swallow it. As a wood preservative, however, it is great stuff. CCA lumber is often referred to also as "Wolmanized" lumber, which is the trademark of the Koppers company, manufacturer of the chemical, which it sells to authorized treating plants.

CCA lumber is made of softwood, usually yellow pine or Douglas-fir, which has been pressure-treated with the chemical described above. It is easily recognized by the green tint it retains until it has weathered a bit. The lumber is subjected to various saturation levels of chemical and is available in several "numbers," or retention levels. Retention refers to the number of pounds per cubic foot of preservative retained in the wood after treatment.

Figure 3-5 CCA, known also as pressure-treated or "Wolmanized" wood, makes a handsome and highly durable deck. Many object to its green look when new, and its more visible grain, but it is an excellent bargain and the longest lasting.

The most densely saturated commercially available wood has a retention level of .60, but this is rarely used for homeowners or builders. It is found in marine bulkheads and similar structures built for frequent immersion in salt water. If you are building at the seashore, where your deck may come in direct contact with the water, you may need .60 wood for the posts, and perhaps other structural members. The most widely used CCA wood, though, has a retention of .40, and this is acceptable for almost any use except directly in water.

CCA lumber rated .40 or better will outlast almost any other wood, including redwood and red cedar. It has been known to resist decay for over 35 years, and the Koppers Company has a written lifetime guarantee for any wood labeled "Wolmanized" or "Outdoor Wood."

There is also a CCA wood rated .25, but this is not really advisable for decks or most other outdoor applications. Wood labeled .25 is recommended by many for any areas that do not come in contact with the ground, but most experts feel that .40 wood lasts much longer for only a small increase in price.

Note that we avoided using "grade" in reference to the retention designations. That's because CCA wood, in addition to having retention numbers, also comes in grades, from 1 to 3. Grade 3 is not seen often and should not be used for decks because of its tendency to warp. Always use 2 grade or better for outdoor projects. Most lumber yards carry 2 grade only.

Deckboards and railings should be built of knot-free 1 grade CCA lumber. Grade 2 .40 grade CCA is the most widely used and is most widely available. It can be difficult to locate 1 CCA and, to make matters worse, most CCA manufacturers do not label the grade on their lumber. A trusted dealer or experienced wood-buyer can tell the difference, but most of us can't. To help the consumer

Figure 3-6 CCA lumber is usually stamped with useful information, such as the retention number (see text). This is stamped "0.40 retention."

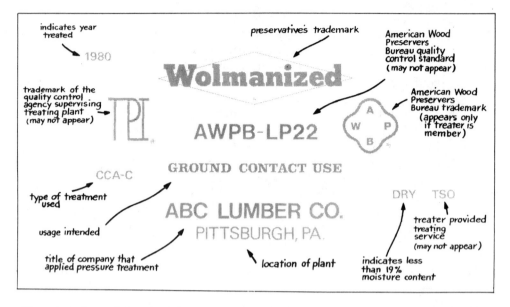

Figure 3-7   Some of the other information you may find stamped on CCA. Note the use of "ground contact" instead of 0.40 retention number. Not all information appears on all lumber, as noted.

with this problem, Koppers has designated their "Outdoor Wood" trademark to mean 1 grade, kiln-dried after treatment (KDAT) for nominal one- and two-inch lumber. It costs more than CCA not so designated, but anyone who wants top-grade lumber may find it worthwhile to look for this stamp.

Although it doesn't have the grade stamped, CCA does have a stamp giving the retention number. If it is kiln-dried after treatment, which is preferred for decks, "KDAT" or "DRY" should be stamped on the lumber, too. But remember, the trademark "Outdoor Wood" includes both kiln-drying and .40 retention. All properly treated pressure-treated lumber should also carry a stamp showing "AWPB," as shown in Figure 3-7, which means that the wood has been approved by the American Wood Preservers Bureau.

Price-wise, with the same cautions as above, 1 grade .40 CCA costs about the same or a little less than "common" red cedar. Grade 2 .40 CCA is about 55 cents a board foot, or $4.25 for an eight-foot 2 × 6.

Just as with redwood and red cedar, you can mix CCA grades, and CCA can be mixed with the other woods. This author personally feels that CCA doesn't blend well with redwood and cedar, but it can be done. Frequently CCA is used for the underlying structure, especially where it is hidden, with redwood used for the more visible members such as deckboards and railings.

We would also recommend .60 CCA where there is good possibility of prolonged and direct contact with water, especially salt water. If you are planning a deck on a barrier island, for example, there is no question that the posts should be built of .60 CCA. If there is little or no prospect of storms or tides washing around the joists and deckboards, you can probably use redwood or red cedar—or .40 CCA for that.

Because of its green tint, CCA doesn't look as nice as redwood or red cedar when it is new. Eventually, it acquires the same silver-gray hue that the other woods do, but this takes at least a few months and can be a year or longer. That initial pride you usually take in a new project is diminished somewhat by this, but remember that you are building for the long term.

We have been informed that, because of the green color, CCA is not a big seller in western parts of the continent. Recognizing this, manufacturers have introduced a gray-colored pressure-treated wood that looks something like weathered redwood or cedar. This author has not seen it, and it is certainly a rarity in eastern states. One wonders why gray CCA is not more widely available.

In this author's opinion, the color and grain of CCA are less attractive than redwood or red cedar. The durability and cost saving in using CCA makes it a very practical choice, however. CCA lumber can be stained, painted, or otherwise finished just like normal pine and is undoubtedly the best choice if you plan on adding some kind of finish anyway. (See Chapter 12 on this.)

One thing that has been a concern about CCA is its possible toxicity. The chemicals used in CCA have been certified by the EPA as a pesticide. Under normal use for decks, there should be no particular problems. See pp. 62-63 for potential hazards, nonetheless, if you plan on using pressure-treated wood.

If you must, for the sake of economy, use untreated wood other than redwood or red cedar, it is highly advisable to treat the wood prior to assembly. The wood should be *soaked* in preservatives, not just coated. If the wood is already assembled, then coating will do some good, but this is considerably less effective than soaking. Chapter 12 also addresses preserving methods.

FASTENERS AND OTHER SUPPLIES

As soon as your plan is complete, or even before, you should start thinking about ordering your supplies. Watch for sales in the newspapers, which may save you a bundle. Lumber, of course, is your primary material; you will also need plenty of nails and other fasteners.

Posts should be anchored to footings or pedestals as discussed in the following chapter. "Teco" fasteners can be used for this, as well as for other purposes. Many building codes specify joist hangers or similar metal fasteners (Figure 3-8) for use on the ends of beams or joists. Code or not, it is a good idea. These fasteners are indispensable for attaching the ends of joists and beams to the house or to each other. The usual alternative, toenailing, is not acceptable in many building codes and is not as strong when used alone.

Whatever else you need, you will need a great number of nails. These should always be corrosion-free, either hot-dipped galvanized, aluminum, or stainless steel. Buy them in 50-pound boxes, at least for the deckboards, to save a few dollars. In addition to, or perhaps instead of, "Tecos," you will probably also need a number of metal plates, angle irons, bolts, nuts, and washers.

EPA PRECAUTIONS—PRESSURE-
TREATED WOOD

The Environmental Protection Agency has issued guidelines for the use and handling of pressure-treated wood. There are actually three sets of guidelines for the various types of pressure treatments. Since the most common type of pressure treatment is with inorganic arsenic, only those guidelines will be given here. If your pressure-treatment happens to be with pentachlorophenol or creosote, consult the separate guidelines for that type of wood.

Below are the EPA precautions as listed in the guidelines issued by the American Wood Preservers Institute:

- Wood pressure-treated with waterborne arsenical preservatives may be used inside as long as sawdust and construction debris are cleaned up and disposed of after construction.
- Do not use treated wood under circumstances where the preservative may become a component of food or animal feed. Examples of such sites would be structures or containers for storing silage or food.
- Do not use treated wood for cutting-boards or countertops.
- Only treated wood that is visibly clean and free of surface residue should be used for patios, decks, and walkways.
- Dispose of treated wood by ordinary trash collection or burial. Treated wood should not be burned in open fires or in stoves, fireplaces, or residential boilers because toxic chemicals may be produced as part of the smoke or ashes.
- Avoid frequent or prolonged inhalation of sawdust from treated wood. When sawing and drilling treated wood, wear a dust mask. Whenever possible, these operations should be performed outdoors to avoid indoor accumulations or airborne sawdust from treated wood.
- When power-sawing or machining, wear goggles to protect eyes from flying particles.
- After working with the wood, and before eating, drinking, and use of tobacco products, wash exposed areas thoroughly.
- If preservatives or sawdust accumulate on clothes, launder before reuse. Wash workclothes separately from other household clothing.

ARSENIC IN WOOD AND FOOD

Arsenic has a long history as a means of getting rid of inconvenient people, such as wives, husbands, and kings. Lavinia the Poisoner used it to polish off those who would deny her son the crown of Rome. Even used with kindness, as in "Arsenic and Old Lace," it did the job.

When we hear that the CCA preservative in pressure-treated lumber has arsenic as a main ingredient, some of us are understandably astonished. But be not afraid. Properly handled, arsenic is harmless in CCA and is commonly found in nature—even in foods. You've never eaten arsenic? Want to bet?

Here is the arsenic concentration found in many common foods, as determined in 1977 by the National Academy of Sciences.

Shrimp	19.90 PPM	(parts per million)
Oysters	2.00 PPM	
Tomato	1.49 PPM	
Mushrooms	0.66 PPM	
Potato	0.63 PPM	
Rice	0.40 PPM	
Clams	0.36 PPM	

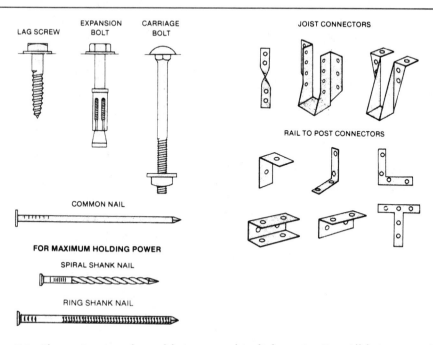

Figure 3-8 The most commonly used fasteners used in deck construction. All fasteners must be rust-proof, either hot-dipped galvanized, stainless steel, or aluminum. (*Courtesy Koppers Co.*)

Standard and lag screws may also be necessary, depending on the type of construction. All of these should be galvanized or stainless steel. You may also want to use exterior construction adhesives in some applications. If your plans have been drawn up by professionals, the fasteners for all the main joints (except for nails) should be clearly specified on the plans.

It is usually a good idea to go over your plan carefully with your building supply dealer well in advance of construction. If you order everything from the same supplier, he or she should be more than willing to give you advice and assistance. When your order is large enough, the dealer may well give you a discount, too, of 10 percent or more. You should certainly ask for it.

Shop around the various lumber yards and building supply houses for the best deal. Ask about prices and discounts ahead of time. Make sure that you specify the lumber quality. If you aren't sure yourself, ask for recommendations. When comparing prices, don't mix apples and oranges. A dealer that gives you a good price for 2 grade lumber isn't doing you any favors as opposed to someone with a higher price for 1 grade, or clear all-heart, for example.

Your dealer may give you a better price if the entire order can be delivered at one time. There is no problem with this if you have the room to store it. The materials should all be weather-resistant anyway and can be stored outside. There will be a lot of lumber laying around, though, so you may want to order in stages, especially if you're building a large deck.

Ordinarily, lumber should be ordered in long lengths—one 16-footer, rather than two eight-footers, for example. You are almost always better off cutting than piecing boards together. If you have a lot of lumber all the same size, then it may be best to order to size, as when you have deckboards all 12 feet long. Then get the required number of 12-foot boards.

GENERAL RULES FOR OUTDOOR CONSTRUCTION

Chapter 5 gives details of the various types of connections and joinery you will need in your deck construction. Before you even begin on-site work and other preparatory work, though, it helps, for buying purposes, to have an overview of what connects to what. Here, we will list some general rules that apply to virtually any deck or outdoor project (and most other woodworking).

Fasteners

- Always use corrosion-resistant, nonstaining hardware.
- Always fasten a thinner member to a thicker member.
  1. A nail should be long enough to penetrate the receiving member twice the thickness of the thinner member. For example, with a board 3/4 inches thick, the nail should penetrate the other board at least 1-1/2 inches (2 1/4 inches overall). In other words, the nail should be a 7d nail, which is rare, so 6d or 8d nails are ordinarily used.

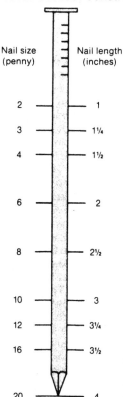

Nail size (penny)

Nail length (inches)

2	1
3	1¼
4	1½
6	2
8	2½
10	3
12	3¼
16	3½
20	4

Figure 3-9 Sizes of common nails and their "penny" designations ("d"). An 8d nail, for example, will be 2½ inches long. Hot-dipped galvanized nails are common nails, as shown. Other types of nails, such as finishing nails, will be different lengths. (*Courtesy Koppers Co.*)

2. A screw should be long enough to penetrate the receiving member at least the thickness of the thinner (attaching) member. In decks, for example, attach a 3/4 deckboard to a joist or beam with a screw at least 1-1/2 inches long.

- To reduce splitting of boards when nailing:
  1. Blunt the point of the nail.
  2. Predrill (ideally, 3/4 of the nail diameter).
  3. Use more nails of a smaller size.
  4. Allow more space between nails.
  5. Stagger nails in each row.
  6. Place nails no closer to the edge than half the thickness of the board and no closer to the end than the thickness of the board. In other words, for 3/4-inch lumber, don't nail any closer to the sides than 3/8 inch or closer to the ends that 3/4 inch.
  7. For boards eight inches wide or more, stay as far away from the edges as possible.

- Always use at least two nails at each joint of every board. Use three nails for boards eight inches or more.

- When using lag screws:
  1. Use a plain, flat washer under the head.
  2. Predrill the hole and turn all the way in, but don't overturn.
  3. Do not countersink. (This reduces wood thickness.)
- When using bolts:
  1. Put flat washers under both nut and head of machine bolts and under the nut of carriage bolts. In softwoods, use a larger washer under the bolt head.
  2. Holes must be drilled the exact size as the bolt diameter.

Lumber

- If possible, when wide boards are required, use quarter-sawn boards (cut vertically or from edge grain). They shrink, swell, and cup less than flat-sawn boards.
- Never use wood in direct contact with soil that is not designed for this. Use pressure-treated lumber, redwood, or red cedar.
- Allow sufficient clearance (at least six inches) of all framing lumber from the ground and plants and other vegetation to avoid damage from moisture.
- Wherever possible, slope flat boards (e.g., cap rails) to provide natural drainage.
- When you have a choice, prefer rectangular lumber to longer, flatter boards (e.g., prefer a 3 × 6 to a 2 × 8).
- If and when you use non-weather-resistant lumber, soak the wood in preservative and dip the ends in the same solution after cutting and before attaching.

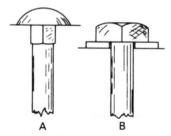

A   B

Figure 3-10 Machine bolts (right) are often used for joining larger pieces of lumber. At left is a carriage bolt, which resists turning because of the squared section under its head. Washers are used under machine-bolt heads to prevent its digging into the wood.

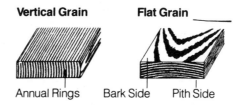

Vertical Grain   **Flat Grain** _____

Annual Rings   Bark Side   Pith Side

Figure 3-11 Wood cut vertically or radially at left is less prone to warping. If you use the more common flat-grain boards, nail them "bark-side-up" so that, if warpage occurs, they will "crown" in the center and allow better drainage. (*Courtesy California Redwood Association*)

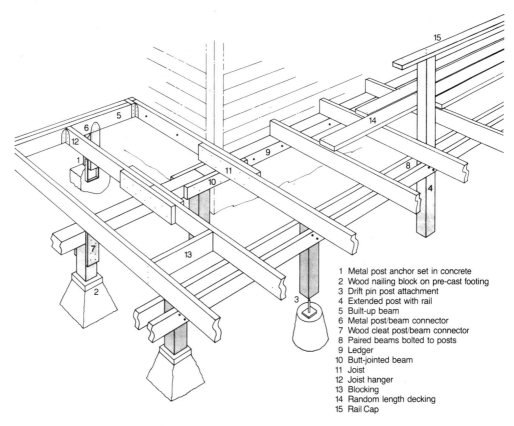

1 Metal post anchor set in concrete
2 Wood nailing block on pre-cast footing
3 Drift pin post attachment
4 Extended post with rail
5 Built-up beam
6 Metal post/beam connector
7 Wood cleat post/beam connector
8 Paired beams bolted to posts
9 Ledger
10 Butt-jointed beam
11 Joist
12 Joist hanger
13 Blocking
14 Random length decking
15 Rail Cap

Figure 3-12 An illustration of the more common terms used in deck construction, and examples of how and where they are used. (*Courtesy California Redwood Association*)

4

Site Work and Other Preparation

The first step in building your deck is a detailed plan, based on your rough design. You may be able to do this yourself, especially if the deck is low and not too elaborate. More complicated plans should really be drawn up by an architect or an engineer experienced in deck or home construction.

If you do draw your own plans, remember that these will have to be submitted to the local building department, so draw them neatly and with some degree of finesse. Use graph paper and a scale of 1/4 inch or 1/2 inch to the foot. Measure accurately and specify dimensions, type and size of lumber, etc. There are books on drawing up plans, if you have no inkling as to how to go about it.

Most building departments are lenient with homeowners who draw their own plans and will make any needed corrections with no ill will. Others can be very tough. You will have to find out from people who work there, neighbors, contractors, and others about that. Do as good a job as you can, showing by your plans that you know what you're doing, and the average building inspector will approve your plans without too much trouble.

When decks are high or could otherwise present safety problems, it is almost mandatory to have a professional draw up the final plans. He or she will be familiar with local building codes, zoning, and other ordinances that may affect your home.

Whichever method you choose, the final scale drawings will almost always have to be approved by the local building department. Many people think that they can skip this step, thereby saving time, trouble, and an increased assessment. Quite often, frankly, they do get away with it. This is a short-sighted view, however, since building inspectors can often help you in pointing out errors and poor design factors. Furthermore, if you get caught, building departments tend to take a harsh attitude about approving the project later. You may have to tear down the entire deck just to satisfy a requirement for deeper footings, for example, or put in larger posts.

You may think that because your deck is located at the rear of your house, no one from the town will see it. But some municipalities have helicopters for that very purpose. More often than not, though, it's a jealous or spiteful neighbor who blows the whistle on the permit-avoider. Save time and future problems by being upfront to begin with.

There is one way to build a deck legally without getting a building permit. In most jurisdictions, decks are covered by the building code only if they become "part of the house." In practice, this means attachment to the house. Detached construction, such as a poolside or freestanding deck, does not normally require a building permit.

SITE WORK

Assuming that you have your detailed plans, and that all necessary permits have been acquired, you can finally begin work. The first step is to lay out the overall dimensions on the ground beneath the deck. Using powdered chalk, a garden hose, or something else that can simply form an outline of the perimeter, establish what preparatory site work must be done.

With the outline established, you can determine exactly what needs removal or relocation, and what grading must be done. If the deck will be ground-level, all the vegetation must be removed to eliminate potential high moisture content. This will also help prevent wood rot.

There is not much other site work to be done for a ground-level deck (but see pp. 18–19 and 245–249 on utilities). You should provide a three-inch bed of tamped sand below the deck surface to provide drainage and help control weeds. If the soil is poorly drained, an additional three inches of gravel may be needed.

Use a vegetation killer to kill the grass, weeds, or whatever is growing beneath a planned ground-level deck to prevent the vegetation from growing back. Another method is to lay a polyethylene or asphalt felt membrane over the soil, punching a few holes in the surface so that the cover doesn't become a drainage problem. This must be done later, though, after the framework is complete and before the deckboards are laid.

For a high-level deck, site work will depend on what you will do with the space below. What can happen to vegetation below a deck was covered in Chapter 1. It is best to kill it all off and replace the vegetation with gravel, pine bark, or some other type of mulch. You should at least remove all sun-loving

Figure 4-1   A high deck will cast vegetation-killing shadows beneath it. You may as well face the inevitable and kill off grass and plantings before you build. Gravel, pine bark, or some other mulch can be added later under the deck.

plants and replant them elsewhere. If you want, you can probably leave the grass and see what happens. Quite probably it will remove itself after a season or two for lack or sunshine.

If you insist on keeping the area grassy, check local extension agents, nurseries, or garden supply houses to see which grasses are shade-tolerant, then plan to sow new grass if necessary (after the deck is finished). For whatever other purpose, determine whether regrading is in order. If so, it should be done before you start the deck. A new carport, for example, will require almost level ground. Any extensive grading should be done prior to construction.

Plantings that do not require sun can possibly be left in place, as long as you have some way of watering them. When the deckboards are spaced apart, as normally, enough rainfall may get through to provide some moisture for the plants. Otherwise, a sprinkling system should be considered.

If the deck is to serve also as a roof for a garage, carport, or living area below, the deck should be treated as part of the house drainage. Gutters and downspouts should be installed, or some type of drain system installed near the perimeter of the deck.

Where the deck needs to be drained, a method must be devised to carry water away from the site and prevent soil erosion in the drainage area. This can usually be accomplished with drain tile laid in a shallow ditch (Figure 4–2). Run the tile to the main drainage system or some other area where erosion will not be a problem. Perforated tiles are the easiest to use, but you can use regular drain pipe with asphalt felt covers as shown.

It should not be necessary to bring in the bulldozer when building a high deck with no special plan for the below-deck area. You should be able to dig the holes for the post footings with only minor grading, if any. It is best not to disturb the natural landscape any more than you must.

Whenever there is any possibility of disturbing underground utilities such as electrical or plumbing lines, make sure you mark their location, even if you are only digging shallow holes for footings. Have an electrician relocate any underground service lines that might be in the way. If there are other underground wires, such as those leading to pools, garages, or other outbuildings, you may be able to do these yourself—if you know what you are doing (see Chapter 11).

Plumbing lines may have to be relocated, too. Avoid this wherever possible, but if you must excavate in their vicinity, check with a plumber and the water or sanitation department. You may be able to relocate these, maybe not.

You may also want to provide any necessary underground wiring and plumbing for your deck at this stage. This is more likely for ground-level decks than higher ones. Utilities can be run above ground when the deck is high enough. Make sure you have provided for these utilities in your plan and prepare for them before you start building.

LAYOUT

Start out by establishing a convenient straight line to serve as your measuring guide. For attached decks, this is usually the side of the house to which the deck will be bolted. Since "straight" lines are rarely true, however, run a line

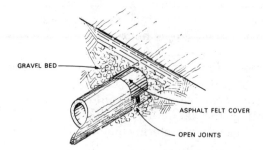

GRAVEL BED

ASPHALT FELT COVER

OPEN JOINTS

Figure 4-2 If there is a potential drainage problem under the deck, drain tile should be laid in a bed of gravel before construction.

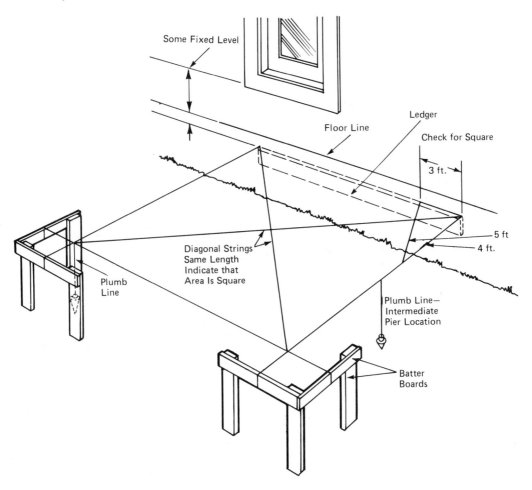

Figure 4-3 Batter boards ensure square corners. Erect them as shown, using the 3-4-5 system discussed in the text. To double-check for square, run diagonal lines between corners as shown.

alongside the house and make any adjustments necessary to make sure that you really have a straight line.

When the deck is detached, pick out one corner where you want the deck to start, then run a line along one edge to the next corner. Drive stakes in at the ends and proceed as follows. Once you have a straight, true, starting line, begin the rest of the measurements. You can choose the perimeter of the deck, the substructure, or whatever is most convenient. If exact measurements are given for each post location, it is best to begin the measurements there.

The most accurate method of measuring is to erect batter boards as shown in Figure 4–3. These should be outside of the actual measuring lines. It doesn't really matter how far outside, as long as they are all the same distance away, but four feet out from each edge is the usual distance.

To ensure square corners, the "3-4-5" method is used. This is based on the mathematical formula for a right triangle. If one side is three feet (or inches, for that matter), the other is four feet (or inches, millimeters, or whatever), and the hypotenuse (diagonal) is five feet (or whatever), the right angle formed at one corner will be exactly 90°, or square. These distances are often doubled to 6-8-10 as shown in Figure 4-4.

For squaring the corners, nail lines between batter boards in each direction. Add the distance from the actual perimeter to the nail, then measure off three feet (plus distance to the batter boards) in one direction, then four feet in the other. Install temporary stakes at each point. Measure the distance between the two stakes, and if it isn't exactly five feet, adjust one or other of the lines until it is precisely five feet.

Mark the location of the new line and move the nail to the new position if necessary (and it probably will be). Double-check the new angle with a carpenter's square, and make any necessary adjustments.

Proceed to the next corner post (or edge of whatever it is you are using as a benchmark), and repeat the procedure for all four corners. When you're sure it's right, then check it one more time by measuring from one corner to the other on the diagonal. Do the same thing for the other diagonal. These lines should be exactly equal. If they aren't, go back and try again. Make sure this job is done right. (It's much easier, by the way, with a helper to hold the string while you measure and mark.) "Unsquare" corners can cause a lot of grief during the entire construction project.

All of this assumes, of course, that you are building a rectangular deck. Even if you aren't, though, there should be several right angles somewhere, probably between posts. These should be your starting points. If you lay out the right angles correctly, the odd angles or rounded edges will be much easier.

Measurements should be "o.c." or "on center," if you are using the posts themselves for your baselines. Your plan will (or should) show the exact distance from the center of each post to the next one. As each post center is located, set a stake at that exact position.

Locating post centers is not difficult (if you are careful) when the terrain is reasonably level. With a steep slope or bumpy terrain, it may be better to attach

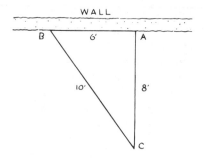

Figure 4-4 You can double the 3-4-5 dimensions as shown to get the same result. These are better for large decks.

the ledger board to the house and measure out from there as discussed in the following chapter. Instead of using this method to determine post height, measure down with a plumb line to establish each post location.

Where there is even a slight slope involved, make sure that your measurements are perfectly horizontal. If your rule is dipping to make even a slight diagonal line, you will not be measuring at a right angle, which can throw off crucial distances by an inch or more.

DIGGING THE POST HOLES

After grading, layout, and any other site work has been done, foundation work is next. At each post stake, dig a hole as wide and deep as required. The size of the holes depends on the type of footings you will be using. Minimum, however, is two feet, if you are putting the posts directly into the ground. The best rule of thumb is that one-third of each post should be in the ground.

For most types of hole-digging, it is easier to use a post-hole digger than a spade or shovel. A scoop-type digger (Figure 4-6) is fine for most soils, but clayey soil may require an auger-type digger. You can rent these, but if you use the scoop variety, you will probably find that you can buy one for what it costs to rent it. Sometimes the lumber dealer will have a "loaner."

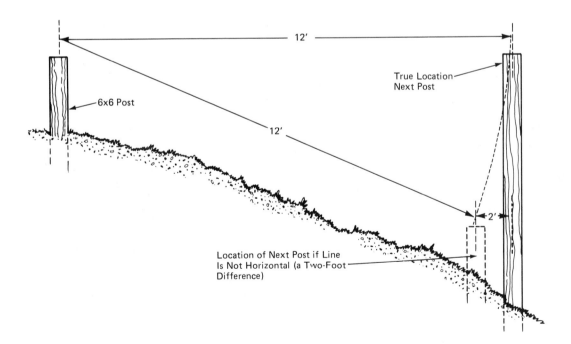

Figure 4-5 When laying out on sloping ground, make sure that your measurements are horizontal by using a line level and plumb line to locate the next post. In the drawing, note that both lines are 12 feet long, but the dotted-line post would be 2 feet too close to the first post (see text).

Figure 4-6 Post-hole digging is hard work, but it is easier when you use a digger made for this work. The poles of the clam-shell type shown here are pulled apart to bring up the dirt (A). The poles are pushed together when digging in (B).

This is not exactly fun time in the grand adventure of deck-building. Site preparation involves a lot of heavy, dirty, muscle-wrenching work. Those with bad backs and hearts should try to find a healthy friend or family member. Otherwise, hire a laborer with a strong body.

FOOTINGS

It is possible, though unlikely, that footings will not be necessary. If there is no chance of freezing, the ground is flat and well-drained, and the deck not too high, you may be able to simply lay some 4 × 4s or pedestals on the ground and build up from that. Even if it seems okay to you, the building code is likely to require footings.

In the vast majority of cases, some type of footing is required to support the posts or poles that transfer the weight load to the ground. It is also possible to insert the posts deeply into the ground and hope for the best, but footings ensure that your posts will stay where they are supposed to be. Shortcuts are not recommended here and are sure to be frowned upon by your building department.

For a low-level deck on level ground, it may be easier to simply dig a trench and pour a continuous footing, the same way you would for a house.

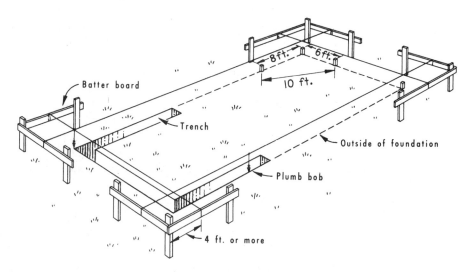

Figure 4-7 A continuous footing may be used when the posts are low and set close together. Lay out the footing and dig the trench as shown. Concrete is then poured all at one time into the trench.

This is more work and takes more concrete than using individual footings for each post, but it might be the better method if your deck is designed with a lot of low posts spaced fairly close together.

Concrete work can be complicated and would require another entire book. There are lots of these around, if you need them. Footings of this type, however, are easy to do and don't require any fancy finishing. All you have to do is dig down below the frost line (usually four feet or more in Northern climates) and lay a six-inch bed of gravel below the bottom of the footings.

Continuous footings should be at least 8 inches deep and 16 inches wide. You don't need forms for these footings, unless the ground is crumbly or you aren't too steady with your spadework. Using a square-end spade for neat sides, just dig out the earth and use that for your forms.

Where forms are necessary, use 1 × 8 lumber to form the sides and stake every four feet around the outside of the forms. Rent a portable mixer, use premixed concrete, or make your own using a 1:2:3 formula—one 90-bag of concrete to 2 parts of sand and 3 pounds of aggregate (gravel). Mix thoroughly with five gallons of water.

If you have a lot of concrete to pour, and can bring a "cement" truck up to the forms, bring in some ready-mix from a concrete supplier and pour it into the trench. Level and finish the top of the concrete with a wooden hand float.

INDIVIDUAL POST FOOTINGS

When you have more widely spaced posts, it is easier to pour or buy individual precast footings, available from most masonry dealers. If your deck is a low one, all that is necessary is to dig out the ground for each footing, put in some gravel as described above, then lay or pour the footings on top of the gravel.

Footings should be below frost level where required in the Snowbelt. Minimum size is 12 × 12 square and 8 inches deep, but 16 × 16 is usually recommended. When posts are more than 6 feet apart, 20 × 20 × 10-inch footings are preferred. Check your local building code for compliance.

Another type of below-grade footing is the poured-in-place type shown in Figure 4-9. In such construction, the posts are prealigned, plumbed, and supported above the excavated hole. Concrete is then poured below and around the bottom end of the post as shown. A minimum of eight inches of concrete below the butt end of the post is advisable. Pressure-treated lumber (.60 retention) is highly recommended for this type of construction.

It is evident that, to use this method of pouring footings, you will have to purchase your posts ahead of time. It is also wise to cut them to size beforehand, too. It is difficult enough to cut 4 × 4s or larger lumber on the ground, much less try to trim them to size when the tops are in the air. Take great care, then, in sawing and setting the posts to the proper height. If you want to allow some leeway, cut them a little long, if anything. Whatever you do, don't leave them too short. (If you aren't sure of proper post height, see the next chapter.)

Posts can be supported while pouring by using temporary bracing as shown in Figure 4-10. Stake the ends of the braces solidly in the ground to help resist movement. Don't remove these braces until construction is complete. They will help to keep things steady while you work.

Many builders are turning to "sonotubes" (rigid circular forms) to pour footings. You can even carry the sonotubes up the bottom of your framing, so that the concrete tubes serve not only as footings, but do the work of ordinary posts. Consult local concrete dealers about the use of sonotubes.

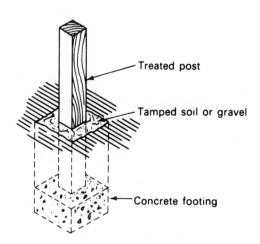

Figure 4-8   Individual post footings can be poured or bought precast. They should be a minimum of 12 × 12 inches and 8 inches deep. Sixteen-inch-square footings are the norm.

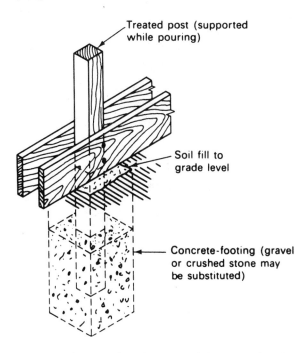

Treated post (supported
while pouring)

Soil fill to
grade level

Concrete-footing (gravel
or crushed stone may
be substituted)

Figure 4-9 Footings can also be poured in place around the posts. Though this gives very strong support, it requires that the posts be installed and braced ahead of time, which could be a problem as described in the text.

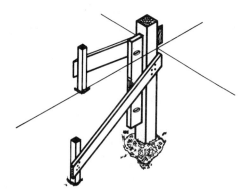

Figure 4-10 Poured-in-place posts should be plumbed and braced with stakes driven into the ground as shown. (*Courtesy TECO*)

Another construction technique is to keep the posts entirely above ground. Although the posts may need extra bracing in this method, they are more resistant to decay than when they are embedded in the soil. When built above ground, the bottoms of the posts rest on deep pedestals or piers with the tops at least six inches above grade.

For reasonably low decks, the ends of the posts are set on pedestals, as shown in Figure 4-11. The piers in turn rest upon footings, which should be

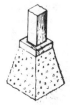
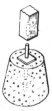

Figure 4-11 Precast piers or pedestals are often used to keep deck posts away from the ground. Low-level decks can be attached to pedestals by toenailing to the nailing block as shown at left, or by the use of a "drift pin" at right. Higher decks or decks exposed to uplift drafts should be attached with connectors (see Figure 4-13). (*Courtesy California Redwood Association*)

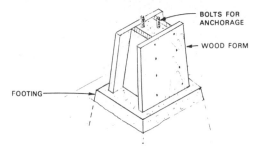

Figure 4-12 Making your own forms and pouring your own pedestals will save money if you have a lot of piers to buy.

extended below the frost line where required. Precast pedestals are usually available from concrete suppliers. You can make your own reusable forms like those shown, however, extended at the sides, which are easily knocked apart after the concrete hardens. Double-headed nails can also be used for easy removal.

ANCHORING POSTS

Posts set above grade should be anchored to footings or pedestals whenever the deck will be significantly higher than ground-level. This is important not only to resist lateral movement but also uplift stresses, which can occur during high winds. These anchorages should be designated for good drainage and freedom from contact of the end-grain of the wood with dampness. Any metal fasteners should be hot-dipped galvanized or otherwise corrosion-free.

Some methods of properly anchoring the posts to the footings or pedestals are shown in Figures 4-13 and 4-14. At least a portion of these anchors must be embedded in the concrete after pouring. Be sure you know what member goes into the concrete with the type anchor you are using, and embed that part before the concrete sets up.

| Place base over anchor bolt. | Place washer on top of base and over bolt. | Apply nut. Do not tighten. | Place support in base as shown. | Nail post. Plumb and tighten nut with wrench. |

Figure 4-13 Teco post anchors should be used for high decks and wherever there is a chance for uplift stresses. When footings are poured, insert a "J-bolt" into each footing so that it protrudes one inch above the concrete and is in the center of the post. Install anchors as shown.

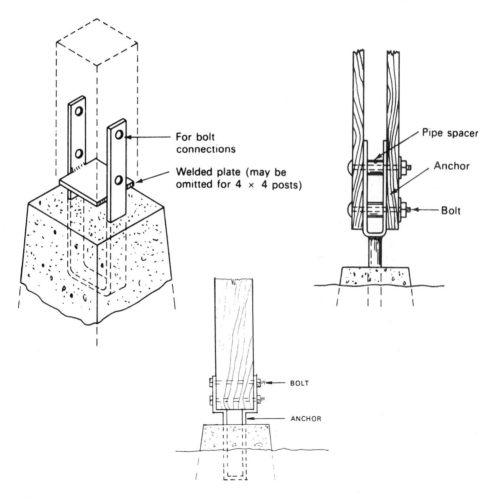

Figure 4-14 Some other methods of anchoring posts securely to the footings. You may not find exactly the same hardware, but the important thing is that part of the anchor is embedded into the concrete.

81

CREATING NEW ACCESS

The ideal means of access for any deck is through sliding or swinging glass doors. As discussed earlier, a regular door will do, but sliding doors look better, even if they often get stuck or off track. (Regular applications of WD-40 or silicone can help that.) Sometimes, there is no door to the deck at all, which means you have to make one anyway.

Installing a sliding door is no job for an amateur, or even for many experienced do-it-yourselfers. The main problem is that the wall you are cutting into is almost certainly a load-bearing wall. You will have to remove some studs, even for a regular door, and this must be done with great care to avoid creating a sag or even the collapse of the entire wall.

Then, assuming that you have adequately braced that part of the structure that has been held up by the removed studs, electric, heating, and plumbing lines may need to be relocated. (Be sure to determine the location of any lines—especially wiring—before you randomly cut into the wall.) You will also have to calculate the size of the header that will absorb the load formerly supported by the studs.

We don't pretend to be engineers or architects. I know experienced contractors, for example, who say that there is no need to brace a six-foot opening—and others who worry so much they use steel lally poles. Each house is different, and there are few general uses to go by. All advice here goes without a guarantee.

At first blush, this seems to be a good place to apply the rule of thumb set forth on p. 42. Where you have a six-foot opening, use a six-inch header. But exterior walls carry the weight of the roof and everything else above them, so it is very wise to play it safe.

Though they may be slightly oversized, construct any header of at least two 2 × 10s on edge, and use 2 × 12s for any opening beyond seven feet. Assuming that the wall is made of standard 2 × 4s, you'll also need a piece of 1/2-inch plywood in between the 2 × 10s. (Two 2 × 10s on edge are only three inches wide, while the studs are 3-1/2 inches.) Older houses may have different dimensions, so always measure first.

Make up the header as soon as you know exactly what size it should be and have it waiting to hoist quickly into the opening. Bracing is only temporary and not really strong enough to carry that load for too long.

Sliding door manufacturers will have packed installation instructions with the unit. (If not, don't buy it.) One very important bit of information is the "rough opening," which you will have to prepare yourself.

When you know how big the opening has to be, the first step is to determine the position of the studs and other framing. After deciding where the door should go, use a stud-finder, or otherwise figure out where the studs are. Since you will be ripping out part of the wall anyway, you can drill some holes or pull off some of the wallboard to get a better picture.

Figure 4-15 To cut out an opening for sliding doors, locate studs and mark opening. Cut away wallboard, etc. (A) and set up bracing (B). Remove existing framing (C), put up header and jack studs (D). Install door frame, partially screwing it into the framework (E), level and plumb, using shims as necessary (F). Tighten screws and insulate between frame and opening. (Read text carefully if you want to try it.)

Measure the distance of the opening, and jockey the dimensions around so that there will be at least one existing stud beside the opening. When you know exactly what is to be removed, take off all the wall covering inside and outside of the framing. (Try to do this in warm weather, and have a tarpaulin or sheet plastic handy to cover the opening in case of rain.)

The key part is coming. Now you must shore up the joists or whatever framing is *supported* by the studs within the opening. You may think that you can brace the header above the opening and prevent future problems. But what happens when you have to put in the new header? The braces are in the way.

The easiest way to brace the joists that rest on the wall plate is to run a 2 × 4 underneath them as shown in Figure 4-15B. Then wedge a 2 × 4 tightly between the floor and the brace at each end. Make sure that the braces run as close to the opening as possible and are tightly secured. Nail the ends to the floor or ceiling, if necessary. For wider openings, you may need lally poles for bracing.

Now you can start removing the existing studs. With standard eight-foot ceilings, the door plus the header will probably take up the entire opening, so rip out the existing studs completely. For high ceilings, cut studs off to the required height, leaving the "cripple" ends.

You should have your new header already assembled and a helper waiting. Also measure and cut the "jack studs" or "trimmers" before taking out all of the old studs. Lift the header into place between the end studs and wedge the jack studs in at each side underneath the header to help hold it in place. Make sure everything is plumb and level and shim if necessary. Nail in the jack studs and toenail the header to the adjacent studs. Secure with appropriate connectors.

Figure 4-16 Install the sliding door per manufacturer's instructions, making sure to check movement and make any necessary adjustments. (*Courtesy Andersen*)

After installing the header, you can relax a little (assuming that the house doesn't fall down). From there on, install the frame of your sliding door according to manufacturer's instructions. Be sure to level, plumb, shim, and caulk as directed.

In most cases, there is a stationary door and a sliding door. Install the stationary door first, as directed, then tip in the sliding door and push to close position. Install the head stop, if any. Attach handle and other hardware, check the movement, and make any adjustments.

Pack strips of insulation into the opening between the door jambs and the side studs. Attach molding, trim, etc. Open and close the door a few times, just to prove what a wonderful job you did. If it wasn't so wonderful, make further adjustments as recommended by the manufacturer. When it's finally over, you will have a convenient and good-looking access as shown in Figure 4-17.

It is much less of a problem to install a standard exterior door for deck access. Many people prefer it, in fact, to a sliding door. Locate an existing

Figure 4-17 When it's finally finished, your sliding door will give you good-looking and convenient access. (*Courtesy Andersen*)

window (high enough to walk under), remove it, then take out the framing underneath the window header. Reframe all around for the door, using the same header for your new door.

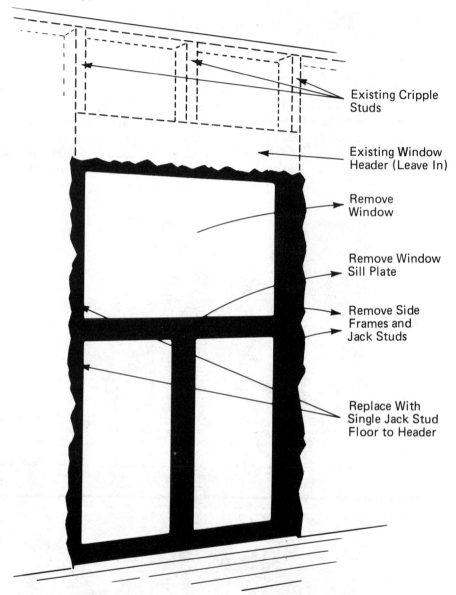

Existing Cripple Studs

Existing Window Header (Leave In)

Remove Window

Remove Window Sill Plate

Remove Side Frames and Jack Studs

Replace With Single Jack Stud Floor to Header

Figure 4-18 It is considerably easier to install a regular door for deck access. Find an existing window, remove it and the framing beneath the header. Use the same header, which will support the wall meanwhile, for your door.

5

Construction Details

Now the fun begins. There will be moments when it will seem anything but fun. Everybody makes mistakes somewhere along the line. By careful reading, planning, and measuring, you should be able to keep them to a minimum, however. And, you will find that there is a lot of pleasure in using your own hands (plus a few more, with luck) to build a handsome and functional edifice of your own.

Meanwhile, there's work to be done. If you embedded the posts in concrete, and installed them firmly and plumb, as discussed in the previous chapter, the first step is already done. Otherwise, the first step is usually to measure and install the ledger board, which is used as a baseline for the other work.

If the posts are in, and you will be attaching railings to the posts, or using any plan whereby the posts extend above the deckboards, there is no great rush to saw the posts to size. This can be done in the later stages, when you have a deck to stand on and work from.

There are decks, however, in which there is no ledger board, such as freestanding decks, and other occasions when the posts must be measured and cut to their proper height at this time. In any case, this section will describe how to measure and cut posts to height at this point.

When the main structural components (joists or beams—in rare cases, deckboards) are to be fastened on top of the posts, they must be cut to the proper height before attaching the rest of the structure. If your plans don't specify, or

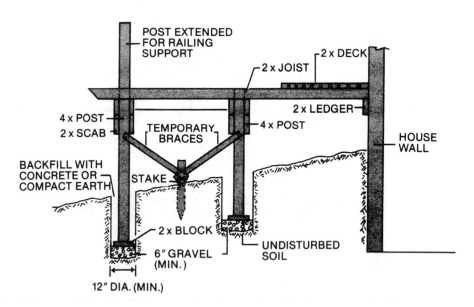

Figure 5-1 Typical high-deck construction, as described in detail throughout this chapter.

you don't really know just how high the posts should be, there are a couple of ways to do this.

Many like their decks level with the door opening, but it is usually better to have at least one step down onto the deck from the entranceway. Even for level decks, though, start an inch down from the entrance to allow for drainage. Upsloping decks, of course, will of necessity have steps up. In any case, when there will be steps up or down, figure on six inches for every step if not specified on the plan. (Or see pp. 90–91 for determining the exact height.) To the total step height, add the thickness of each piece of lumber between the top of the post and the top of the deckboards. This will be the proper distance between the level of the entranceway and the top of the post. (Remember to use actual, not nominal, sizes.)

As an example, suppose you are working on a deck with 2 × 6 joists connected directly to the top of the posts and 2 × 4 deckboards laid on the wide side. Assume one step down from the entrance. To compute post height, allow six inches for the step, plus 5-1/2 inches for the joists, and 1-1/2 inches for the deckboards. That's 6 + 5-1/2 + 1-1/2 inches, or 13 inches total. With spaced deckboards on a small deck, we won't need to slope for drainage. The top of the post should be 13 inches down from the entrance level.

Make a mark on the house where the top of the deckboards will be (p. 101), then pick one post, preferably close to the entrance, for your "base post." Measure over to this with a line and line-level, or use a straight piece of lumber on edge with a carpenter's level, to get a perfectly horizontal line from the entrance level to the post. Measure down from there the required height (13 inches in our example). You can also measure down 13 inches on the side of the house, and run the line out from there, but the house siding may interfere with accurate measuring.

Whichever way you accomplish it, mark the line on your base post, then use the same method for marking the other posts. With spaced deckboards, you don't necessarily have to allow for drainage, although it isn't a bad idea to do so on general principles.

If you're making a solid decktop, you *must* allow for drainage—at least 1/8 inch per foot toward the drain side. In our example, starting from the house and draining away from it, assume that the master post is one foot away from the benchmark on the house.

Using the same sample dimensions as before, add an extra 1/8 inch, or 13-1/8 inches for the master post. The outside posts, if four foot distant, should be an extra 1/2 inch lower, or 13-5/8 inches down from the entrance level. (It is obviously simpler to rely on spaced deckboards, but check local codes.)

When using the ledger board as your baseline, determine its location first as discussed before. You don't necessarily have to lag it in at this time, but secure it firmly with nails before using it as your base for measuring. Follow the same procedure with lines and levels, allowing for drainage as necessary. Remember that post height will now be measured from the top of the ledger board, which is ordinarily the bottom of the deckboards. Make the necessary adjustments accordingly, subtracting 1-1/2 inches for the deckboard height, making the top of the post 11-1/2 inches.

The easiest way to cut off the post tops is with a chainsaw or "sawz-all." Be sure that you cut them off level. To ensure this, mark the post on at least two adjacent sides and cut carefully. If you aren't too handy with a chainsaw, a portable circular will do the job, but you may have to make two or more cuts. Take your time and make your cuts square and level.

While accuracy is very important, especially at this stage of the game, realize that this is not work that requires fine tolerances. If you cut one side of the post 1/16 inch lower than the other, it won't be a disaster. You can live with small errors, but not big ones, such as cutting the post an inch too low.

When the posts are high, sawing off the ends can be very tricky. Make sure that the posts are braced, and use a ladder, or scaffolding if need be, to get to the top. In the case of high posts, it may be easier to cut them to size beforehand, as discussed previously.

ATTACHING THE DECK TO THE HOUSE

When the deck adjoins the house, the connection there must be firm and sturdy. Ordinarily, the "ledger" beam or board is lag-bolted to the frame of the house as described later. This may also serve as a joist when the joists run parallel to the house (Figure 5–3—right). If the joists rest on beams, the beams, of course, are first connected to the house (Figure 5–2).

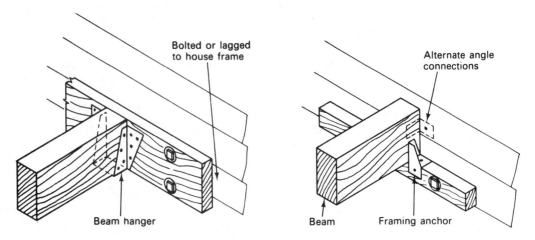

Figure 5-2 Where deck beams run at right angles to the house, they are attached with beam hangers to a header or ledger (left), or they can rest on a bolted ledger with additional support at top from a framing anchor or angle iron (right).

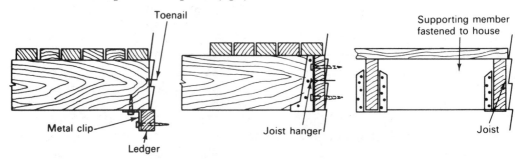

Figure 5-3 Joists connected to the house without beams below can rest on a small ledger, connected with metal clips or angle irons, as at left. Top is toenailed as shown. Better construction is shown at center, with a same-size ledger beam, and supported by a joist connector. Right drawing shows construction with joists running parallel to the house.

When there are no beams, and the joists run perpendicular to the house, they can be attached to a ledger board with joist hangers (Figure 5–3, center), or they can rest on top of a ledger board and be toe-nailed at the top as shown in Figure 5-3, left. Beams and joists are connected to the ledger in the same basic way, except that beams have larger and stronger connectors.

In most cases, the ledger is located about an inch below the inside floor level to allow for drainage away from the house. Inside floor level is easy to determine when using an existing entrance. Simply measure down from the top of the door threshold to the top of the floor. Then transfer this measurement, plus one inch, the height of the step or whatever, to the outside of the house. (See below and Figure 5-4.)

The baseline is a little more difficult to establish when there is no existing door, with the opening to be cut out later. To establish the correct height with

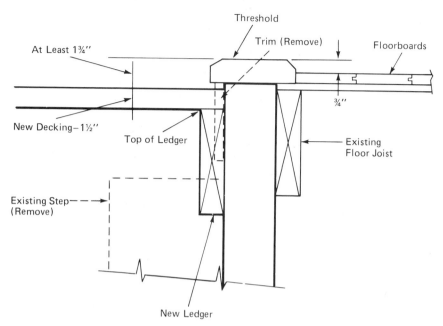

Figure 5-4 To determine height of ledger from door opening, find height from top of floor to threshold, measure same distance down on outside, add one inch for drainage plus height of deckboards (see text).

no door opening, measure down from an existing window to the floor below. Transfer that measurement to the outside of the house, add another inch (or more with steps), then subtract the depth of the deckboard—ordinarily 1-1/2 inches. The top of the joist or beam below the deckboards should be located at this point.

Using a line or regular level, draw or snap a line along the side of the house where the top of the ledger should be. In some cases, you will be able to bolt the ledger to the floor framing of the house. If not, the ledger should be attached to other house framing with lag bolts spaced every two feet. Two-inch lumber requires 3/8 × 4-inch lag bolts. Use 3/8-inch carriage bolts of appropriate length to attach the ledger to the floor framing. Alternate the lag bolts from top to bottom of the ledger.

The ledger should be either a little shorter or a little longer than the actual deck dimension (Figure 5–6). When using joist hangers on the outside joists, you will need about two inches on each side to nail the hangers. If you nail or lag the outside joists or beams to the ledger board on each side, subtract the width of the joist of beam from the desired dimension. In other words, if you nail outside 2 × 8 joists to the ledger, cut the ledger 1-1/2 inches shorter on each end.

Homes that are built of brick, block, or stucco can present special problems. In most cases, you will be unable to nail the ledger board to the side of the house because of the thickness of the masonry. Drill holes every 18 inches to 2 feet in the ledger board and hold the board against the side of the house. Mark

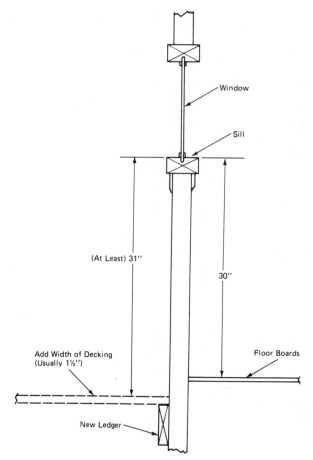

Figure 5-5 When there is no door to measure from, measure up to top of window sill from floor, transfer that to outside, then proceed as with door measurement.

where the holes are with a pencil or punch, then drill holes into the masonry to hold an expansion anchor 3/8 × 4-1/2 inches long. Insert the expansion anchors into the holes and screw expansion or lag bolts through the ledger board into the anchors.

The ledger board is an important structural member and should remain intact for at least as long as the deck. To ensure against rot at this important juncture, it is wise to install aluminum or galvanized flashing above the board.

BEAMS AND JOISTS

Most smaller decks will have only one layer of framing between the posts and the deckboards, as in the example given above. Large decks, or decks with wide spans, may have an intermediate "beam," which is connected to the posts. The joists are then attached to the beam. (The "layers" may be even greater for truly complex structures.)

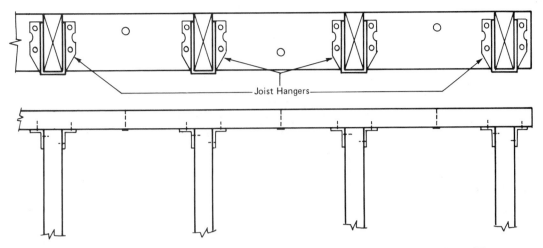

Cut Ledger About 2″ Longer on Each End to Allow Room for Joist Hangers at Outside Joist— OR

A

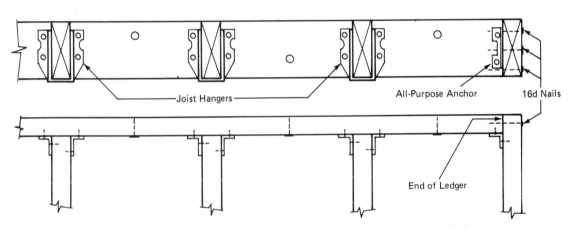

Cut Ledger 1½″ Shorter at Each End to Allow Outside Joist to Butt Against End of Ledger

B

Figure 5-6 When using joist connectors, ledger must be cut either two inches long (A) to allow room for outside connectors, or three inches short (1½″ at each end) when outside joists are nailed into the side of the ledger (B).

In the interest of completeness, each type of construction and its connections is discussed here. Those with simpler, direct joist-to-post construction need not be concerned with the more complicated beam-to-post and post-to-beam details.

Since each deck is different, though, and there may be some of the following connections that apply to yours, you should at least skim through these

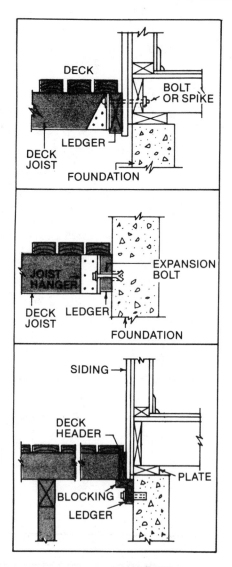

Figure 5-7 With wood siding, ledger is bolted to inside floor frame (top). Center and bottom drawings show means of attaching to concrete and other masonry. See text for details.

pages to see what does and what does not apply. Even simple multilevel decks may use some of the methods described.

If you do have beams, they may be attached to the posts in any one of the ways shown in Figures 5-8 through 5–10. Beams may be a single piece of lumber, usually nominal four-inch lumber, or two pieces of nominal two-inch lumber. The double two-inch beams may be spiked together every 12 inches, or connected on both sides to the post as shown in Figure 5-8.

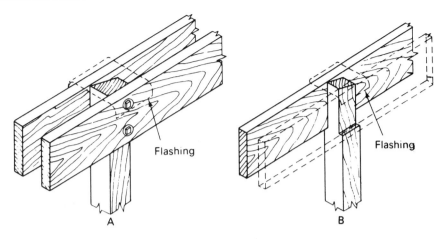

Figure 5-8 Two approved ways to make post connections when a double beam is used. Notching (right) increases beam capacity.

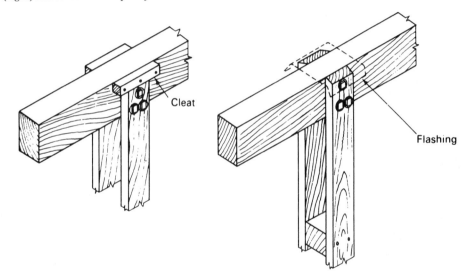

Figure 5-9 Ways to attach double posts to single beams. Flashing and cleats are designed to protect exposed end grain.

Posts also can be connected to the beams on each side as shown in Figure 5-9. This type of construction can be used to attach the various levels of multilevel decks, but should not be employed for posts into the ground.

As you can see in Figures 5-10 and 5–11, various methods can be used to attach the beams to the posts. For attaching nominal four-inch beams or "double joists" with Teco fasteners, use either post-cap or double tie-down anchors, one on each side (Figure 5–10). Other methods (Figure 5–11) are angle irons fastened with lag screws, 1/8 × 3-inch preformed metal straps, or cleats cut from 1 × 4 lumber or 3/4-inch exterior plywood.

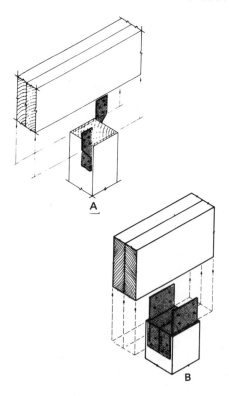

Figure 5-10 Some of the commonly used beam-to-post connections. (A) uses two all-purpose anchors. A single connector is used in (B). Both are available from Teco dealers.

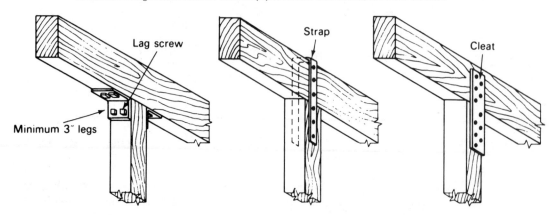

Figure 5-11 Three other approved methods of connecting single beams to single posts.

For metal straps, use 10d ring-groove nails for 4 × 4s, or 1/4-inch lag screws for larger members. Attach wood cleats to both sides of the posts with 8d annular nails. Each framing member should receive 5–6 nails on each side. If the "deformed shank" nails recommended are not available rust-free, use common hot-dipped galvanized.

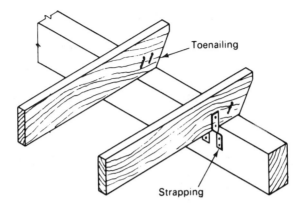

Figure 5-12 Joists are sometimes toenailed, but it is better—and codes may require—use of metal connectors or straps as shown at right.

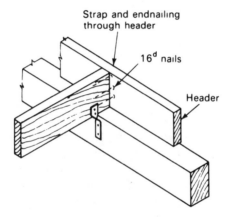

Figure 5-13 When a header is used at the end of a joist on top of a beam, strap the joist to the beam, nail through the header, and overlap the header by half its width to provide a drip edge.

When beams are spaced two to five feet apart and typical deckboards are used, they can be attached without intermediate joists. The beams both support the deckboards and are used to fasten them. In some cases, joists will be needed as a "layer," for extra strength, between the beams and the decking.

There are several ways to attach nominal two-inch joists to larger beams. They may be toenailed, using two 10d nails on each of the joists, and this may suffice for many applications and building codes. Strapping, though, is much stronger, and may be required whenever there are uplift stresses in high wind areas. This is illustrated in Figure 5-12.

Teco connectors, or 24- to 26-gage galvanized strapping, are recommended in addition to toenailing. Attach with 8d galvanized nails. When a header is used at the joist ends, as shown in Figure 5-13, nail the header into the end of each joist and strap it to the beam. Have the header overhang the beam by one half of its width to provide a good drip edge.

Joists located between beams and flush with their tops may be connected in either of two ways (Figure 5–14). A 2 × 3 or 2 × 4 ledger can be spiked to the beam, as shown at the left of the diagram. Joists are cut to fit between the beams, then toenailed to the beams at each end and on top of the ledger. Small metal clips can be used for greater strength.

It is easier, however, to use joist hangers as shown at right in Figure 5-14. The hanger is first nailed to the joist, either with nails provided with the hangers or 8d galvanized nails. (Those with portable drills may find that rust-proof screws work even faster. Screws are quite expensive, though.) The joist is then located in place and nailed to the beam in the same manner.

BRACING

Bracing is not ordinarily required, even on sloping or bumpy terrain, as long as the height of the posts is five feet or less. For higher posts, or when the deck is freestanding, it is good practice to brace the posts to provide lateral resistance. This is not as important when the posts are embedded in the soil and on concrete footings, but it is especially recommended when the posts rest above ground directly on concrete footings or pedestals. Bracing for decks serves the same purposes as bracing in house-framing.

Most decks rely on the stability of the house structure itself. Free-standing decks do not have this advantage, and unless they are on or close to the ground, some type of bracing is required. Horizontal bracing is normally not required, but it is not a bad idea to use galvanized steel bridging between joists, particularly when the deck is a large one. Large, complicated decks should be referred to an architect or engineer to determine what type of bracing, if any, is advisable.

Some of the various ways to brace the posts of a high deck are shown in Figures 5-16 through 5–21. When the posts are eight feet high or less, 2 × 4 lumber is sufficient for braces. Higher posts require 2 × 6s. They should be securely fastened with lag screws or bolts (and washers).

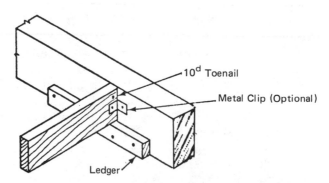

Figure 5-14 When smaller joists are connected flush with the top of larger beams, the easiest way of connecting them is with joist hangers (right). You can also rest the joist on a ledger, toenail and strap as shown at left.

Figure 5-15 A portable drill can be used to drive in rust-proof screws instead of nails when attaching joist hangers. Most people find it faster, and it works especially well in tight corners.

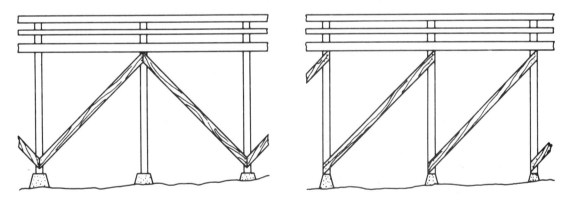

Figure 5-16 Two of the ways to brace high decks up to 14 feet in height.

The "W" type of brace shown in Figure 5-16 (left) is lagged to posts near top and bottom on alternate diagonals, butting against one another at the centerline. A similar method is to use the simpler single braces shown at right, which are just about as strong, but not quite as sturdy-*looking*.

Cross-bracing (Figure 5–17) is even stronger, particularly when the two braces are joined at the center with bolts. For moderate heights, bracing at every other "bay," as shown, is sufficient. High posts should have such braces at each bay.

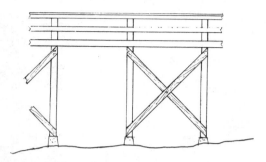

Figure 5-17 Cross-bracing is stronger than the methods shown in Figure 5-16, especially if the braces are joined at the center with bolts.

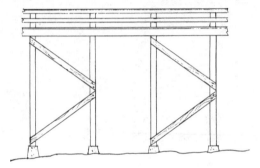

Figure 5-18 Braces over 14 feet in height should be doubled as shown as explained in text.

When the posts are about 14 feet or higher, it is difficult and not very effective to extend the braces from the top to the bottom of the next brace. Double braces, as shown in Figure 5-18, are recommended for very high posts.

Posts that extend five to seven feet above the ground can be strengthened adequately with partial braces such as those shown in Figure 5-19. The plywood gussets shown at left not only serve as braces, but as post-to-beam connectors as well. Use 3/4-inch exterior plywood and several alternating rows of 10d galvanized nails as shown. The top edge of the gusset should be protected by an edge or header member that extends above the plywood.

Dimension lumber (2 × 4s) can also be used for partial bracing, as shown at right in Figure 5-19. It is best to use the braces shown when there are deckboards or other structural members located above the braces. End-grain should not be exposed horizontally to the elements, if it can be at all avoided (see the following paragraph). If there is no alternative, use vertical cuts as shown by the dotted lines.

Braces should be fastened to avoid exposure of the end-grain and to minimize the possibility of trapped moisture at the connection. Figure 5-20 shows two ways of cutting the ends of braces, with the one at the bottom being much superior. Figure 5-21 shows the same relationship with regard to brace joints. The top connection is a good one, but may trap moisture in the tight space

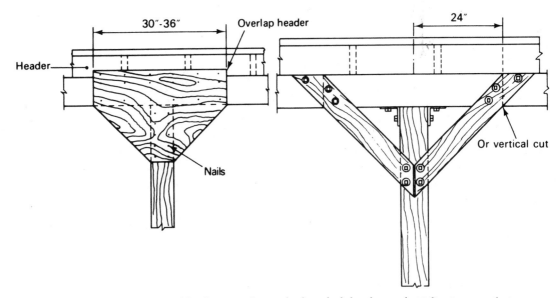

Figure 5-19 Partial braces like these can be used when deck levels are about five to seven feet above ground.

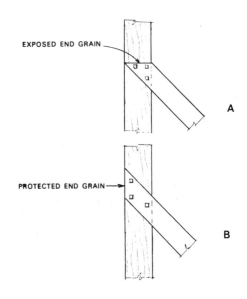

Figure 5-20 The ends of braces should be cut as in (B) to protect the end grain. Do *not* cut as in (A).

between. The slight gap shown in the bottom diagram allows moisture to escape and is less subject to strain from expansion and contraction of the wood.

FASTENING DECKBOARDS

Practically all deckboards are laid flat, or with the long side horizontal. It is possible, and structurally stronger, to lay the deckboards on edge, or vertically.

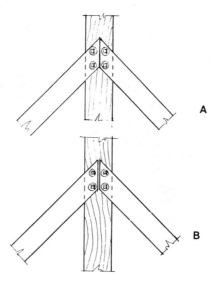

Figure 5-21   When joining braces, allow a slight gap, as in (B), to avoid trapping moisture. Joint A is not a bad one, but B is better.

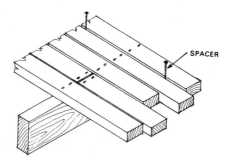

Figure 5-22   The usual method of attaching deckboards, with two nails at each end and joint.

It is even possible to use 2 × 2s, but these structurally weak boards require so much extra bracing they are rarely used. Two-by-three lumber is sometimes laid, too, but it is much more common and sensible to use 2 × 4s, ordinarily laid flat.

No matter what type of deckboards are used, there are certain fundamental rules for fastening them:

• Use hot-dipped galvanized nails or rust-proof screws, flat or oval head. Nail at a slight angle to prevent loosening, or use rust-proof annular or spiral-groove nails if available.

• Use two fasteners at each joint for 2 × 4 or 2 × 3 lumber laid flat. Use one fastener per joint for 2 × 2s or 2 × 3s laid on edge. (Screws *must* be used for 2 × 4s on edge.) The California Redwood Association, however, recommends one fastener only with redwood deckboards at each joint, staggered as shown in Figure 5-23.

- Nail size can be somewhat mystifying. According to general woodworking rules, nails should be three times the size of the wood being nailed. This would mean fastening nominal two-inch deckboards with 4-1/2-inch nails (20d) or larger. But there are other factors such as spacing and wood species. According to the Department of Agriculture, where deckboards are spaced 1/8 inch apart, 8d nails are allowed. If spacing is 1/4 inch use 10d nails; 3/8-inch spacing requires 12d nails. The California Redwood Association recommends 16d for deckboards. When in doubt, this author says to use 12d nails.

- If using screws, they should be three inches long for flat 2 × 4 or 2 × 2 deckboards. For 2 × 3s on edge, use 4-1/2-inch screws or five-inch nails. Five-inch screws are required for 2 × 4s on edge.

- Flat decking should always be laid "bark side up," as discussed on p. 67. That way, when the boards get wet, and a slight crowning or "cupping" occurs, the center of the board will be raised up and drain off the edges. Laid "bark-side-down," any warping will raise the edges, making drainage more difficult.

- All end joints must be made over a joist or beam. When using decking on edge, join ends over a double joist or four-inch beam. Otherwise, use nailing cleats as shown in Figure 5-24.

- Predrill all screwholes and nailholes at the ends of the board. When using dry or dense wood, which tends to split, it may be advisable to predrill all holes, as recommended by the California Redwood Association.

SPACING AND CUTTING DECKBOARDS

As indicated above, spaced deckboards make drainage much easier, and the deck usually looks better. Spacing can be between 1/8 and 3/8 inch. You can stretch to 1/2 inch, but beware of high heels. A 12d nail makes a good spacing

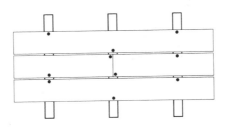

Figure 5-23   The California Redwood Association believes that one 16d nail at each joint permits more natural movement and recommends the pattern shown.

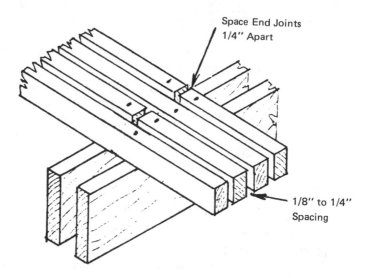

Space End Joints
1/4" Apart

1/8" to 1/4"
Spacing

Figure 5-24 Nailing 2 × 2 or 2 × 3 deckboards on edge. (Screws must be used for 2 × 4s on edge.) Try to have boards meet over double joist as shown. When boards meet over a single joist, nail cleats underneath. There isn't enough nailing room otherwise.

Figure 5-25 Predrilling nailholes avoids splintering, especially at the deckboard ends.

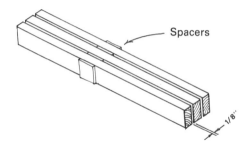

Figure 5-26 On-edge deck is difficult to space, so permanent spacers of tempered hardboard should be used every four feet. Attach with waterproof adhesive.

Figure 5-27 When deckboards are flush with, or extend beyond, the framing, they can be left uncut until the deck is finished. At that time, they can be trimmed neatly and cleanly with a circular saw.

template. Simply place the nail between the deckboards. It's about 3/8 inch wide. If deckboards contain a lot of moisture—as many CCA boards do—it is advisable to butt them together. They will open up as they dry out.

On-edge decking is more difficult to space, and spacers should be permanently attached to the deckboards every four feet to keep the boards vertically aligned. Use tempered hardboard such as Masonite for spacers, and set them in waterproof construction adhesive to prevent water retention.

Deckboards that are laid flush with or beyond outside framing edges can be left uncut until all of them are in place. Waste ends can then be cut off evenly with a circular saw. If you are laying diagonal boards, start with the longest lengths in the center, then work to the outside. Here, you should cut off the longer scraps as you go along, at least in the rough, and use them as you find a shorter place for them.

If the fascia or outside header is level with the top of the deckboards, decking must be cut to fit as you proceed. Examples of this are shown on pp. 102.

6

Railings, Benches, and Stairs

It's starting to look like a real deck! But not quite. What's missing, of course, are all those nice little amenities that lend that touch of class—and comfort. Indeed, if your deck is a high one, it looks (and is) positively dangerous around the edges. What the deck needs at this point are railings or benches.

High decks mandate railings, and strong ones. Very low decks may need nothing to make them safe, but they do look a little bare without something to set them off from the rest of the landscape. Benches, or even planters (Chapter 9), will suffice here.

If the deck is exactly at ground level, you need nothing at all, although there may be a "missing" feeling when you step from the deck to the grass. Usually, some visual setting off of the deck perimeter is required for esthetic reasons.

Any deck edge that exceeds three feet in height *must* be guarded by a railing to prevent injury. Your local code may demand them for even lower heights. Perimeters less than a foot or two don't need railings. Falls from that height will not cause serious injury. Deck edges between one and three feet high may be a safety problem, but any injuries are usually minor. Whether you build railings around this type of deck is a personal and family choice. If you have small children, for example, it may be essential that you build sturdy railings. And always check your building codes.

Figure 6-1 High decks such as this need good, strong railings to prevent falls and make the occupants feel safe.

Figure 6-2 Low-level decks don't really need railings, although they often look naked without something. Here, the bench gives the redwood deck a finished look and provides seating.

Figure 6-3 Seating and railings can be combined, as here. These Wolmanized lamp posts combine lighting and structural support, in addition to serving as railing posts.

When you do have a choice of railings or benches, which do you build? Again, this is a personal choice. You may wish to combine both railings and benches as shown in Figure 6-3, or you may prefer nothing at all. Visually, however, a naked edge, even though it isn't particularly dangerous, makes many people nervous and gives them a feeling of insecurity.

Benches are a nice addition for that in-between position where you have a naked edge that is safe enough, but just a little scary-looking. In that situation, you should build benches with backs, which will further allay that nervous feeling about being on the edge.

Where the deck is really low and doesn't give you qualms about being up in the air, backless benches are the better choice. They provide seating, for one thing. Backs may be more comfortable, but they can also obstruct the view.

On the other hand, when the view may not be so great, as it isn't for the deck shown in Figure 6-4, a closed or lattice railing can serve as a fence. The people who built this deck put it in front of the house, mainly because they wanted to tie two somewhat awkward front entrances together. But the street was quite close, and they wanted to at least partially block it out, without creating a visual barrier. Hence, the use of lattice.

If you intend to use railings, benches, or anything above the deck such as fencing, it is a good idea to design the deck so that the framing posts also serve as supports for the railings (or whatever). This not only saves on materials and

Figure 6-4 This small deck has an attractive lattice railing that doubles as a privacy fence. Note the finials on top of the posts, which lend a nice touch.

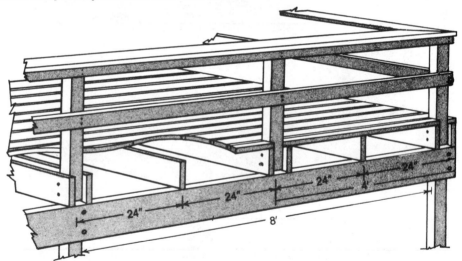

Figure 6-5 Post design that incorporates railing supports with deck structure.

time, but makes it easier to cut the posts off to the proper height. You can cut them while standing on the already completed deck, instead of mid-air.

RAILING POSTS

The key members of a railing are the posts. Posts must be large enough and strong enough to support a lateral load of 20 pounds per linear foot. They must

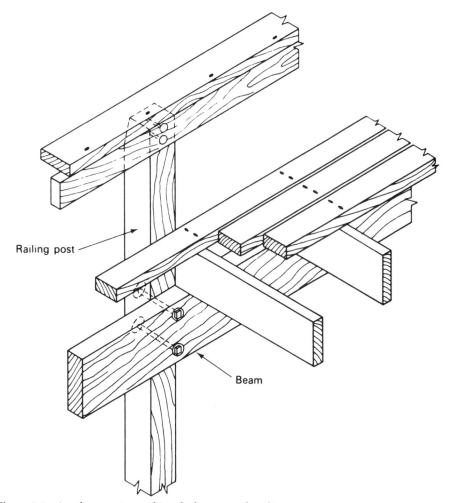

Figure 6-6   Another way to combine deck posts with railing posts.

be rigid and spaced properly to resist such loads. Remember that people often lean, and even sit on, deck railings. Posts are the main supports for the railings and should be designed with care. Unless they can withstand the loads, the rest of the railings are structurally useless and dangerous.

Posts can be extensions of the structural supports as discussed before and can also do additional duty as part of benches or similar edge structures such as fences. Note in the photo (Figure 6-3) that the laminated structural posts serve double duty—and more—supporting deck, railing, bench, lamp, and fence in foreground. Figures 6-6 and 6-7 show how to utilize structural deck posts for railing supports.

Some other ways of attaching railing posts are illustrated in Figures 6-8 and 6-9. Structurally, posts must be spaced no more than four feet apart when 2 × 4s are used for horizontal top rails, or no more than six feet apart when 2 × 6s or larger rails are used. Railing heights vary from 30 to 40 inches, with 36 inches

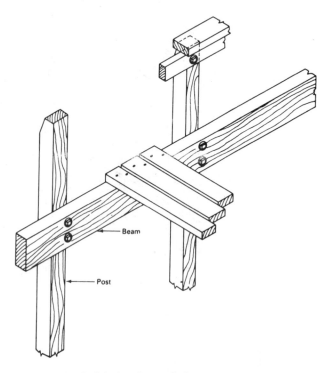

Figure 6-7 Still another method of deck-rail post design.

the norm. If benches or wind screens are also attached, the railings should be higher.

Building codes may specify both the height and maximum openings of deck railings (in addition to a lot else). They should be carefully consulted in this regard as elsewhere. If there is any chance of small children playing on the deck, the deck should be designed so that they will not fall through the openings. This is particularly true for high decks, of course. You may wish to consider temporary measures, though, such as clear plastic, chicken wire, or lattice, which can be removed when the kids grow up or are no longer around.

If the railing posts are not part of the structural posts, they must be self-supporting. When railings run parallel to a joist or beam, one of the methods shown in Figure 6-8 can be used. In the construction shown in A, the posts must be built of 2 × 6 lumber for spans four feet or less, of 2 × 8s or 4 × 4s for spans four to six feet, and from 4 × 6 or 3 × 8 timbers if from six to eight feet apart. Each post should be bolted to the support member with two 3/8-inch or larger carriage bolts.

Smaller, baluster-like lumber is used for posts in the example shown in Figure 6-8B. These are made from 2 × 2s or 2 × 3s spaced from 12 to 16 inches apart. In this type of construction, the top row of fasteners consists of 1/4 inch or 3/8 inch bolts or lag screws. The bottom row can also be bolts or screws, but

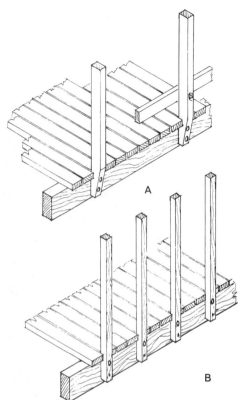

Figure 6-8 Fastening 2 × 6 or larger railing posts to joists of deck with carriage bolts. See text for details.

12d or larger nails can be used, instead, if you prefer. Larger spans or larger posts require two bolts in each baluster.

When either of these railing types are used, a space 1/8 inch to 1/4 inch should be allowed between the ends of the deckboards and the edges of the posts to prevent moisture concentration. Predrill holes as necessary, particularly for the thinner lumber sizes.

If the railing runs at right angles to the joists or beams, one way of attaching the posts is shown in Figure 6-9. A double post is shown, but single posts or balusters can be attached as well. Follow the guidelines above generally for spacing and attaching these posts. Since spacing of the posts will depend on the spacing of the joists and method of attachment, there are no cut and dried rules. When in doubt, make it stronger. Or consult experts as discussed previously.

Some other general rules:

- Don't mount posts on deckboards unless that is the only way you can do it. Posts mounted this way are structurally weak and subject to high moisture concentration where the bottoms of the posts rest on flat deckboard

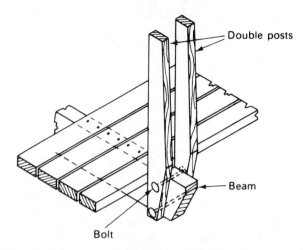

Figure 6-9 When the railing runs at right angles to the joist, the post can be attached as shown, using two bolts at each joint and 2 × 6 lumber.

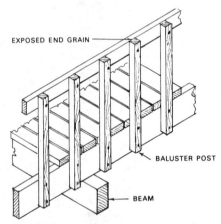

Figure 6-10 Drawing shows how *not* to build baluster-style railings. See Figure 6-11 for improvements.

surface. If you *must* attach the posts this way, use the connectors mentioned in Chapter 2 for better strength.

- Design your railings so that the tops of the posts are covered by the top rail or a cap rail. Here again, the top of the posts expose the end-grain to heavy moisture concentration as shown in Figure 6-10, which is an example of how *not* to build a railing. Also note the inferior connections (all nails) and the squared-off beam end. Figure 6-11 shows how to improve this railing design, with a cap rail over the post tops, bolts instead of nails, and the tapered-under beam end to expose less of its end-grain.

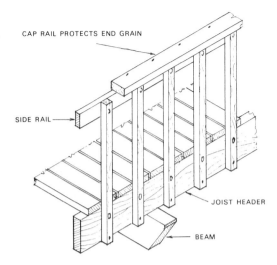

CAP RAIL PROTECTS END GRAIN

SIDE RAIL

JOIST HEADER

BEAM

Figure 6-11 Proper design for baluster-type railings, with suggested improvements described in text.

RAILING CONSTRUCTION

The railings themselves (horizontal braces) are ordinarily built of 2 × 4 lumber. One rail along the top, along with a cap rail, is sufficient for low railings and spans of less than two feet. Higher railings, or spans more than two feet apart, may require another horizontal rail (or more, for high railings).

All the railings may be of 2 × 4s as long as the span between posts is four feet or less. Use 2 × 6s for horizontal members when posts are spaced over four feet apart. Cap rails are usually built of 2 × 4s, but it is not a bad idea to make them of 2 × 6s. Cap rails are often used for setting down plates and drinks, and even sitting—on low decks anyway. Setting them at a slight pitch will allow better rain run-off. Routing or attaching molding at the edges gives the cap a distinctive touch, if you want to bother. Miter the corners for better looks and attachment, and round off sharp edges.

The upper or top rail should always be bolted to the posts. Any other side rails can then be nailed, using two 12d nails at each post. Splices must be made at post centers, which is a problem when using balusters or any lumber less than nominal two-inch. There is not enough room to make a strong connection.

With posts less than two inches wide, the use of a double post (Figure 6-13) at splice points is advised. In addition to providing enough nailing room, using double posts means that the ends of the side rails can be spaced about an inch apart. This allows for faster drying after a rainstorm. If you do go to double posts, plan your work so that all splices can be made at the double post.

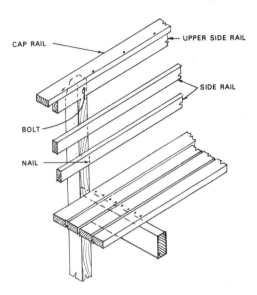

Figure 6-12   Suggested side rail construction for high-level decks. Upper rail should always be bolted to the post. The other side rails can be nailed with two 12d nails at each post. Note cap rails at top.

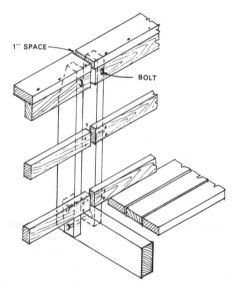

Figure 6-13   When railings are spliced at a post, there isn't quite enough room for the fasteners. It is best to double the posts as shown when splices must be made.

When the cap rail is mounted in addition to a top rail outside of the posts, as shown in most construction here, it is good practice to nail the cap rail into the side rail. Use 12d nails spaced 12 to 16 inches apart. In some designs, however, such as that shown in Figure 6-14, the top rail is attached directly to the top of the post, serving double duty as a cap rail.

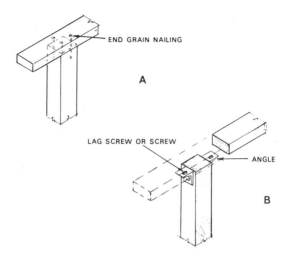

Figure 6-14 It is best to use top rails in addition to a cap rail, but sometimes a cap rail also serves as a top rail. If so, avoid simply nailing into the top of the post (A). Angle irons (B) have better holding power.

If you nail a cap rail directly into the top of the post (A), you will be nailing into end-grain, which is not a good idea. Nails in end-grain usually loosen and fall out in time. It is much better, although more difficult, to use galvanized angle irons or other connectors to attach the cap rail to the post (B). Use 1-1/2-inch lag screws through each hole in the angle iron.

Angle irons or galvanized connectors should also be used when the horizontal railing members are flush with the outside of the posts as shown in Figure 6-15 E and F. Several methods of attaching the rails are shown, with the bottom three (D–F) being the best. Dadoing is ordinarily good joinery, but in exterior work, dadoes form little pockets for collecting moisture. This is not so serious for pressure-treated and other rot-free woods, but it is much better to avoid moisture traps if possible.

If you do use dadoes, the type shown in C is preferred, since there is less chance of moisture collecting at the bottom. Making this type of cut accurately, however, can be difficult and time-consuming. The type of joint shown in D is a good one, as long as the wood block is lagged into the post as depicted. The rail should be spaced slightly away from the post and be screwed into the cleat.

BUILDING BENCHES

Benches are usually built at the perimeter of a deck, but they can be built anywhere, really. When the deck is a large one, benches provide visual distinctions among the various areas, as well as places to sit, relax, converse, or read. They don't necessarily have to be built in. Freestanding benches, though, should be built to blend in with the style of the deck itself.

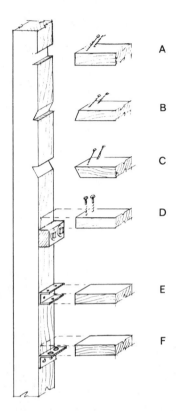

A

B

C

D

E

F

Figure 6-15 Another way to attach rails to posts is to butt them flush with edges. Shown are bad, fair, and good ways of doing this, in descending order, bad at top and best at bottom (see text).

As with railings, benches can be designed to utilize the structural posts as supports. They can be built along with the railings—or instead of them—using the same structural supports. They can be backless or be built with backs that also serve as railings. Planters or other amenities can be built in along with the benches (or railings). The combinations are endless and limited only by your imagination.

Basically, bench design falls into two general categories: high-deck (with back) and low-deck (without a back). There is no reason why you can't use a high-deck style on a low deck, if it looks all right, or vice versa, as long as safety needs are factored in. And there is no reason why you can't alter any design, or start a design from scratch, with the same caveats.

High-Deck Benches

The basic high-deck bench shown in Figure 6-16 is designed to provide both utility and protection. This type is ordinarily built along the perimeter instead of a railing. As can be seen, the back of the bench *is* a railing, and should follow the structural guidelines given for railings.

The backs (vertical supports) of high-deck benches should be spaced no more than six feet apart, and are bolted to the joists or beams in the same way as

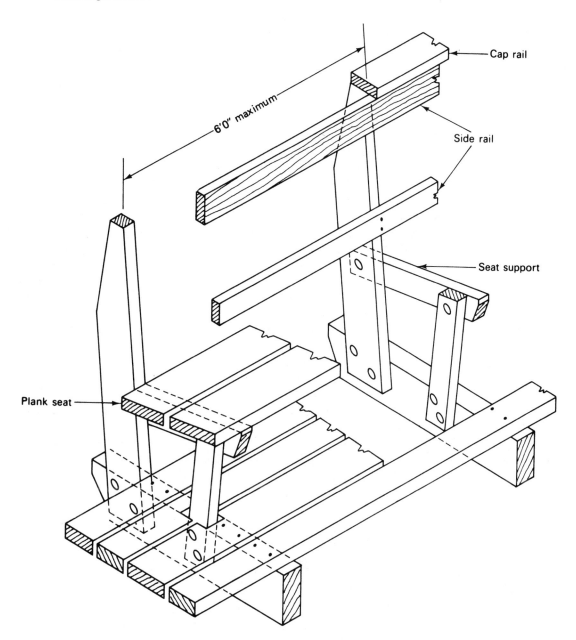

Figure 6-16   Approved construction design for high-level benches.

railing posts. In the design shown, the posts are bolted to extensions of the joists. (See the section above on railing posts for other methods of attaching the posts.) As with railings, the bench posts can be supported by extending the structural deck posts.

Low-Deck Benches

Low benches are also used primarily at the perimeter of the deck, but they can also be used to set off designated areas or provide seating wherever desired. The same or similar design is often adapted as steps between multilevel decks. This design is particularly suited for multiple deck elevations that are from 12 to 16 inches apart.

Since there are minimal safety considerations in this type of construction, the homeowner has a free hand in making his or her own design. Building codes are not ordinarily a factor. You can build low-level benches out of anything, and any way you please. As discussed throughout, the style should blend in with the deck itself. There are some structural considerations to follow, however, if only to ensure that the benches don't fall apart. Here, too, the structural posts can also serve as supports for the benches, if designed that way from the outset. When using nominal two-inch lumber, the maximum span between supports should be six feet.

When fastening benches to the deck, follow the same guidelines as for attaching railing posts above. Again, this is not a critical consideration for low decks, but there is no reason to build in benches that will fall apart. By the same token, rules for spans, fastening, and avoiding exposure of end-grain should be followed as previously described.

Just as for railings, it isn't a good idea to attach the bench posts to the deckboards. Moisture buildup is too often the result. Some methods of attaching low-deck posts are shown in Figure 6-17. At left, the support is a single 2 × 10 in the center of the bench bottom. The design at right uses double 2 × 4 supports. Cleats of 2 × 3 or 2 × 4 lumber are bolted to the posts, and the benches are nailed to the cleats. The benches themselves are usually made of 2 × 6s, although 2 × 4s or 2 × 8s can also be used.

Other bench designs, some with plans and instructions, are shown in Chapter 9. Many of those shown are free-standing, but can easily be incorporated into the structure itself.

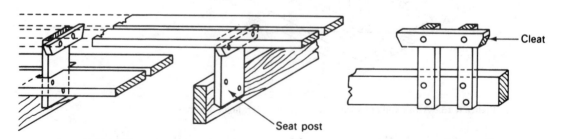

Seat post

Cleat

Figure 6-17   Several of the various ways to build low-level benches. See text and Chapter 10 for more.

Whether your deck is a high or low one, stairways are often needed to get from one level to the next. If the deck is relatively low, stairways can take the form of one or more smaller levels, as shown in Figure 6-18. When proceeding from one section to another of a multilevel deck, the steps between can themselves be in the form of low-level decks.

For low- and multilevel decks, there is a wide latitude in the type of steps leading from the ground or to another level. As long as the steps are sturdy, conform to the style of the deck, and generally follow the non-moisture-trapping tips given for general deck construction, they should be fine. In general, steps for these types of decks should be considerably wider than the steps ordinarily used for stairway construction.

When the deck is high, the only step you might need is the one leading from the house to the deck—if any. This is the case for a privacy deck, for

Figure 6-18 With a multilevel deck, stairs should be wide, and can be in the form of minidecks as shown. (*Courtesy California Redwood Association*)

example, leading off a bedroom, which you intend to reserve for sunbathing, reading, or other types of "quiet time." Very often, however, especially for decks designed for multiple purposes, entertainment, or extensive-use "outdoor rooms," true stairways will be needed to get from the deck to the ground, to a patio, or from one level to the next. This type—a "stairway to the stars," more or less—should be built with greater care in design and execution. Poor construction can, in fact, be dangerous.

In general, such stairways consist of several elements with which you should familiarize yourself. The parts you step on are called "treads," and the treads are connected to side sections called "stringers" (or sometimes "stair carriages"). In general construction, "risers" usually connect the treads with each other. These are the vertical pieces between the treads, but they really have little structural purpose, and are omitted in most exterior designs.

Inside the home, there are usually walls on each side of the stairway, with hand railings on one or both sides. Deck stairways may have a wall on one side, but rarely on both. Instead, to provide safety and support where needed, railings must be built "from scratch." Your stairway may or may not need railings, depending on height from the ground.

Stairway Design

Stairways should be designed to go along with the other aspects of deck design as closely as possible. Use the same type of wood, for example, and adhere to the same type of railing design as for the regular deck railings. Try to use the same size boards for the treads as you do for the deckboards.

If you are fortunate enough to have your plans drawn up by a professional, you don't have to worry about the next section. Just follow your plan. If you already know about tread-to-rise relationship, you can skip this part also. If not, there is a somewhat tedious lesson to be learned.

The relation of the tread width ("run") to the height of the risers (whether actually built or not) is important in determining the number and dimensions of the steps required—which you need to know before building them. This in turn is determined by the total length (total run) of the stairway, which is determined by the total "rise" (see Figure 6-19).

In other words, the first "step" in step-building is to find out the distance between the top of the deckboards to the ground or next level, wherever the stairs lead to. This is the "total rise." For ease of ascent, engineers have determined that the rise of each step times the width (front-to-back measurement) of the tread should total between 72 to 75 inches. Some stretch the ratio to 77 inches total.

For example, when the height of each rise is eight inches, which is maximum for a rise, the stair tread should be nine inches front to back ($8 \times 9 = 72$). When the rise is 7-1/2 inches, the width of the stair tread should be 10 inches (7-1/2 $\times$ 10 = 75).

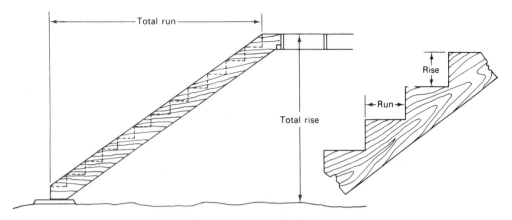

Figure 6-19 "Run," "rise," and "total" for each.

Exterior stairs are usually a little wider in tread and lower in rise, if possible. The ratio is often more like 7:11 (77 total) or 6:12 (72), but this can be difficult to achieve. When you use six-inch risers, for example, you greatly extend the "run" and may run out of room. Here's how it works.

The first thing you have to do is determine the total rise, which you do by measuring from the top of the deck to approximately the place where the stair will end. In Figure 6-19, for instance, assume that the total rise is 100 inches. To achieve an ideal outside stair tread of 12 inches, you have to divide 100 by 6 (the other half of the 6 × 12 = 72 ratio). Dividing 100 by 6, you get almost 17 (steps). Each step is 12 inches, which means that the total distance from the front of the top step to the front of the bottom step (total run) is 232 inches, or almost 17-1/2 feet. That's a long stairway, and impossible if there is a wall or some other obstruction in the way.

You can try some other combination, beginning with eight-inch risers, the maximum. But we can tell you that the best combination for a high stairway like this is a 7-1/2-inch rise and a 10-inch tread (75 multiplied). This comes out just a little less than 13 steps. That's a better number than most of the others (if you aren't superstitious).

Therefore, for a rise of 100 inches, we opted for 13 steps, with each riser 7-1/2 inches high, and each tread 10 inches in width (7.5 × 10 = 75). Since you now know that your risers will be 7-1/2 inches and your treads 10 inches wide, you also know that the total run will be 120 inches. (You count from the front of the top step, which means you deduct it from the total.)

Now that the math is all done, we can get on with building the darn things.

Stringers

All stairways are built with stringers as the main support. They are built in pairs before attachment and should be three feet or less apart. Normally, 2 × 12s are used for stringers, but 2 × 10s are adequate for narrow and shorter stairways. To determine the length of the stringers, lay out the dimensions of the total rise and run, then measure the distance between the top of the deckboards and the bottom of the lowest stair. This hypotenuse is the length of the stringer. (If it's easier, measure the actual distance.)

Stringers can be dadoed or notched as shown in Figure 6-20, which is commonly done for inside stairs. It is easier, and better outside construction, to leave the stringers as is and use cleats as shown in Figure 6-22 and discussed later.

Stringers must be well secured to the framing of the deck. They are normally supported by a ledger (Figure 6-21, left) or by bolting to an extension of a joist or beam (Figure 6-21, right). At left, the stringer is notched at the bottom and rests on a 2 × 3 or 2 × 4 ledger. The stringer is attached to the ledger with small metal clips or by toenailing. It is also toenailed to the joist or beam at the top. When attaching to a beam or joist extension as shown at right, use at least two 1/2-inch bolts for fastening each stringer.

The bottoms of the stringers should be anchored to a solid base, such as a slab or concrete, and be isolated from sources of possible moisture. This can be done by metal anchors thick enough to raise the stringer off the concrete. Another method is to bolt the stringer to pressure-treated wood rated for contact with the ground.

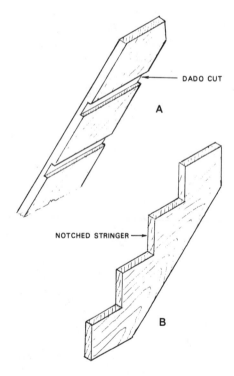

Figure 6-20 Typical indoor stair stringers are either dadoed or notched. Avoid this for outdoor stairways.

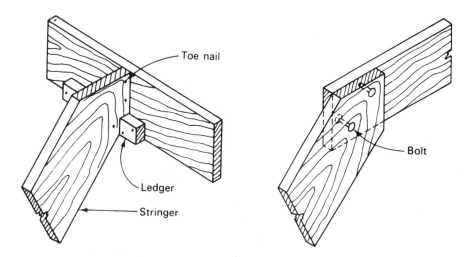

Figure 6-21 How to attach stringers to the deck. At left is detail for attaching to right-angle joist; at right, attachment for parallel joists.

Tread Supports

Notching and dadoing commonly provide tread support for indoor stairs. Both methods, however, expose end-grain and trap moisture. While this is not a major problem with decay-resistant woods, it is better and easier to use tread supports as shown in Figures 6-22 and 6–23.

The cleats (or ledgers) are made from 2 × 4 lumber and extended to form tread supports in Figure 6-22. The cleats can be sloped back gently to allow better drainage. The diagram above left shows single 2 × 10s or 2 × 12s attached to the supports with three 12d nails or three-inch screws at each stringer.

Since wider boards are subject to warping, the drawing below right shows a somewhat better method. Here, two treads, with a space between, are substituted for a single tread. This type of tread, however, must not be used on wide spans, especially if 2 × 4s form the treads. When using 2 × 6s, do not exceed 42 inches in width.

Another method for attaching cleats is shown in Figure 6-23. This is simpler, if not as attractive, and should be used only with decay-resistant woods. Here, cleats are attached to each stringer with three or four nails, and the treads are nailed directly to the cleats with no extension.

If there will be no interference with railings on either side, the cleats in Figure 6-22 can be bolted to the outside of the stringers, as well as the inside. Do this, however, only when the spans are relatively small.

Stairway Railings

As previously mentioned, railings are necessary when there are unprotected sides of a stairway and are required by most building codes, if not by common

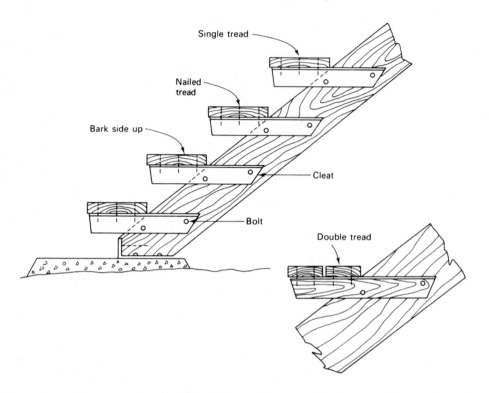

Single tread

Nailed
tread

Bark side up

Cleat

Bolt

Double tread

Figure 6-22 The approved method for outdoor stair construction is to use cleats, with treads nailed to both sides. Even better, since it minimizes warping, is the double-tread shown at right. Note steel plate at bottom, which protects end-grain from concrete.

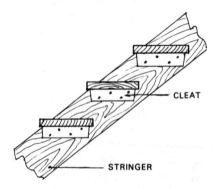

CLEAT

STRINGER

Figure 6-23 Cleats can also be nailed to inside of stairs with rot-resistant wood. Treads go directly on top.

sense. Wherever possible, they should be similar to the deck railings in design and construction.

A few examples are shown in Figures 6-24 and 6-25. Figure 6-24 shows 2 × 4 posts for spacing three feet or less. Three by fours or 2 × 6s are used for spacing three to six feet. The other members are built of 2 × 4s. Bolt or lag screws should be used at all joints.

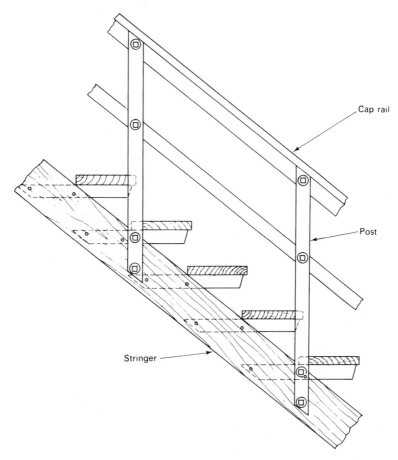

Figure 6-24 Stairway railings are built similar to regular railings. With 2 × 4 posts, spacing should be three feet or less.

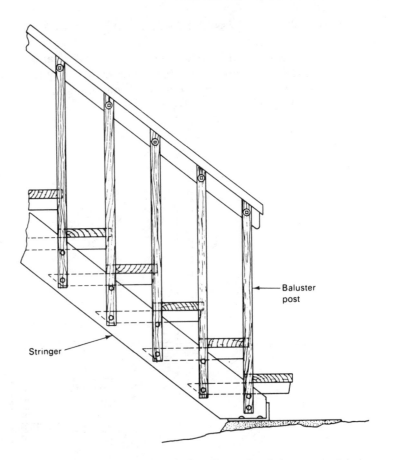

Figure 6-25 Balusters can be used, also, as in deck railings. One baluster per stair is usual construction.

Figure 6-25 shows baluster construction, with one at each step. Follow the same general rules as with the techniques discussed under regular railing construction. Balusters should be bolted at both top and bottom.

Single cap rails can be used at the top of either type of railing, instead of the side rail plus cap, but here too, it is best to attach the cap with clips or angle irons to avoid unreliable end-nailing.

7

Low-Level Designs and How to Adapt Them

We've stated before that the best way to design a deck is to call on a professional to devise the best possible layout for your particular site and needs. When you can afford it, a landscape or house architect, or a well-experienced contractor, will design a deck that is particularly suited to you and your family. While true, this also takes quite a chunk out of your building budget.

There are a lot of people (such as freelance writers) who can't afford this type of help, however. If you're reasonably skilled at construction, and have a good eye for what does and does not fit into the landscape, you can do the designing and building yourself. Or you can perhaps do one or the other.

In any case, it helps to have some sort of model to start with, something to study and either copy step by step or adapt to your own specifications. This chapter outlines several plans for low-level decks, with at least general instructions, for copy or adaptation. For specifics on connections, hardware, etc., not shown in the plans, refer to previous chapters. (Plans for high-level, multilevel, or some other types of decks are given in the following chapter.)

There may be nothing here to help you, or there may be something exactly suited to your needs. Those who already have a specific plan in mind may wish to skip these chapters entirely, but you may just find some tips that will prove helpful. If you're still looking for a type of deck that is just right for you, and

Figure 7-1   The bare walls, dull grass, and ugly stoop of this house badly needs something to spruce it up. Redwood deck in "after" photo does the job.

have only a vague plan in mind, we suggest that you at least browse through this and the next chapter for some ideas.

As mentioned in the previous chapter, the precautions suggested for avoiding end-grain exposure, moisture-trapping, etc., are not as vital when using pressure-treated, redwood, or other weather- and insect-repellent woods. Some of these plans were themselves adapted from wood manufacturers or organizations that represent them. If you are not using this type of lumber yourself, it is wise to follow the recommendations in the previous chapter, and adapt the plans as suggested there.

SIMPLE, LOW-LEVEL PLANS

The low-level plans shown on these pages are very versatile. Most can be built either attached or freestanding. They can be easily modified to a gently rolling landscape or as a section of a multilevel deck. Some types can be combined, although the previous cautions about keeping the same general style should still be kept in mind.

The deck shown in Figures 7-1 through 7-6 can be built by anyone but a rank amateur at construction. Note how it transforms the dull backyard into a pleasant spot, ideal for barbecuing, among other pursuits. The plans shows the deck attached to the house, but you can make it freestanding, part of a multilevel, or whatever.

As shown, this deck is built of redwood. Construction heart-grade redwood is used for the framing, with construction common grade for the deckboards. (You can see the difference for yourself in the photos. The deckboards contain streaks of light-colored sapwood, the framing members don't.)

This sample plan is for a 10 × 12 foot area, using 4 × 4 posts attached to precast pedestals. For the attached deck shown, five pedestals are needed, one at each outside corner, one at the center of the ouside edge, and one each along the sides at the halfway point between the house and outside corner. For a freestanding deck, add three more piers—two each at the inside corners, and one in between—and eliminate the bolted ledger.

In the version shown, a 2 × 12 ledger is attached to the house. On both deck sides, 2 × 12 "skirtboards" (outside headers) are lagged either to the pedestals, as shown in the photos, or to the posts, as shown in the plan, depending on height and grade. Then, 2 × 6 joists are attached to the ledger and the outside skirtboard using joist hangers.

The joist hangers are set far enough below the skirtboard to allow for the deckboards to line up level with the top of the 2 × 12s. In this case, nominal 2 × 4 redwood was used for deckboards, so the joists were located 1-1/2 inches below. Along the side skirtboards, 2 × 4 ledgers are bolted, also 1-1/2 inches below the top. Figure 7-4 shows a handy tip. Instead of measuring down for each joist or side ledger, use a scrap of deckboard to determine the correct

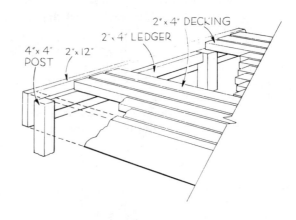

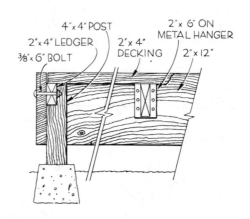

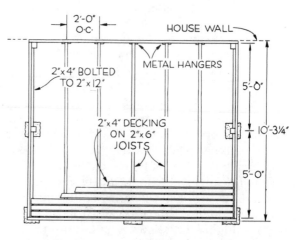

Figure 7-2 Plan shows deckboards over top of posts and inside "skirtboards" (outside headers).

Figure 7-3 In this construction, where deck is close to the ground, skirtboards are attached directly to the wooden inset of the pedestals.

Figure 7-4 Joists are attached to skirtboards with hangers, leveled and plumbed. Easy way to position joists to leave room for decking is to use a piece of deckboard for measuring.

height. Simply scratch or draw a line along the bottom of the deckboard and attach to the top of the joists at that line.

As noted in the plan, joists are spaced two feet apart, with deckboards running at right angles to the joists. Since deckboards here go inside the skirtboards, they must be cut before nailing. Space deckboards with a 16d nail, also used for fastening. With this type of small, spaced-board deck, it isn't really necessary to allow for drainage, but it's never a bad idea. Allow 1/8 inch per running foot, away from the house.

ADAPTING—AN EXAMPLE

Just to show how adaptation works, let's change the dimensions of the previous deck to a slightly smaller size (roughly 8 × 10 feet) and also make it freestanding, instead of attached to the house. The style and general construction techniques are the same.

Note that, with the eight-foot dimension, we have been able to eliminate the extra set of pedestals and/or posts along the shorter sides. If this deck were attached to the house, you'd need only three, instead of six, pedestals.

MATERIALS LIST—8 × 10 FREESTANDING DECK

Description	Quantity	Size	Length
Construction heart redwood			
Posts	6 pieces	4 × 4	varied
Skirtboard	2 pieces	2 × 12	10 feet
Skirtboard	2 pieces	2 × 12	8 feet
Ledgers	2 pieces	2 × 4	8 feet
Joists	4 pieces	2 × 8	8 feet
Construction common redwood			
Deckboards	26 pieces	2 × 4	10 feet
Other materials			

Quantity	Description
1 lb.	16-penny nails
8	2 × 8 joist hangers
10	3/8 × 6-inch lag screws
10	3/8 × 6-inch carriage bolts, washers and nuts
6	Concrete footings with nailing blocks

Figure 7-5 Ledgers are bolted deckboard-width to the skirtboards, and decking is cut to size before installation, since it goes inside skirtboard.

Figure 7-6 Nail deckboards to joists after predrilling. The California Redwood Association recommends one 16d nail for each joint.

135

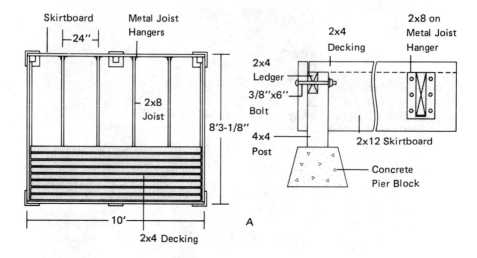

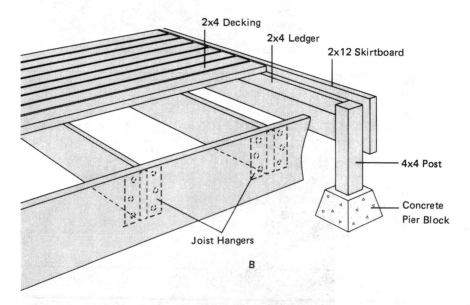

Figure 7-7 Adapting the previous plan to a smaller, freestanding deck. Note that the two intermediate pedestals along the sides have been eliminated, but three more piers along the edge have been added to make deck freestanding. Thicker joists are needed because of longer span.

Furthermore, we have lost two side pedestals, which bore some of the weight of the deck and its "live load." Since there is now a wider span for each joist, we will use 2 × 8s instead of 2 × 6s. That makes up for the lost pier support (pier pressure?).

To build this particular deck, you will need the materials shown in the accompanying Materials List. Keeping in mind the general instructions in the previous chapters, here are the steps to building this deck:

- Lay out and measure for placement of the concrete piers and footings (if necessary). Attach the posts to the piers and cut the posts to height. Since the deckboards are laid on top of the posts, allow 1-1/2 inches extra for them (cut them 1-1/2 inches below the final height).
- Note that the plan shows the side dimensions measuring a little more than eight feet—8 feet 3 inches to be exact. That's because the 10-foot front and side skirtboards overlap them at each end. Add 1-1/2 inches for the width of these two boards, and you add another three inches to the dimension. Measure the eight-foot boards to see if they are exactly eight feet, which is rarely the case. Cut them to size, if necessary.
- Although you can attach the 2 × 4 side ledgers later, it is easier to nail them before the skirtboards are attached. Cut and attach the 2 × 4s 3-1/2 inches less on each side than the skirtboards, since they butt up against the posts, and the skirtboards do not. Also, set the 2 × 4s 1-1/2 inches below the top of the skirtboard, so that the top of the decking will be level with the top of the skirtboards. (Use a scrap piece of deckboard to measure as shown in Figure 7-4.)
- Use five 3/8 × 6-inch carriage bolts to attach each 2 × 4 ledger to the side skirtboards. Put one each about 2 inches from the ends, and the other 3 about 27 inches apart. Attach the eight-foot skirtboards to the posts with 3/8 × 6-inch lag screws, one at each post. Lag in the two 10-foot skirtboards, overlapping the ends of the other skirtboards.
- Attach joists to front and back skirtboards on 24-inch centers, using metal joist hangers at each end. These should also be attached a deckboard width below the top of the skirtboards to leave room for the 2 × 4s.
- Cut the ten-foot 2 × 4s to exactly nine feet nine inches (or a trifle less), and lay these deckboards on the joists. Determine the best spacing when the outside pieces are aligned exactly along the inside of the skirtboards. When everything looks right, attach the decking with 16d nails. Predrill holes at the end of each board to prevent splitting. Nail at a slight angle for better holding power.

PARQUET DECKS

Parquet decks are almost infinitely adaptable. They can be laid out by themselves on level or slightly sloping ground, in a random pattern, in a neat arrangement on a separately constructed framework, put down as a pathway, between different levels, or be used as the floor of a high deck (with a proper understructure, of course).

Figure 7-8 Parquet decks are useful anywhere and are especially nice around the pool.

One of the nice things about parquets is that you can build the components during the cold months and rainy days, and save them up for good weather. Once you've built the parquets, they can be laid down quickly to form a beautiful deck.

There are many ways to build a parquet deck, and the variety leaves your imagination free to explore, expecially if you build each parquet as an independent unit. They can then be put down directly in a bed of sand or gravel. You can more or less freelance your way as you go along, adding a unit here and there, skipping shrubbery in between, going up or down in grade, and so on. This type of construction, however, must be made completely of rot-free materials, since there is a lot of ground contact.

Making uniform parquet units is a little trickier than it looks. One way of ensuring uniform dimensions is to build a framing jig, as shown in Figure 7-9. These are made three-feet square (A) or two or four foot (B) in the examples, but the same principles apply to any size units.

The problem arises when you attempt to have the same spacing between units. If you butt all the deckboards against the ends of the jig, there will be no spaces between adjoining units. This is okay, construction-wise, but the parquets look better when they are spaced the same way at the edges as the rest of

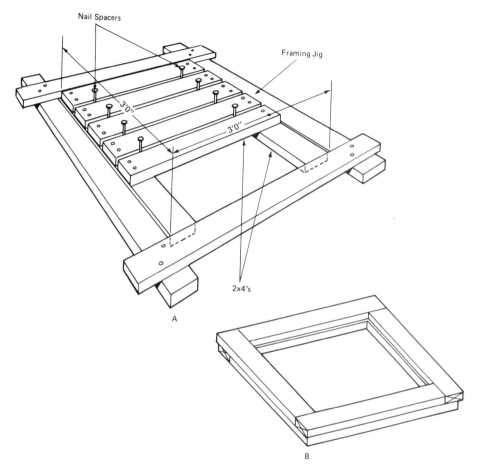

Figure 7-9 Two different kinds of nailing jigs for parquet decks. You can choose among several sizes, as discussed in the text.

the deckboards. The problem is compounded by the nominal vs. actual size situation discussed at length in prior chapters.

A 2 × 4, as we all know very well by now, is actually 1-1/2 by 3-1/2 inches. (There are exceptions, so it doesn't hurt to measure and be sure.) To further complicate the problem, a popular lumber for making parquets is "5/4" or radius-edge decking, so-called because it is slightly rounded at the edges. These nominal 1-1/4 × 6-inch boards (hence 5/4) are actually 1 inch thick and 5-1/2 inches wide.

Figure 7-9A shows nine 2 × 4 deckboards (9 × 3-1/2 inches) for each three-foot unit, but there is actually only 31-1/2 inches of wood, with 4-1/2 inches left for spacing. The simplest spacing is to allow 1/2 inch between each board. (This is, truthfully, a little wider than recommended, since half-inch spacing may catch high heels and be tripped over more easily than the preferred 1/8 inch–3/8 inch, but it's the only practical way to work out this spacing.)

But you also want 1/2-inch spacing between the end boards of each unit, which means that the outside deckboards will have to be spaced half that distance, or 1/4 inch from the edges, so that there will be a total of 1/2 inch when they abut each other. That also means that the length of the deckboards should be 35-1/2 inches, not 36 inches, to allow 1/4-inch spacing at each end (for 1/2-inch spacing when these two abut each other).

This sounds more complicated than it really is (honest). If you'd like to keep the same spacing all around, the best way to comprehend is to build a couple of units and butt them together. You'll see that it works out.

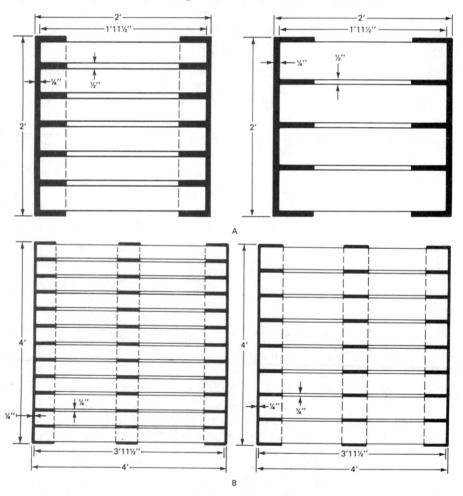

Figure 7-10 How to lay out parquet units for Jig A in Figure 7-9. The two-foot units in layout A can accommodate six 2 × 4s or four 2 × 6s. The four-foot jigs can also be used for 2 × 4 or 2 × 6 parquets.

In any case, the best way to build individual parquets is to make one of the framing jigs illustrated. The inside diameter of jig A is made of 1-inch lumber exactly 36 inches on each side. Cut the two supporting frames of 2 × 4s, exactly 36 inches long, and butt these against the inside of the jig. Cut your deckboards (35-1/2 inches), and lay them out with 1/4 inch all around and 1/2 inch between. Nail the deckboards to the frames with 8d nails, set the unit aside, and start another. Keep going until you have as many parquets as you need.

Jig B is designed for use with either 2 × 4s or 5/4 × 6 lumber, and can be adapted for squares 2 × 2 or 4 × 4 feet. See the accompanying charts for making the frames, using four pieces each for both the upper and lower frames. The top larger frame is designed to give you a shelf of 1/4 inch all around for easier alignment. You don't have to measure each time.

With this framing jig, the deckboards are cut and placed upside down in the smaller bottom frame, then the stringers (two for 2 × 2 squares and three for 4 × 4s) are set at right angles along the edges of the top frame, and nails are driven through the stringers into the deckboards. See the charts and diagrams for further information. Again, this sort of thing is easier to do than explain. Just try it, and we think it'll work out.

Parquets in a Frame

This is somewhat a misnomer, since the word "parquet" implies individual units. But the deck looks like a parquet deck, and is built in much the same way. The deck must be level in this situation, so either find level ground, or regrade to make it level. If you want to build a similar deck on sloping ground, you will have to provide posts and other support for it, as described in previous chapters.

Figure 7-11 shows a deck 10-foot square. The squares are 30 inches o.c. in the diagram, but can be altered as you desire. To build a larger or smaller deck, add or deduct squares as necessary.

Again, we have a problem with edges, as described previously. If you have ever built a wall, you know that the outside studs are moved in by half the width of the stud, because you are measuring from the outside edge to the center, instead of from center to center.

In the construction shown here, the edge frames are brought in 1-3/8 inches on each side to allow for half the width of the framing members. If you didn't do this, you'd have the outside parquets landing on the center of the outside frame, instead of going to the edge. (Most of us have had the experience of putting up drywall or paneling on a newly built wall and finding that the edges wind up in the center of the end studs, instead of butted against the adjoining wall. This is a similar problem.)

The actual distance *between* the boards as shown in Figure 7—11, is 26-1/2 inches for the middle parquets (30 inches o.c.) and 24-3/4 inches at the edges. For skeptics, the only answer is to try out both ways and see what happens.

MAKING FRAMING JIGS FOR 2 × 2
AND 4 × 4 SQUARES

Materials for the jigs

	For 2′×2′ Block		For 4′×4′ Block	
Type of deckboards	2″×4	5/4″×6″	2″×4″	5/4″×6″
Bottom frame (4)	2′3″	2′4 1/8″	4′3″	4′ 4 1/8″
Top frame (4)	2′3 1/2″	2′4 7/8″	4′3 1/2″	4′ 4 7/8″

Materials for each parquet

	For 4′×4′ Block		For 2′×2′ Block	
Type of deckboards	2″×4″	5/4″×6″	2″×4″	5/4″×6″
Deckboards				
Length	1′11 1/2″	1′10 3/4″	3′11 1/2″	3′10 3/4″
Number	6	4	12	8
Stringers				
Length	2′0″	1′11 3/8″	4′0″	3′11 3/8″
Number	2	2	3	3
Approx. spacing	1/2″	3/8″	1/2″	3/8″

All number sizes nominal.

For the 10 × 10-foot deck in the diagram, cut five 10-foot rails out of 2 × 4 stock and lay them flat. Cut ten pieces 26-1/2 inches long and toenail them between the three center rails with 8d nails. Cut ten more pieces 24-3/4 inches long and use them between the end and adjacent rails. If you are laying the frame anywhere but directly on ground level, use angle irons or some similar strong hardware to attach these.

Cut the deckboards into 30-inch sections (128 of them for the 10 × 10 deck shown). Attach to the frame with 12d nails. As shown, there are eight deckboards for each parquet, using a 12d nail for even spacing.

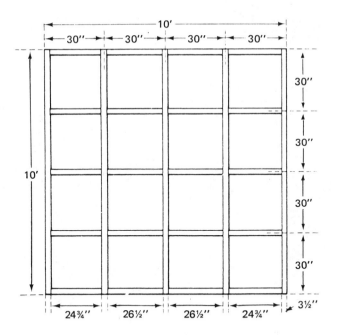

Figure 7-11 Framing a solid deck made of 30 × 30 inch parquets.

DECK OVER CONCRETE

Concrete makes a decent enough patio, but plain "gray" concrete gets a little boring after awhile and often cracks badly or deteriorates in time. One way to improve the looks of your backyard is to cover the concrete with a wooden deck. This redwood deck is a relatively easy deck to build, mainly because the concrete itself provides the support system for the deck. If it fits your plan, a similar design can be used for matching cabinets, counter top, bench planters, and windscreen (Figure 7-12).

It is theoretically possible to simply nail deckboards to the concrete, but the concrete must be completely level, which it rarely is. When concrete has been recently poured, special masonry nails can be pounded in fairly easily, but nailing can be devilish when the concrete ages and hardens completely. Furthermore, you'll need a large number of expensive masonry nails to attach the individual deckboards to the concrete.

To avoid all of these problems, "sleepers" are used between the concrete and deckboards. These flat-laid 2 × 6s or 2 × 8s are attached to the concrete on 24-inch centers, preferably at right angles to the house for better drainage.

There are several ways to attach wood to concrete, with masonry nails probably the worst (unless the concrete is freshly laid, which is unlikely in this instance). The easiest and fastest method is to rent a power hammer (Figure 7-14) from a local rental agency. Follow the directions that come with the tool.

Figure 7-12 A deteriorated concrete patio is transformed into an attractive deck with garden-grade redwood.

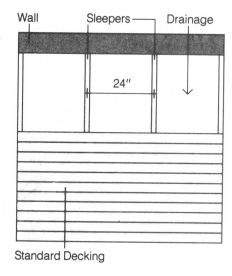

Wall Sleepers Drainage

24"

Standard Decking

Figure 7-13 The plan for a deck over concrete is simple, since the concrete provides a solid base. Heartwood "sleepers" are laid on two-foot centers.

Figure 7-14 Use a power hammer to nail sleepers to concrete.

You can use short lengths of wood for sleepers, if you want, since the structural strength of the deck is supplied by the concrete. Lay the sleepers in place and check them for level. If the slab is cracked or uneven, you may have to shim under them as shown in Figure 7-15. Use rot-resistant lumber for all sleepers and shims.

When the sleepers are leveled and firmly attached to the concrete, all that remains is to lay the deckboards and trim. In the photos, the two-level patio was made into a two-level deck, using diagonal deckboards. When laying deckboards diagonally, it is a good idea to start in the center with the longer boards, cutting them as you go along, then using the scraps near the edges. Use 12d nails for decking here, since longer nails will only hit the concrete.

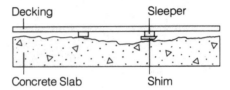

Figure 7-15 Level the sleepers, if necessary, with shims, also rot-resistant heartwood (or CCA).

Figure 7-16 Construction common (garden-grade) redwood 2 × 6 lumber is laid diagonally here. Start with the longest boards in the center, using scraps cut off later at the edges.

In the photos, "garden-grade" construction, common, and merchantable grades were used for the decking, borders, and steps. Deckboards are 2 × 6s, with 2 ×8 lumber used for most of the fascia boards.

FREE-FORM DECK

You're on your own for this type of deck. A free-form deck can be beautiful, but it may turn out pretty badly, too. There is something very graceful about a deck with long, curving edges, and it is ideal for a site with casual landscaping. You can design a deck that fits right into the setting without disturbing any more of the shrubbery than you want to (Figure 7-18).

The best advice we can offer is to study the design shown here, then adapt it as necessary. The basic features of construction are shown, with some sections for further guidance. If the plan shown fits pretty well into the site you have in mind, it's rather easy to build. It can be altered, of course, anyway you see fit, but there are no guarantees that it will look good or be properly framed.

Those with a good feeling for design and some skills at filling in construction detail should feel free to make their own adaptations. Those without

Figure 7-17 Completed deck and accessories make a pleasant spot to spend leisure days.

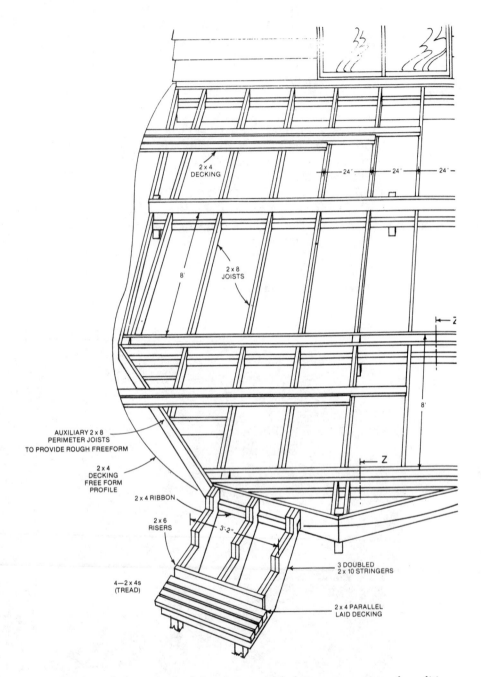

Figure 7-18 Free-form deck can be copied as is, or modified to meet a variety of conditions. Follow the same general techniques used here for adaptation, but don't go too high with a freelance job like this.

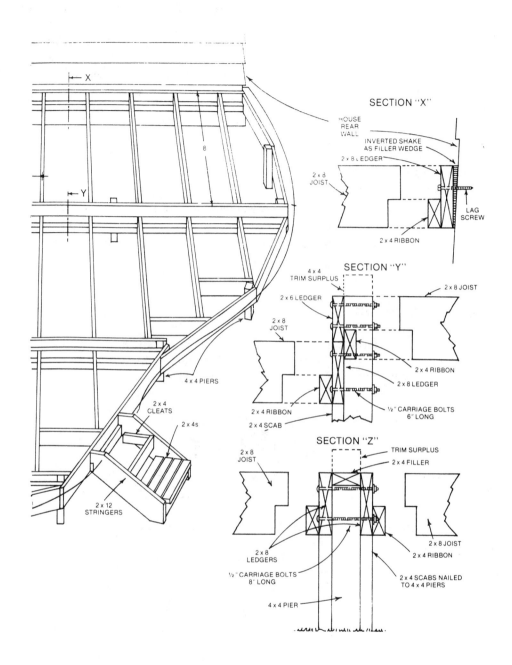

SECTION "X"

HOUSE REAR WALL

INVERTED SHAKE AS FILLER WEDGE

2 x 8 LEDGER

2 x 8 JOIST

LAG SCREW

2 x 4 RIBBON

SECTION "Y"

4 x 4 TRIM SURPLUS

2 x 6 LEDGER

2 x 8 JOINT

2 x 8 JOIST

2 x 4 RIBBON

2 x 8 LEDGER

2 x 4 RIBBON

2 x 4 SCAB

½" CARRIAGE BOLTS 6" LONG

SECTION "Z"

2 x 8 JOIST

TRIM SURPLUS

2 x 4 FILLER

2 x 8 LEDGERS

2 x 8 JOIST

2 x 4 RIBBON

½" CARRIAGE BOLTS 8" LONG

2 x 4 SCABS NAILED TO 4 x 4 PIERS

4 x 4 PIER

X

Y

8

4 x 4 PIERS

2 x 4 CLEATS

2 x 4s

2 x 12 STRINGERS

should probably stick to a more basic design. Free-form decks allow a lot of artistic license, which is good—if you're good at it. By the same token, a free-form deck can wind up poorly supported or just plain ugly. You've been warned.

For the 16 × 20-foot deck shown, the following materials are needed. All numbers are approximate, depending on terrain:

- 12 4 × 4 posts, length to fit
- 30 2 × 8 × 12 feet joists
- 96 2 × 4 × 16 feet decking
- 112 lin. ft. 2 × 4 "ribbon" board (small ledgers)
- 24 lin. ft. 2 × 6 ledger board
- 112 lin. ft. 2 × 8 ledger board
- stair stringers, risers, etc. to fit

OTHER LOW-DECK DESIGNS

By now, you should have a pretty good idea as to how a low-level deck is put together. We devote the last pages of this chapter to several more adaptable designs, which are pretty much self-explanatory.

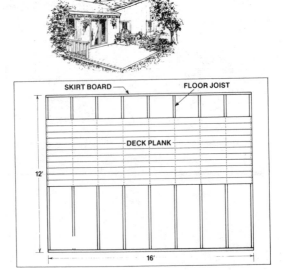

Figure 7-19 A very simple, but good-looking deck, which is easy to build. This patio deck can go directly on the ground, being made of Wolmanized wood, but it can be raised up, too, as shown in Figure 7-20.

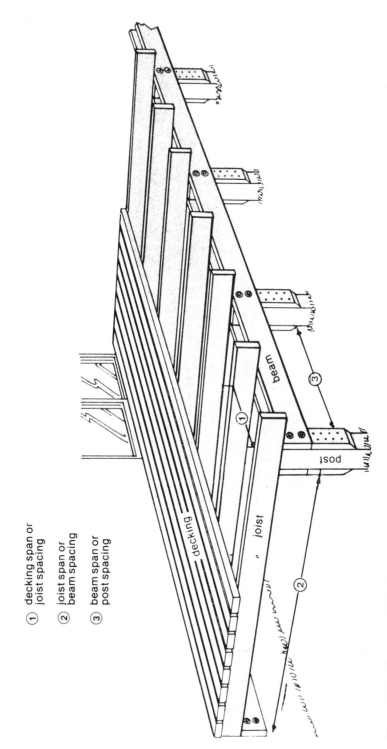

① decking span or
   joist spacing

② joist span or
   beam spacing

③ beam span or
   post spacing

decking

joist

beam

post

Figure 7-20 The same deck as Figure 7-19, but raised up off the ground on 4 × 4, cleated posts.

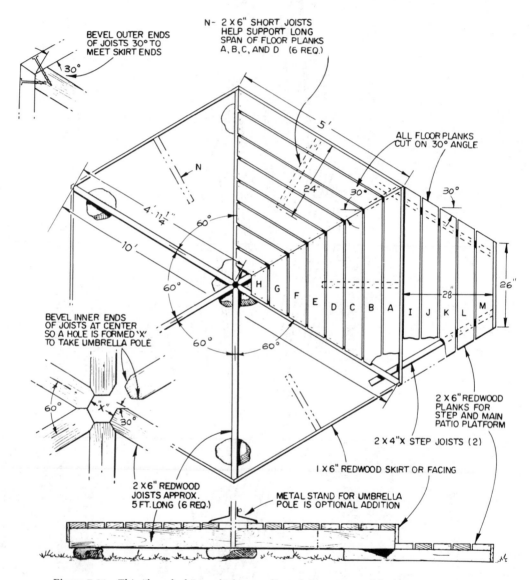

BEVEL OUTER ENDS
OF JOISTS 30° TO
MEET SKIRT ENDS

30°

N- 2 X 6" SHORT JOISTS
HELP SUPPORT LONG
SPAN OF FLOOR PLANKS
A, B, C, AND D (6 REQ.)

5'

ALL FLOOR PLANKS
CUT ON 30° ANGLE

N

24

30°

30°

4-11¼"

60°

10'

60°

H G F E D C B A I J K L M

26"

BEVEL INNER ENDS
OF JOISTS AT CENTER
SO A HOLE IS FORMED 'X'
TO TAKE UMBRELLA POLE

60°

60°

28"

60°

X

30°

2 X 6" REDWOOD
PLANKS FOR
STEP AND MAIN
PATIO PLATFORM

2 X 4"X STEP JOISTS (2)

1 X 6" REDWOOD SKIRT OR FACING

2 X 6" REDWOOD
JOISTS APPROX.
5 FT. LONG (6 REQ.)

METAL STAND FOR UMBRELLA
POLE IS OPTIONAL ADDITION

Figure 7-21   This "hex deck" is a little complicated, but very good-looking. It is small enough to warrant a little time to study and build it.

152

DIAGRAM SHOWS CUTS TO BE MADE TO OBTAIN ALL PIECES FOR PATIO

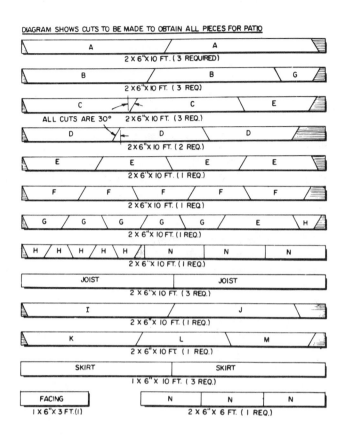

A   A
2 X 6"X 10 FT. (3 REQUIRED)

B   B   G
2 X 6"X 10 FT. (3 REQ)

C   C   E
ALL CUTS ARE 30°   2 X 6"X 10 FT. (3 REQ.)

D   D   D
2 X 6"X 10 FT. (2 REQ.)

E   E   E   E
2 X 6"X 10 FT. (1 REQ.)

F   F   F   F   F
2 X 6"X 10 FT. (1 REQ)

G   G   G   G   G   E   H
2 X 6"X 10 FT. (1 REQ.)

H   H   H   H   H   N   N   N
2 X 6"X 10 FT. (1 REQ.)

JOIST   JOIST
2 X 6"X 10 FT. (3 REQ.)

I   J
2 X 6"X 10 FT. (1 REQ.)

K   L   M
2 X 6"X 10 FT (1 REQ.)

SKIRT   SKIRT
1 X 6"X 10 FT. (3 REQ.)

FACING   N   N   N
1 X 6"X 3 FT.(1)   2 X 6"X 6 FT. (1 REQ.)

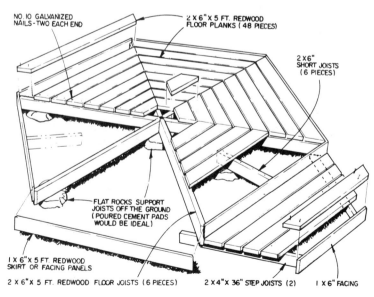

NO. 10 GALVANIZED
NAILS - TWO EACH END

2 X 6"X 5 FT. REDWOOD
FLOOR PLANKS (48 PIECES)

2 X 6"
SHORT JOISTS
(6 PIECES)

FLAT ROCKS SUPPORT
JOISTS OFF THE GROUND
(POURED CEMENT PADS
WOULD BE IDEAL)

1 X 6"X 5 FT. REDWOOD
SKIRT OR FACING PANELS

2 X 6"X 5 FT. REDWOOD FLOOR JOISTS (6 PIECES)

2 X 4"X 36" STEP JOISTS (2)

1 X 6" FACING

153

Patio Deck

This is a very simple deck plan using 5/4 lumber as discussed before. It can be built directly on the ground as shown in Figure 7-19, or be raised slightly as in Figure 7-20. As shown in Figure 7-19, it is 12 × 16 feet, which uses nine 12-foot 2 × 6s for joists and two 16-foot 2 × 6s for skirtboards. The deck consists of 26 pieces of 16-foot 5/4 × 6 planking.

If posts are used, four 4 × 4s are cut to length as needed, and two 16-foot 2 × 8s are bolted to the posts on each side to serve as a beam. Additional beam support is provided by 2 × 4 cleats nailed to the posts as shown in Figure 7-20.

Free-Standing Hex Deck

This is a fairly small but elegant deck, preferably made from redwood. The hexagonal deck shape is ideal for use with a large umbrella, but can be used without, too. It is shown resting on large rocks, but small posts or pedestals can be used instead (Figure 7-21).

With its 30° angles, our hex deck can be a little complicated to build, but the cutting diagrams help save on lumber costs. Study the plan carefully before you build, and lay out the lumber before you start cutting. If you don't plan on using an umbrella, simply butt the ends of the 30° cut joists together.

8

Multilevel, High-Level, and Other Designs

As discussed at length (*ad nausem?*) in previous chapters, the greater the height in deck design, the greater the need for sound engineering and construction. When a deck is at truly dangerous heights, we strongly recommend that the final plans be drawn up by an architect or engineer.

This isn't to say that you can't make the basic design yourself. It's your deck, after all. You can probably go at least as far as making a scale drawing as discussed on p. 69. Using the tables on pp. 43–49, a knowledgeable do-it-yourselfer can no doubt do a perfectly creditable job of "specing" the beams, joists, and other parts of the structure.

But you may just make one little error that can cause serious injury or death. We're talking *high* decks, now, we hasten to remind you. Most decks, even moderately high ones, are not that dangerous. But virtually all municipalities have building departments and inspectors. No matter how good you are, or what book or other background material you have read, building departments may cast a jaundiced eye on self-drawn plans, especially where there are potential hazards.

The attitude of such public officials is that they are paid to protect the public, so why take a chance? You, after all, may sell the house tomorrow. So

Figure 8-1 This deck starts out low next to the house, but winds up quite high on the outside, because of sloping ground. Note the use of lattice to help disguise the understructure. Made entirely of Wolmanized wood.

even if *you* don't worry about it, the next occupant might. And you should not, after all, take any chances yourself, especially when it involves your family.

Furthermore, we have to face the fact that building department employees are often local politicians. They have their own axes to grind, and—let's be honest—friends and voters in the construction industry. They can make it tough for do-it-yourselfers. We take jobs away from contractors. Building departments may demand professionally designed plans no matter how good your own plans are—just to keep the local engineers in business. There are a lot of in-laws out there.

All that aside, it is certainly a wise practice to talk to the building department when you plan any exterior project, and it is a must if you are building a high deck. Bring at least a rough plan with you, and ask for advice. Nothing succeeds like making a public official feel that he or she is important.

Let's start off slowly, with a plan that doesn't present any safety hazards—unless you really louse it up. Sure, some little kid can fall and hurt himself, but not seriously. There are no inherent safety hazards in the following deck.

Here is a very flexible deck that can be modified quite easily to fit existing terrain and varying size conditions (Figures 8-2–8-4). It is built extra strong, as multilevel decks should be. It is also a very attractive deck, one that any homeowner can be proud of—especially when you can say "I did it myself."

The version shown here is made of redwood, with all supporting members built of construction-grade heartwood, and the rest either construction heart or construction common. It is built similar to the pyramids, with each level resting firmly on top of the one beneath (Figure 8-3). The basic design shown applies to each level and can be infinitely adapted to suit individual situations.

The 4 × 4 posts are set five feet apart o.c., and are attached to concrete pedestals with wood blocks and metal post connectors. The beams are constructed of double 2 × 6s nailed together to form a 4 × 6. These are attached to the posts using appropriate metal connectors. Joists are attached to the beams with joist hangers where they end up at a beam or another joist, and with U-shaped Tecos where they run on top of a parallel member.

As shown in Figure 8-4, add extra nailing blocks at outside corners and provide an additional diagonal joist so that the deckboards will be properly braced. An alternate herringbone pattern is also shown. Decking consists of 2 × 4s attached with 16d nails. Turn 2 × 4s on end at the sides to serve as fascia boards. See appropriate sections of this book for seats, planters, and other peripherals.

Figure 8-2 Here is a handsome multilevel deck, with decking, fence, planters, and everything else except supporting members built of construction-grade redwood. See text and accompanying drawings for construction details.

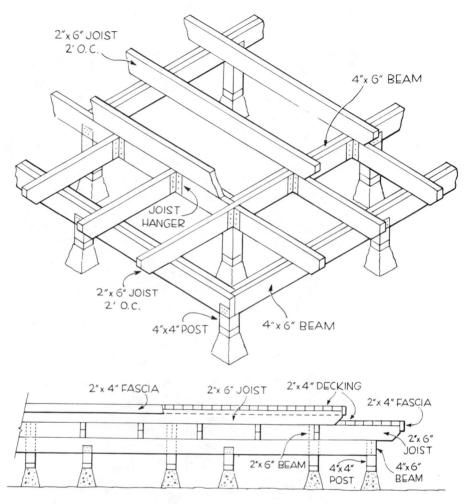

Figure 8-3 Construction design is similar to the pyramids, almost as durable. Use the same pattern to design a multilevel deck to fit your own homesite.

Figure 8-4 Install an extra joist at all corners as shown at left to provide extra support and nailing surface. Diagram at right shows how to run deckboards in herringbone pattern.

The deck illustrated in Figures 8-5 and 8-6 is perfect for sunning. It features a partial cantilever, which can be tricky, but if you follow the structural details shown, it should be strong and safe. When freelancing your own design, make sure that it conforms to local building codes and have the structure evaluated (at minimum) by a professional. In general, you can safely cantilever out from the beams 18–24 inches, but always check this sort of construction with a professional or building inspector.

Four-by-four posts support this deck, which is a little less than 12 × 12 feet in both directions. Structural rigidity is enhanced by the 4 × 6 beam running on top of the posts. The single beam is attached with U-shaped hangers in the main diagrams. An alternate choice is shown in the inset, with double 2 × 6s being attached on each side of the posts with ⅜ × 6 inch carriage bolts.

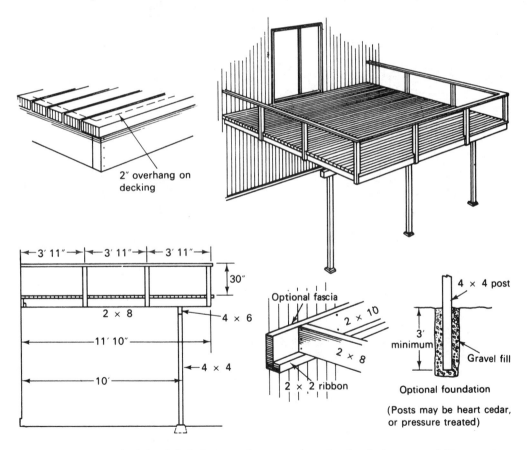

Figure 8-5 Basic high-level deck design and some construction details (see text and Figure 8-6). (*Courtesy Western Wood Products Association*)

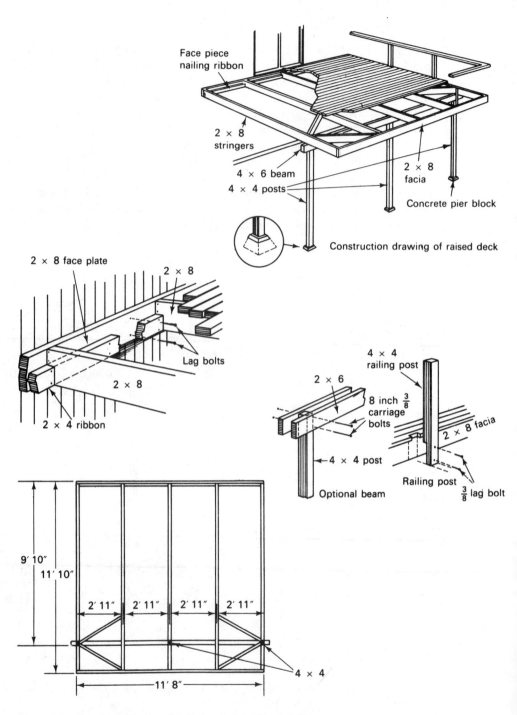

Face piece
nailing ribbon

2 × 8
stringers

4 × 6 beam

4 × 4 posts

2 × 8
facia

Concrete pier block

Construction drawing of raised deck

2 × 8 face plate

2 × 8

Lag bolts

2 × 8

2 × 4 ribbon

2 × 6

4 × 4
railing post

8 inch $\frac{3}{8}$
carriage
bolts

2 × 8 facia

4 × 4 post

Optional beam

Railing post
$\frac{3}{8}$ lag bolt

9′ 10″

11′ 10″

2′ 11″ 2′ 11″ 2′ 11″ 2′ 11″

4 × 4

11′ 8″

Figure 8-6   Framing and other details for deck in Figure 8-5.

160

Posts rest on piers, or are set into the ground a minimum of three feet as shown in the alternate drawing. The deckboards rest on 2 × 8 joists, with a 2 × 8 face-plate and 2 × 4 ribbon forming the ledger at the house connection. Here, joists are notched to fit the lag-bolted ledger and toenailed. See pp. 92–96 for other types of connections. Metal connectors (not shown) should be used instead of, or in addition to, the toenailing, especially if the deck is very high.

The outside of the deck is cantilevered two feet beyond the beam. Extra support for the cantilevered section is provided by the diagonal 2 × 8s between the outside joists and the adjacent joists as shown.

Deckboards are 2 × 4s laid flat, and railings are made of 4 × 4 posts and 2 × 4 rails. Higher decks, and any decks where children may play, should have intermediate posts, balusters, or some other form of protection between posts to prevent falls (see Chapter 6).

HIGH DECK WITH STAIRWAY

Figure 8-7 shows a similar deck, but with a stairway and other different details. Size is 10 × 12 feet. Modifications are possible, but stay within similar sizes using the same basic structure. The beam here is composed of double 2 × 10s lagged to each side of the 4 × 4 posts, with 2 × 4 cleats giving additional support.

Terminology in carpentry has never been adequately defined. Note the use of different terms for essentially the same things, even in our diagrams, which are taken from various sources and based on designs by manufacturers and associations throughout North America. Different designers use different words, just as New Yorkers say "soda," Bostonians say "tonic," and most people say "pop."

We hesitate to change the terms used by the designers, but you will notice we often give you alternatives in the text and captions. We are pointing it out so that you won't think you're crazy, or missing something. The "ribbon board" in this plan, for example, is called an outside header, skirtboard, or fascia board by other people.

Some of the difference is understandable but confusing. It often reflects what are really advances in technology. "Ledger," for example, should mean a board that sticks out and that supports something else. Since joist hangers and similar connectors came into use, true ledgers are not used that often. That is why the board that is attached to the house in deck construction is widely called a "ledger board," even though the joists no longer bear directly on top of it.

We don't intend to start a brouhaha about this, just to point out that what is called one thing in one drawing might be called something else in another diagram or other text. Here, for example, the "header" next to the house is usually referred to as a ledger board. But the 2 × 10 header shown actually has a ledger attached, which the joists bear upon, hence the difference.

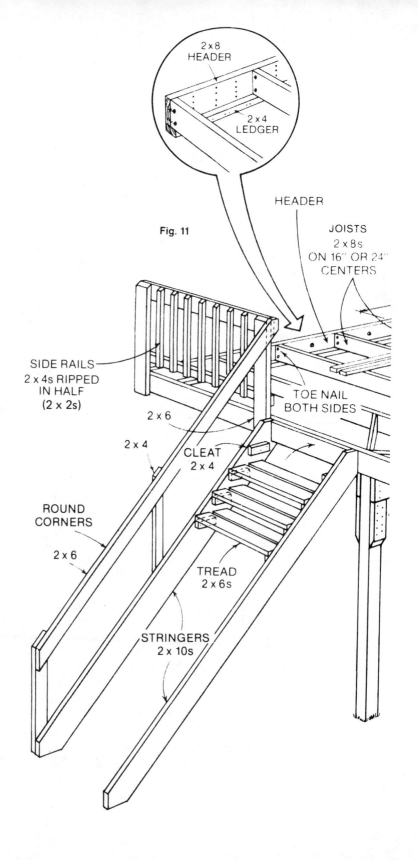

2 x 8
HEADER

2 x 4
LEDGER

HEADER

Fig. 11

JOISTS
2 x 8s
ON 16" OR 24"
CENTERS

SIDE RAILS
2 x 4s RIPPED
IN HALF
(2 x 2s)

TOE NAIL
BOTH SIDES

2 x 6

2 x 4

CLEAT
2 x 4

ROUND
CORNERS

2 x 6

TREAD
2 x 6s

STRINGERS
2 x 10s

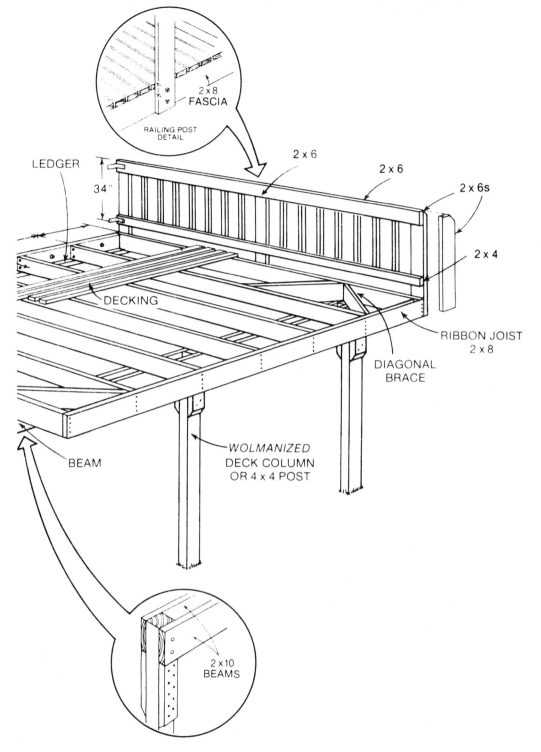

2 x 8
FASCIA

RAILING POST
DETAIL

LEDGER

34″

2 x 6

2 x 6

2 x 6s

2 x 4

DECKING

RIBBON JOIST
2 x 8

DIAGONAL
BRACE

WOLMANIZED
DECK COLUMN
OR 4 x 4 POST

BEAM

2 x 10
BEAMS

Figure 8-7   High-level deck with stairway. (*Courtesy Koppers Co.*)

163

Making up your own specifications for a high deck is somewhat akin to diagnosing your own diseases, but the Teco company has compiled some very useful aids for just this purpose. The basic design is a safe one, with small one-foot cantilevers and no innovations that can lead to difficulty.

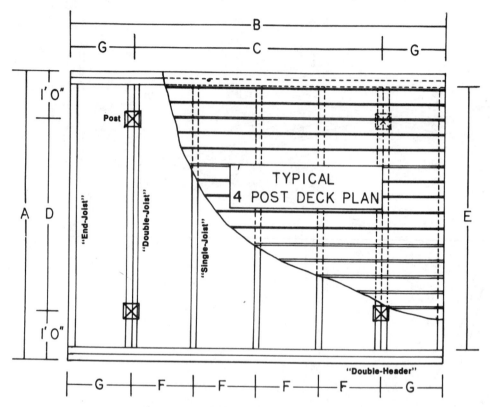

TYPICAL
4 POST DECK PLAN

("Deck Depth" is the shorter dimension.)

WORKING DIMENSIONS
4-POST SUPPORT SYSTEM

6^{FT}x6^{FT}	6^{FT}x8^{FT}	6^{FT}x10^{FT}	8^{FT}x8^{FT}	8^{FT}x10^{FT}	10^{FT}x10^{FT}
A = 6'0"	A = 6'0"	A = 6'0"	A = 8'0"	A = 8'0"	A = 10'0"
B = 6'0"	B = 8'0"	B = 10'0"	B = 8'0"	B = 10'0"	B = 10'0"
C = 4'0"	C = 5'4"	C = 6'8"	C = 5'4"	C = 6'8"	C = 6'8"
D = 4'0"	D = 4'0"	D = 4'0"	D = 6'0"	D = 6'0"	D = 8'0"
E = 5'6"	E = 5'6"	E = 5'6"	E = 7'6"	E = 7'6"	E = 9'6"
F = 1'0"	F = 1'4"	F = 1'8"	F' = 1'4"	F = 1'8"	F = 1'8"
G = 1'0"	G = 1'4"	G = 1'8"	G = 1'4"	G = 1'8"	G = 1'8"

If you follow the recommendations given in Figures 8-8 (four-post system) and 8-9 (six-post system), along with their accompanying charts, you shouldn't get into too much trouble. If the edges of the deck, though, get much higher than 8-10 feet, this author would feel a lot better if he checked out the specs with a qualified engineer.

For not-too-awfully-high decks, though, these are excellent guidelines. Once the approximate size and style of the deck has been established, find the size here that's closest, and follow the specifications given in the charts. Posts are usually 4 × 4, but I would go to 4 × 6s or even 6 × 6s if the deck was large and high. Note that the six-post design should be used for any deck that is over 10 feet in depth (from the house to outside edge).

To use these guidelines, check the distances marked by the letters on the plan, and find the lumber for that particular span. In the four-post system, for example, with an 8 × 10 deck, if you want to determine how far you can build out sideways from the posts, look under "G." You will see that it is one foot eight inches. To determine the size joists needed, look under "Materials.' Joists should be 2 × 6s, eight feet long.

ROOF-TOP DECKS

Roof-top decks are somewhat unusual, but are often the only way to take advantage of a good view or a cramped homesite. They are extremely popular in

MATERIALS – 4 POST SYSTEM

LUMBER AND DECK NAILS REQUIRED FOR THE FOLLOWING DECK SIZES:

6' x 6' DECK		8' x 8' DECK	
4	4' x 4" x LENGTH POSTS*	4	4" x 4" x LENGTH POSTS*
4	2" x 6" x 6'0" HEADERS	4	2" x 6" x 8'0" HEADERS
9	2" x 6" x 6'0" JOISTS	9	2" x 6" x 8'0" JOISTS
20	2" x 4" x 6'0" DECKING	27	2" x 4" x 8'0" DECKING
4	LBS 10D GALV. NAILS	6	LBS 10D GALV. NAILS
6' x 8' DECK		**8 x 10' DECK**	
4	4" x 4" x LENGTH POSTS*	4	4" x 4" x LENGTH POSTS*
4	2" x 6" x 8'0" HEADERS	4	2" x 6" x 10'0" HEADERS
9	2" x 6" x 6'0" JOISTS	9	2" x 6" x 8'0" JOISTS
20	2' x 4" x 8'0" DECKING	27	2" x 4" x 10'0" DECKING
4	LBS 10D GALV. NAILS	6	LBS 10D GALV. NAILS
6' x 10' DECK		**10' x 10' DECK**	
4	4" x 4" x LENGTH POSTS*	4	4" x 4" x LENGTH POSTS*
4	2" x 6" x 10'0" HEADERS	4	2" x 8" x 10'0" HEADERS
9	2" x 6" x 6'0" JOISTS	9	2" x 8" 10'0" JOISTS
20	2" x 4" x 10'0" DECKING	33	2" x 4" x 10'0" DECKING
4	LBS 10D GALV. NAILS	8	LBS 10D GALV. NAILS

* Length of posts depends upon height of deck. At least ⅓ of the post should be embedded in the ground a minimum of 24" or more, depending upon local building codes and frost line conditions.

Figure 8-8   Design shown can be adapted to a wide variety of reasonably high decks, but check with a professional before building more than about seven or eight feet off the ground (see Figure 8-9).

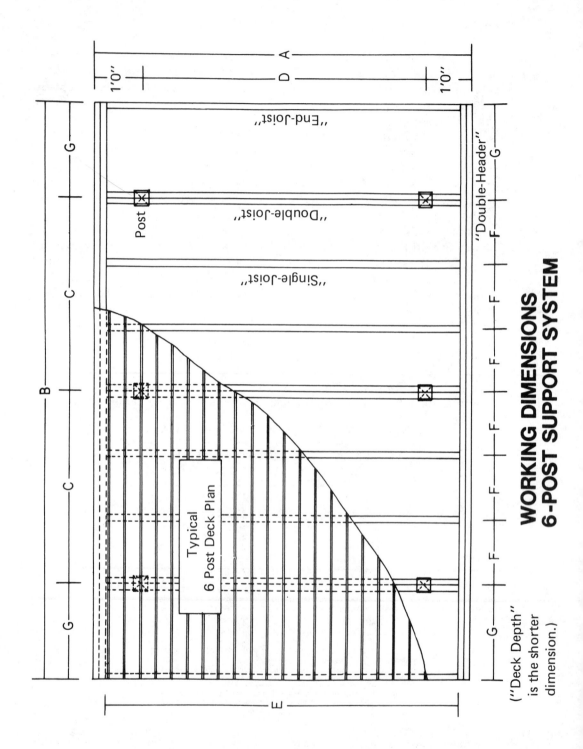

**WORKING DIMENSIONS
6-POST SUPPORT SYSTEM**

Typical
6 Post Deck Plan

Post

"End-Joist"

"Double-Joist"

"Single-Joist"

"Double-Header"

("Deck Depth"
is the shorter
dimension.)

1'0"   D   1'0"

A

8'x12'	8'x14'	8'x16'	10'x12'	10'x14'	10'x16'	12'x12'	12'x14'
A = 8'0"	A = 8'0"	A = 8'0"	A = 10'0"	A = 10'0"	A = 10'0"	A = 12'0"	A = 12'0"
B = 12'0"	B = 14'0"	B = 16'0"	B = 12'0"	B = 14'0"	B = 16'0"	B = 12'0"	B = 14'0"
C = 4'0"	C = 6'0"	C = 6'0"	C = 4'0"	C = 6'0"	C = 6'0"	C = 4'0"	C = 5'0"
D = 6'0"	D = 6'0"	D = 6'0"	D = 8'0"	D = 8'0"	D = 8'0"	D = 10'0"	D = 10'0"
E = 7'6"	E = 7'6"	E = 7'6"	E = 9'6"	E = 9'0"	E = 9'6"	E = 11'6"	E = 11'6"
F = 1'4"	F = 2'0"	F = 2'0"	F = 1'4"	F = 2'0"	F = 2'0"	F = 1'4"	F = 1'8"
G = 2'0"	G = 1'0"	G = 2'0"	G = 2'0"	G = 1'0"	G = 2'0"	G = 2'0"	G = 2'0"

Figure 8-9   Similar plan as in Figure 8-8, but using six posts for decks that extend more than 10 feet from the house. Both plans designed by Teco for use with their connectors.

MATERIALS — 6 POST SYSTEM

LUMBER AND DECK NAILS REQUIRED FOR THE FOLLOWING DECK SIZES:

8' x 12' DECK	10' x 14' DECK
6 4" x 4" x LENGTH POSTS*	6 4" x 4" x LENGTH POSTS*
4 2" x 6" x 12'0" HEADERS	4 2" x 8" x 14'0" HEADERS
12 2" x 6" x 8'0" JOISTS	12 2" x 8" x 10'0" JOISTS
27 2" x 4" x 12'0" DECKING	33 2" x 4" x 14'0" DECKING
7 LBS 10D GALV. NAILS	9 LBS 10D GALV. NAILS
8' x 14' DECK	**10' x 16' DECK**
6 4" x 4" x LENGTH POSTS*	6 4" x 4" x LENGTH POSTS*
4 2" x 6" x 14'0" HEADERS	4 2" x 8" x 16'0" HEADERS
12 2" x 6" x 8'0" JOISTS	12 2" x 8" x 10'0" JOISTS
27 2" x 4" x 14'0" DECKING	33 2" x 4" x 16'0" DECKING
7 LBS 10D GALV. NAILS	9 LBS 10D GALV. NAILS
8' x 16' DECK	**12' x 12' DECK**
6 4" x 4" x LENGTH POSTS*	6 4" x 4" x LENGTH POSTS*
4 2" x 6" x 16'0" HEADERS	4 2" x 8" x 12'0" HEADERS
12 2" x 6" x 8'0" JOISTS	12 2" x 8" x 12'0" JOISTS
27 2" x 4" x 16'0" DECKING	40 2" x 4" x 12'0" DECKING
7 IBS 10D GALV. NAILS	10 LBS 10D GALV. NAILS
10' x 12' DECK	**12' x 14' DECK**
6 4" x 4" x LENGTH POSTS*	6 4" x 4" x LENGTH POSTS*
4 2" x 6" x 12'0" HEADERS	4 2" x 8" x 14'0" HEADERS
12 2" x 6" x 10'0" JOISTS	12 2" x 8" x 12'0" JOISTS
33 2" x 4" x 12'0" DECKING	40 2" x 4" x 14'0" DECKING
9 LBS 10D GALV. NAILS	10 LBS 10D GALV. NAILS

* Length of posts depends upon height of deck. At least ⅓ of the post should be embedded in the ground a minimum of 24" or more, depending upon local building codes and frost line conditions.

Figure 8-9   (Continued)

beach areas, particularly for "second-row" sites or other spots where dunes and other houses block out the waterview.

Before you consider such a deck, check your building department or a qualified engineer to see if the roof can handle the added weight. Additional truss support or bracing may be required. Also be sure that the roof is waterproof before you start to build. If not, hire a professional to do this for you. This is especially important for a flat roof.

Flat roofs, if they are strong and dry enough, need no special preparation. You can, in fact, simply lay deckboards or parquets right on top of the roofing, without nailing if you wish, so that you can take the deck along if you move.

If you have a very steep roof, it is probably impossible to put a deck there. Rooftop decks can usually be adapted, however, to a typical gentle grade. You will have to devise the framework yourself, depending on slope and type of the roof. First, determine the deck level and roof slope, then devise a grid that can be attached to the roof to support and level the deck. Some ways of building a roof deck are shown in Figures 8-10 and 8-11.

For some decks, a gutter system may be needed to carry off any trapped rainwater. Be sure to apply flashing where the deck joins the house. Apply

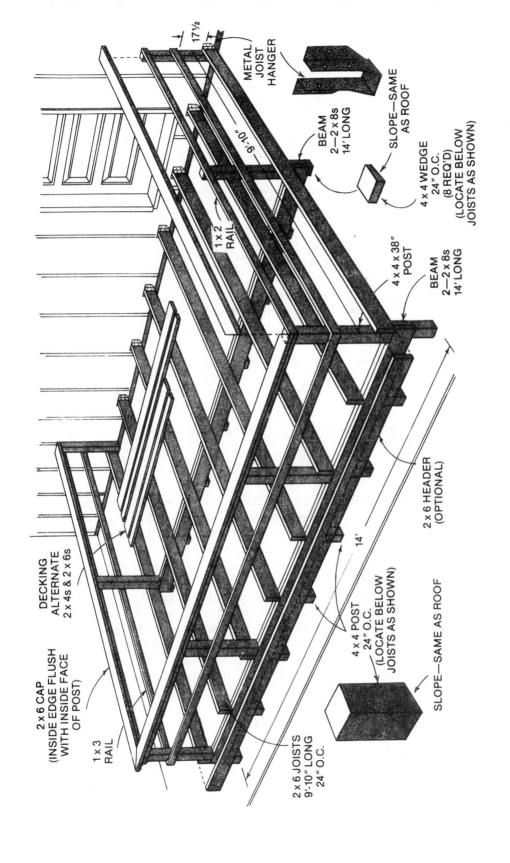

Figure 8-10 A roof-top deck using Wolmanized pressure-treated wood. Posts and other understructure are determined by slope, type, and size of roof.

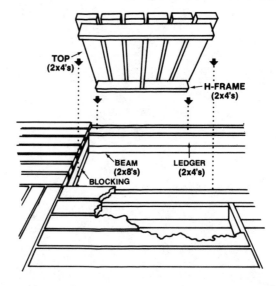

Figure 8-11 Another roof-top deck for redwood, which is ideally suited for this purpose because of its relatively light weight. Here, parquet units are laid into a grid made of 2 × 8 beams, 2 × 4 ledgers and 2 × 4 blocking. Parquets are made of 21-½ inch 2 × 4 frames, with six 2 × 4s forming units 23-½ inches long.

sealant to all post and other roof connections and wherever nails or other fasteners have penetrated the roofing.

DECK WITH FIREPIT

The handsome deck shown in Figure 8-12 combines many of the elements that make up good deck design. It is located directly outside of the recreation room, for easy mingling of indoor-outdoor leisure activities. Access is through sliding-glass doors, with the deck recessed an inch below the inside floor for drainage.

Along the house at the upper right, a built-in wet bar with basic kitchen capabilities avoids long treks to the same facilities inside. To top it off, a good-looking and functional firepit is recessed adjacent to the main deck. Benches along the sides of the firepit provide a conversation pit, in addition to the purely functional cooking aspects. Here, the cook doesn't have to barbecue alone. He or she can be joined by other members of the family or friends while working. The same fire can warm the family on chilly nights, while they sit around chatting about the day's events or the evening's barbecued dinner. Strategically placed lighting enhances the effect.

One somewhat unusual aspect of this deck and accessories is the use of 2 × 4s on edge, instead of flat-laid. The larger deck adjacent to the house follows standard deck construction otherwise.

In the smaller firepit deck (Figure 8-14), the 2 × 4s rest on 4 × 4 sleepers laid in a gravel bed 3-½ inches thick. The version shown is made of untreated

Figure 8-12 An attractive and functional deck, featuring large main section and adjacent firepit, with its own small deck. Western woods were used throughout.

western woods. The 4 × 4s and any other wood in ground contact should be made of pressure-treated lumber. See Chapter 12 for treatment and finishing of the other woods.

Posts are used only for the benches, and the 4 × 4s used here are set into concrete. Benches are built as shown, using 2 × 4s on edge to conform with the deck. The firepit itself is made of 4 × 4 × 16 concrete block, with 2 × 6s bolted to the outside for strength and good looks. When the pit is not in use for cooking or warmth, it can be covered with a homemade "table' as shown in Figure 8-15.

DECK WITH HOT TUB OR SPA

Hot tubs and spas are increasingly popular deck additions, and they are a great way to ensure that the family that "cleans together stays together." A hot tub can also increase the annual use of the deck where the weather might otherwise keep you indoors. You can soak in a hot tub or spa almost any time of the year.

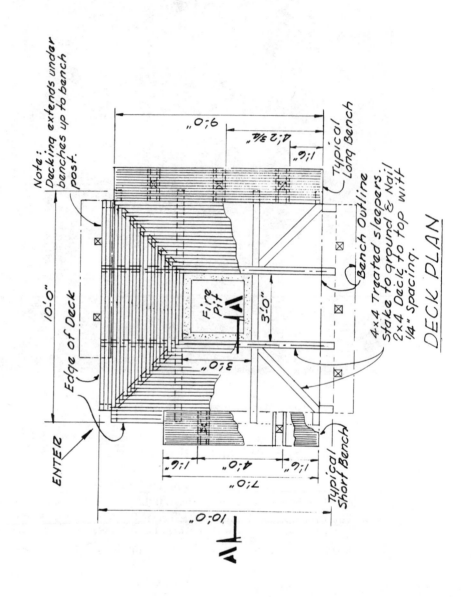

Note: Decking extends under benches up to bench post.

10'-0"

Edge of Deck

ENTER

10'-0"

9'-0"

4'-2 3/4"

1'-2"

Typical Long Bench

Bench Outline

Fire Pit

3'-0"

3'-0"

4x4 Treated sleepers. Stake to ground & Nail 2x4 Deck to top with 1/4" Spacing.

DECK PLAN

1'-6"

4'-0"

1'-6"

7'-0"

Typical Short Bench

172

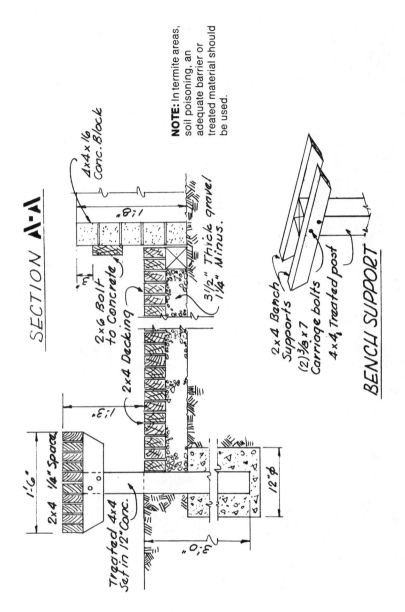

SECTION A-A

4x4x16 Conc. Block

1'-8"

NOTE: In termite areas, soil poisoning, an adequate barrier or treated material should be used.

2x6 Bolt to Concrete

2x4 Decking

3½" Thick gravel ¼" Minus.

1'-3"

1'-6"

2x4 ¼" Space

12" ø

3'-0"

Treated 4x4 Set in 12" Conc.

2x4 Bench Supports

(2) ⅜ x 7 Carriage bolts

4x4 Treated post

BENCH SUPPORT

Figure 8-13 How to build the firepit deck shown in the photo.

173

Figure 8-14 Treated 4 × 4s are laid in the gravel bed, and 2 × 4s on edge are toenailed into sleepers. Note shim for uniform spacing between deckboards.

Figure 8-15 Optional firepit cover, made of 2 × 2 lumber, transforms the firepit into a convenient table.

**Redwood Deck
for Hot Tub**

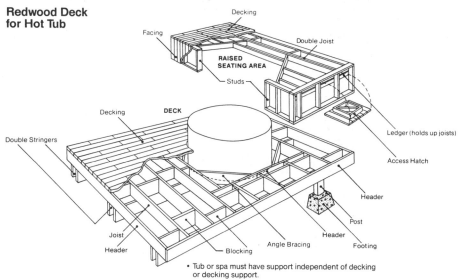

Decking

Facing

Double Joist

**RAISED
SEATING AREA**

Studs

Ledger (holds up joists)

Decking

DECK

Double Stringers

Access Hatch

Header

Post

Joist

Header

Header

Footing

Blocking

Angle Bracing

• Tub or spa must have support independent of decking
or decking support.

Figure 8-16   Redwood deck has hot tub on raised seating area. Overall construction is shown at bottom.

MATERIALS LIST—REDWOOD DECK WITH HOT TUB

Materials list for 12' × 16' deck

		Optional lumber lengths:
Decking	2 × 4-370 lineal feet or 2 × 6-240 lineal feet	
Molding:	1 × 2, 56 lineal feet	
Posts:	9-4 × 4 × height	
Stringers:	4-2 × 10 × 16', 2-2 × 10 × 7', 2-2 × 10 × 2'	9-2 × 6 × 20'
Joists:	6-2 × 6 × 12', 1-2 × 6 × 6', 6-2 × 6 × 26"	(To be cut to dimensions. Cut longer lengths first).
Blocking:	12-2 × 6 × 2'	
Angle bracing:	4-2 × 6 × 3'	
Headers:	2-2 × 6 × 8', 2-2 × 6 × 16'	
Nails:	3# 16d Common, 8# 16d Box (galvanized, stainless)	
Lag screws & washers:	36-3/8 × 4" (galvanized, stainless)	

Materials list for raised seating area (12' × 16' deck)

Facing:	1 × 6 124 lineal feet or 1 × 4 194 lineal feet
Decking:	2 × 6 124 lineal feet or 2 × 4 194 lineal feet

Studwall units

		Optional lumber lengths
Plates:	2-2 × 4 × 12', 6-2 × 4 × 6'	4-2 × 4 × 20'
Studs:	26-2 × 4 × 2'	4-2 × 4 × 8'
Joists:	2-2 × 6 × 12', 2-2 × 6 × 3', 2-2 × 6 × 3'8", 2-2 × 6 × 1'6"	2-2 × 6 × 8'
Ledgers:	2-2 × 6 × 6'	1-2 × 6 × 20'
Nails:	2# 16d Common, 4# 16d Box (galvanized, stainless)	(To be cut to dimensions. Cut longer lengths first).

Materials list for 10′ × 20′ deck

Posts:	12-4 × 4 × height
Stringers:	4-2 × 10 × 20′, 2-2 × 10 × 2′, 2-2 × 10 × 11′,
Joists:	8-2 × 6 × 10′, 1-2 × 6 × 6 × 6′, 6-2 × 6 × 14″
Decking:	2 × 4 = 424 lineal feet; 2 × 6 = 274 lineal feet
Blocking:	18-2 × 6 × 2′
Molding:	60 lineal feet
Nails:	3# 16d common, 8# 16d box (galvanized, stainless)
Lag screws & 48-⅜ × 4″	
Washers	(galvanized, stainless)
Angle bracing:	2-2 × 6 × 3′
Headers	2-2 × 6 × 8′, 2-2 × 6 × 20′

Materials list for raised seating area (10′ × 20′ deck)

Facing:	1 × 6 = 114; 1 × 4 = 178
Decking:	2 × 4 = 138 lineal; or 2 × 6 = 88 lineal
Studwall units	
Plates:	2-2 × 4 × 10′, 6-2 × 4 × 6′
Studs:	24-2 × 4 × 2′
Joists:	2-2 × 6 × 2′, 2-2 × 6 × 4′, 2-2 × 6 × 2′, 2-2 × 6 × 11″, 1-2 × 6 × 3′8″
Ledgers:	2-2 × 6 × 6′
Nails:	2# 16d d C & 4# 16d Box (galvanized, stainless)

Those who savor this idea (and there are a lot of us) should know that hot tubs are an expensive amenity. That isn't just because of the tub itself, which is not cheap, but because of the plumbing, support mechanisms, and other requirements that make the hot tub work. The same is true of "Jacuzzis" or other spas.

If you live in a populated area, there may also be code requirements for drainage and setbacks from rivers, lakes, and streams. Hot tubs are treated much like a built-in pool, with strict electrical codes for any possible hazards nearby, such as outlets or appliances. If you don't already have a GFCI (ground-fault circuit interrupter) installed nearby, you will certainly need one if you install a spa or hot tub (see pp. 240–242.)

A hot tub also needs its own support system. This usually involves a concrete slab with its own footings. Spas ordinarily require a "sand box" below,

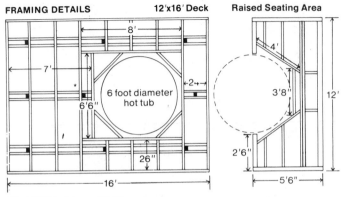

*Post 20" back to next joist.

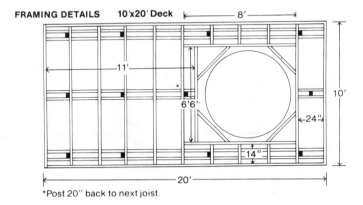

*Post 20" back to next joist.

The raised seating area of the 10'x20' deck is structurally the same as the 12'x16' less 1-foot on either side. Consult cutting list above right.

Figure 8-17 Framing detail for two deck sizes—12 × 16 feet and 10 × 20 feet. Raised seating portion is the same for either deck, except that one foot is deducted from each side for the 10 × 20 deck.

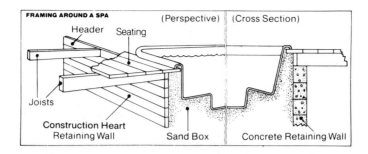

Figure 8-18 If a spa is used instead of hot tub, framing is basically the same, but a "sand box" sits underneath, and retaining walls are needed as shown. Joists and decking should extend under the lip of the spa, but this is more for looks than any special need.

with retaining walls of concrete block or heavy timbers. Check local codes carefully on this, as well as other aspects of construction. In most cases, it is wise to have a professional design and build this part, at least, of your deck complex.

Landscaping is another important part of spa design. Privacy, as well as beauty, should weigh heavily in the factors to consider. Evergreen shrubs and fencing can be used, along with intelligent siting. Seating around the tub should also be provided.

You can add a hot tub to an existing deck, but it's a lot simpler and considerably less expensive to build the spa into the deck at the beginning. It is wise to keep all framing lumber at least six inches away from the outside of the tub, to allow access for repairs. (Decking can be brought up almost to the edges.) An access hatch is provided in the raised design shown, for the same purposes. The raised seating area allows plumbing and accessories to be stored underneath, in addition to providing a convenient place for drying off and sunning.

The redwood deck shown here is built with 2 × 6 decking. Several options are shown in the plans and materials list. You can build either the 12 × 16-foot or 10 × 20-foot versions shown, or adapt them as required. In both plans, the 12 × 16-foot raised seating area is structurally the same, except that the platform is a foot smaller on each side.

Because of constant water contact with the wood in the hot-tub area, all-heart redwood or red cedar should be used, or pressure-treated lumber with .40 retention. It is also wise to apply extra preservatives in that particular area, as discussed in Chapter 12.

POOLSIDE DECKS

Wood decking around a pool makes the pool even more inviting, and gives it a handsome "trim," much like framing does for a picture. It also gives a level, reasonably nonskid surface for poolside activities. For in-ground pools, it is quite easy to level the ground, put in some sleepers over sand or gravel, and nail the deckboards to the sleepers.

Figure 8-19 This deck with spa was cleverly designed to take advantage of maximum sunshine and to ensure privacy on a smallish urban plot. (*Courtesy Southern Forest Products Association*)

Figure 8-20 In-ground pools are easier to beautify than above-ground types. Good-looking design shown uses brick in foreground and redwood decking for other sides of pool and most of backyard. Note both open, screen-type deck covers, and standard roof cover in background.

Figure 8-21 Two views of a superb poolside deck by Goldberg and Rodler of Huntington, New York. Deck is cantilevered over the pool for that feeling of being in the water—but not quite.

Figure 8-22 Less elaborate poolside deck has 2 × 6 decking all around the pool. Tall landscaping helps maintain privacy, essential for pool pleasure. (*Courtesy National Swimming Pool Institute*)

Figure 8-23 Above-ground pools are nice inside, but not too pretty from the outside without decent planning. Here, textured plywood and a second deck surrounding the pool hide the pool structure. (*Courtesy Southern Forest Products Association*)

Figure 8-24 Sloping grounds provide a unique opportunity for creative pool-deck design. Elegant naturalistic landscape blends home easily into its setting. (*Courtesy Koppers Co.*)

Above-ground pools present a more complicated picture. The pool itself, while certainly pleasant inside, may be difficult to fit comfortably into the landscape. In fact, the truth is that an above-ground pool, if simply set on the ground, can be downright ugly from the outside looking in.

The trick is to disguise the underpinnings and exterior of an above-ground pool to blend it better into its setting. Since the pool requires some sort of surrounding surface anyway, this is an excellent time to design an overall deck that not only provides seating and walking room for the pool, but helps hide the not-too-pretty structure of the pool. (See Chapter 12 for landscaping tips.)

If the pool is on sloping ground, one side of the pool can be set into an excavated area, with the outside edge being extended to form the perimeter of the deck. On gently sloping land, another deck, perhaps with a fence or benches along the pool structure, gives continuity.

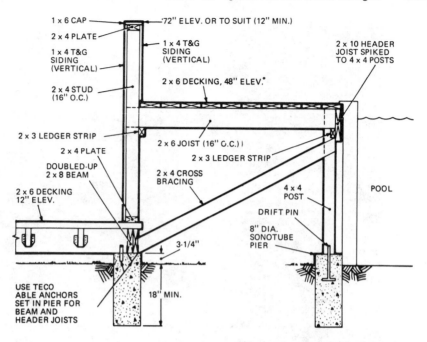

Figure 8-25 Cross-section of double-level poolside deck, with deck hiding the pool's rather ugly structural framing.

On flat ground surfaces, raised or multilevel decks on the exposed sides of the structure will help hide the substructure. Figure 8-25 shows construction details for a two-level deck, one around the pool and another below it.

9

Deck Furniture and Planters

A deck is a deck is a deck. It can do without stairways and benches, even without railings if it's low enough. There are decks that consist of deckboards only—although not too many. Certainly not all decks need covers, benches, planters, or any of the amenities discussed in these final chapters.

All of these things are nice, but in many cases they aren't suitable, or just plain won't fit. The smaller the deck, the less needed to fill it up. But there is one accessory that hardly any deck can do without. That's deck furniture. There has to be something to sit on, lay on, relax on, dream on—besides the deckboards.

If you have built-in benches, that may be all you need. If not, you will either have to build or buy some outdoor furniture. In many cases, it's called "patio" or "lawn" furniture, but it's the same thing, whether it goes on a patio, lawn, deck, driveway, or garage. It's built for outdoor use.

There are numerous types of outdoor furniture on the market today. Redwood, "Adirondack" oak, and other slatted wood are still the old stand-bys, along with rattan, enameled steel, and wrought iron. But there is a lot of competition from newer, high-tech (more or less) materials.

New woven vinyl fabrics and "resin" furniture have revolutionized the market for outdoor furniture, with a much wider variety of frames and fabrics competing with the traditional materials and styles. Many of these are imported from Europe, delighting Americans and raising the trade deficit.

Figure 9-1 This beautiful redwood deck has everything—a large expanse, great view, huge tree, and partial cover for shade—plus a generous variety of furniture, built-in benches, table, chairs, and chaise lounge. (Even a dog, if you look closely.)

Figure 9-2 A deck doesn't have to be large to be nice. This small deck of western woods has—in addition to a lot else including view—a traditional cross-buck table and benches.

Those who haven't looked at outdoor furniture in some time will be pleasantly surprised at the wide variety and the intensity of some of the colors. The bland, quickly faded colors you have been used to are being replaced by vivid bright hues and cool pastels, all made possible by the introduction of new materials and coloring agents.

On the other hand, by far the biggest seller—so far—in North America is "tubular aluminum," those familiar adjustable chairs and chaise lounges that never seem to unfold without crunching a finger, and whose plastic fabric often tears out of the rivets. This type of furniture, however, is inexpensive, lightweight, easily stored, and very handy. For those who have exhausted their savings (and future paychecks) on the deck itself, tubular aluminum is certainly a good way to provide at least temporary seating.

In the middle 1980s, a remarkable item suddenly popped up in discount houses, supermarkets, and hardware stores. This is a smallish outdoor chair made of aluminum with white plastic coating. The seats and back were made of wire mesh also covered with plastic. These chairs were strong, weatherproof, and very inexpensive, and similar material is now being seen for other types of outdoor furniture. It remains to be seen how durable they are, but they were a fine buy at the time.

Fancier, sturdier, and weatherproof aluminum seating is also available in the higher price ranges. These have a baked-on plastic finish that is especially suited to ocean beach areas, where salt air can be more destructive than termites or weather.

As of this writing, the recent craze for PVC outdoor furniture, which is made from the same plastic pipe sold for plumbing, seems to be on the wane. To counter this, manufacturers have come out with new materials and designs specifically targeted at outdoor furniture markets. Best of all, these materials have been coming down in price and are now a good buy.

You can buy PVC furniture readymade, or get some pipe and make your own, as discussed later. The pipe is readily available at plumbing supply houses and larger hardware stores. If you approximate the same sizes (usually 1-¼ inches) as the popular aluminum furniture, "replacement" plastic or webbing for the same type of furniture can often be used for fabric. These materials are readily available in most parts of North America.

Those who are skeptical about the enthusiasm many people show for the new breed of outdoor furniture should note that there are now entire shops devoted to outdoor furniture. There are even several chains that are devoted almost exclusively to outdoor furniture—which is also finding new popularity indoors for the den or family room. One of these, in fact, is called "Deck and Den."

A visit to this type of store will provide an eye-filling array of new styles and materials. A very popular fabric was brought out in the 1980s made of woven vinyl. Known widely by the trade name "Textiline," it is almost impervious to sun, the elements, and salt air. It is extremely durable and dries quickly because of its porous consistency.

Another "hot" new fabric is Zefkrome Acrylic, which bears a marked resemblance to cotton. It is relatively new as an outdoor furniture fabric, but has been used for many years for awnings and sailcloths. See Chapter 10 for more on awning materials.

OUTDOOR FURNITURE YOU CAN BUILD

We were going to call this section "deck furniture," but there is no real distinction between deck furniture and other outdoor furniture. The main characteristic of all outdoor furniture is that it is durable enough to withstand the elements. It is used on decks, patios, lawns—and yes—indoors for dens and family rooms.

Theoretically, you can use any kind of furniture outside—if you weatherproof the wood. But there's a big catch. If you were crazy enough to soak your Chippendale chair in preservative, the wood itself would probably be able to handle it. The chair would still fall apart, though, because those old glues weren't designed for rainstorms.

If you're going to make your own outdoor furniture, there are two main things you have to do—use rot-free wood or soak standard woods in preservatives (see Chapter 12), and use rust-free fasteners and/or waterproof resorcinol glue. Again, you can, in theory, design any style tables, chairs, and benches you wish, but certain types just don't seem to blend in with the outdoors.

The projects shown on these pages are designed specifically for outdoor use. If you want to design your own, you're free to improvise as you wish, but don't follow the same sort of patterns you'd use indoors. They just don't look right, and fancy joinery—dovetailing, for example—is wasted on outdoor furniture. Stick to plain, slatted-type designs. They shed water better, for one thing.

FREESTANDING BENCHES

Most of the benches discussed here can also be adapted as built-ins. The bench shown in Figure 9-3 looks built in, in fact, even though it was designed to be placed anywhere on the deck, or next to a fence, as shown. These benches are very nice to have around when you want extra seating anywhere—even inside—and can be situated around a low-deck perimeter permanently, if you wish.

The benches shown in Figures 9-3 and 9-4 are made of redwood, using 2 × 4 seats to match the deckboards. They can be easily modified for 2 × 6s, or for different dimensions. The frame is constructed of 2 × 12 lumber with 2 × 12 spacers on approximately three-foot centers.

Cross members of 2 × 4 lumber are nailed to the spacers and side frames. Their length depends on spacing of deckboards and overhang desired (if any).

Figure 9-3 A simple, but elegant, redwood bench. It looks built-in, but is actually freestanding.

Nail 2 × 4 fascia boards along the sides and ends. Corners should have an additional 2 × 4 diagonal member to support the ends of the seatboards.

Seatboards are laid out across the fascia and cross members, then nailed when satisfactory spacing is obtained. Use 16d hot-dipped galvanized nails or rust-free screws throughout.

PICNIC TABLE WITH ATTACHED BENCHES

This old favorite (Figure 9-5) can be used not only on the deck, but on a patio or even on the grass in the backyard. It can be made of any of the durable woods discussed in this book, but is designed specifically for Wolmanized wood.

First build the two A-shaped end braces to provide legs and supports for both top and benches. Legs are 2 × 6s, 34 inches long, with a 3-½ inch (60°) diagonal cut at each end to accommodate the slant of the legs.

Seat supports are two 2 × 6s 58-½ inches long. The table supports are two 2 × 4s 29-½ inches in length. Lay each A-frame on a level surface, with the top of the legs flush with the top edge of the table support and 4-¾ inches in from

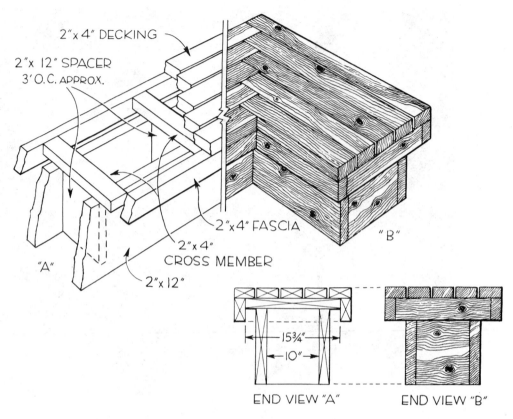

2"x 4" DECKING

2"x 12" SPACER
3' O.C. APPROX.

2"x 4" FASCIA

"B"

"A"

2"x 4"
CROSS MEMBER

2"x 12"

15¾"

10"

END VIEW "A"   END VIEW "B"

Figure 9-4   Plan for building redwood bench in Figure 9-3.

each end. Position the seat support so that the seat edge is 14-½ inches above the bottom of the legs. Assemble each A-shaped end piece with one ⅜ × 3-½-inch carriage bolt through the top of each leg, and two same-size carriage bolts connecting each leg to the seat support.

Temporarily brace assembled end pieces four feet apart on a level surface, then nail top and seat boards to each end piece. Begin with the outside top and seat 2 × 4s at the edges of each support, then nail the other 2 × 4s with even spacing between each board.

Install a piece of 2 × 4 in the bottom center of the table top for a nailing cleat. Cut the 2 × 4 braces to size and nail to the center cleat and side pieces as shown.

TRADITIONAL LOUNGE CHAIR

Here is a comfortable and practical deck chair in traditional outdoor styling that is easy to build. It is made of pressure-treated or other rot-free wood, with slats of nominal one-inch stock and 2 × 4s for legs and arms.

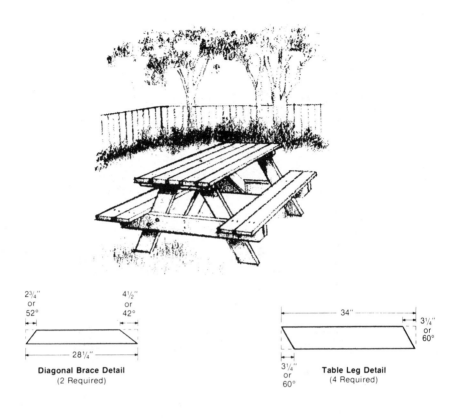

Diagonal Brace Detail
(2 Required)

2¾"
or
52°

4½"
or
42°

28¼"

34"

3¼"
or
60°

3¼"
or
60°

Table Leg Detail
(4 Required)

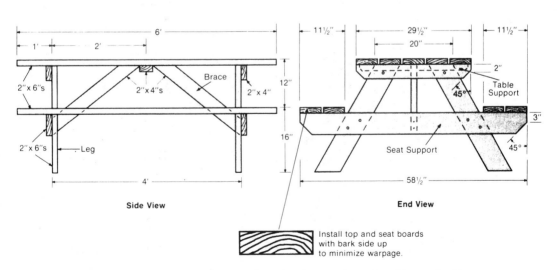

6'

1'

2'

Brace

12"

2" x 6"s

2" x 4"s

2" x 4"

2" x 6"s

Leg

16"

4'

11½"

29½"

20"

11½"

2"

Table
Support

45°

3"

Seat Support

1.1

45°

58½"

Side View

End View

Install top and seat boards
with bark side up
to minimize warpage.

Figure 9-5 A picnic table with built-in benches of Wolmanized wood, and how to build it.

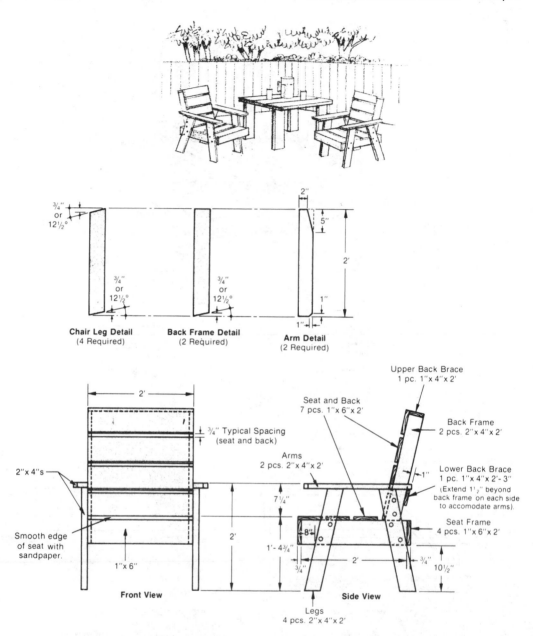

Figure 9-6   This CCA lounge chair is easy to build.

Build the frame first, cutting 2 × 4s to eight two-foot lengths for the legs, arms, and back frame. Trim them as shown in the detail drawings (Figure 9-6).

Cut two pieces of 1 × 6 into two-foot lengths for front and back seat framing. Attach the 1 × 6s to the 2 × 4s with 6d nails. Attach the legs to the seat and back frames with ¼ × 2 = ½-inch carriage bolts, two at each joint as shown. Cut a two-foot piece of 1 × 4 and nail it across the top of the back frame.

Cut seven pieces of 1 × 6 two feet long each. Nail three of these to the seat and four to the back. Secure arms to the tops of the legs with #10 × 2-inch flathead wood screws. Cut another piece of 1 × 4 two feet three inches long and nail to the back of the chair just underneath the arms on each side.

Sit back and enjoy your labor.

SMALL TABLE OR STOOL

This is a very simple project, which does double duty as a small table or stool. The height of the center post is shown as 25-½ inches, but you can raise or lower this to suit your own purposes. Make a few of them for barstools, or just one or two to hold drinks, dishes, ashtrays, or plants.

All you need for each table/stool is one 4 × 4 post, two pieces of 10-foot 2 × 4s, and some 12d nails. Cut the post to the height desired, make four pieces of 18-½ inch 2 × 4s for feet, notch as shown in Figure 9-7, and nail together. Cut out four gussets per the pattern, and attach to the post for strength.

Cut five pieces 11-½ inches long, and two pieces 14-½ inches long from 2 × 4s to serve as a table top. Nail the top pieces together as shown and attach this to the post and gussets. That's it.

Figure 9-7 Here's a simple project that can be used either as a small table, as shown, or as a stool.

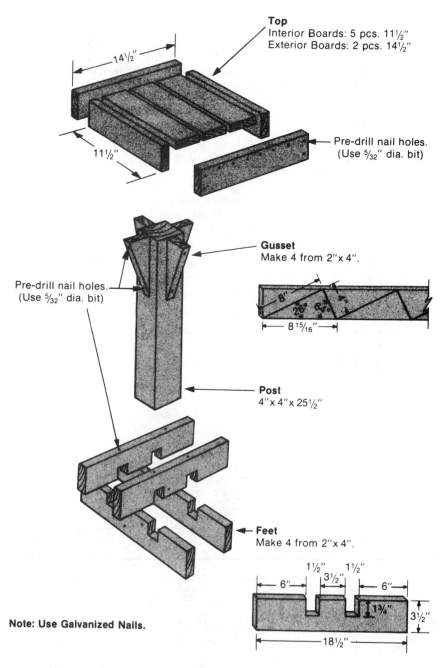

Top
Interior Boards: 5 pcs. 11½"
Exterior Boards: 2 pcs. 14½"

14½"

11½"

Pre-drill nail holes.
(Use ⁵⁄₃₂" dia. bit)

Gusset
Make 4 from 2"x 4".

Pre-drill nail holes.
(Use ⁵⁄₃₂" dia. bit)

8"

26° 6⅜"

8¹⁵⁄₁₆"

Post
4"x 4"x 25½"

Feet
Make 4 from 2"x 4".

1½"   1½"
3½"
6"   6"
1¾"
3½"
18½"

Note: Use Galvanized Nails.

Figure 9-7   *(Continued)*

194

Here's another table, this time a round cocktail table, which can be a planter, too. The plan shows details for using the center of the table as a planter. If you prefer, you can make a planter-less plain table by simplifying the bracing and running the boards all the way across the top.

As shown, the table is four feet in diameter (which you can also alter, if you wish) with a 16 × 16-inch plastic pot in the center for a planter. If you can't find a pot exactly that size, again you alter the plan, but leave a hole 1-½ inch wider than the pot in the center for easy removal.

The table with planter takes one piece of six-foot 4 × 4 for the four 16-½ inch legs, and 10 pieces of eight-foot 2 × 4s for the frame and top. Make the frame or substructure as shown, 48 inches in each direction. Notch as shown (Figure 9-9) for half-lap joints.

Use 16d nails for through-nailing and 8d nails for toenailing, forming the "tic-tac-toe" support grid as shown. Then tacknail a piece of wood across the centerspace, with a nail temporarily set into the exact center of the planter hole.

Use a string compass to draw an arc 23 inches long around the framing. (This allows for a one-inch overhang all around, which you can also modify at your discretion.) Cut off the sections of the 2 × 4s that are outside of the arc, then miter the ends to 45° for a finished look.

Figure 9-8   This round table of pressure-treated 2 × 4s is shown with a planter in the center, but the planter can be eliminated, if desired. See Figure 9-9.

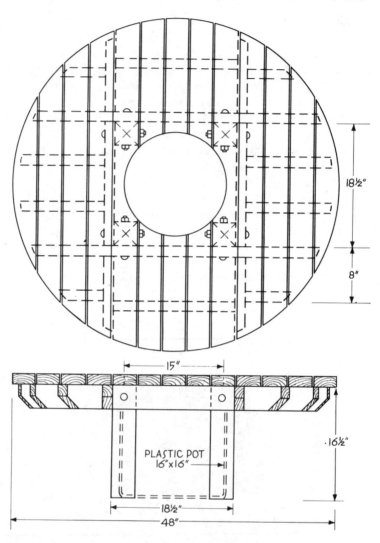

Figure 9-9 Plan for making table-planter in Figure 9-8.

Attach the substructure to the legs with eight ⅜ × 6-inch carriage bolts, two at each side of 4 × 4s as shown. Lay out the 2 × 4 top for best spacing, then use the string compass again with a 24-inch arc to round off the top. (You can nail the boards on first, then cut out later with a portable jigsaw, if that's easier.) Nail the top pieces to the frame with 12d nails.

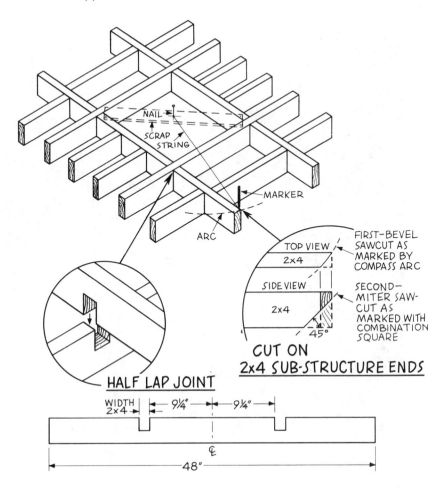

HALF LAP JOINT

CUT ON
2x4 SUB-STRUCTURE ENDS

PLANTER BENCH-SUPPORT

The photo (Figure 9-10) shows a very simple and sturdy foot-square planter, which is made of 10-½-inch 2 × 4s butted alternately and glue-nailed to 2 × 2 supports. The bottom is made of nine-inch 1 × 4s glued and nailed to the bottom of the side pieces. Drill four to six ¾-inch holes for drainage. The planter in the photo is 14 inches high.

Figure 9-10   A planter made of western woods, which can also serve as a bench support as shown in Figure 9-11.

Some interesting variations are shown in the other drawings, and you can come up with more of your own. Figure 9-11, for example, shows how the planters can be enlarged and combined with benches. Make each side 24 inches (22-½-inch pieces), add another layer of 2 × 4s, and cut out sections shown to hold up the ends of the benches. The benches are simply 2 × 4s on edge, with the planters supporting each end. For an eight-foot bench (inside measure) like the one shown, use seven 2 × 4s 8 feet 3 inches long.

You don't even have to bother edge-gluing the 1 × 4s for the bottoms, if this seems like too much trouble. (If you use glue, use resorcinol outdoor glue.) Substitute ½-inch exterior plywood and nail this to the bottoms of the planters instead.

OTHER PLANTER PLANS

Decks are great places for planters, and planters are great projects for decks. They're quick and easy to make, and can often be constructed of scrap wood left

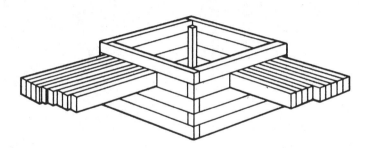

Figure 9-11 Adapting planter in Figure 9-10 for bench support, as described in the text.

over from the deck. Planters add an island of interest in what otherwise might be a rather dull surface. For low-level decks, they can be interspersed with deckboards. And, you can use house plants in lightweight units, which can be brought outdoors in good weather.

Best of all, though, planters (when filled) provide a dash of color and texture. Wood is nice. This author happens to think wood is one of the most beautiful materials around. But wood alone can be a bit monotonous. Add a few flowers or small evergreen shrubs, and the deck can come alive. (Deck planters are an ideal place to show off your bonsai, for example.)

There are a thousand ways to make a planter. There are just two basic rules:

- The wood must be capable of withstanding not only the elements, but the moisture from inside.
- There must be a way of providing drainage.

The easiest way of complying with the first rule is to use redwood, red cedar, or .40 CCA. But you can also make planters out of regular wood if you dip it in preservative or paint it. Exterior-graded plywood is good planter material, but it should be painted for looks, if nothing else.

Drainage is easily provided by either leaving spaces between the bottom pieces, or drilling several holes through them. You can also build a planter that

is really only a shell, then put plastic or clay pots inside. Be sure that there is some method of providing drainage, however. Some suggestions for building planters are shown in Figures 9-12 through 9-16. There is no special trick to building any of them, unless mentioned in the caption.

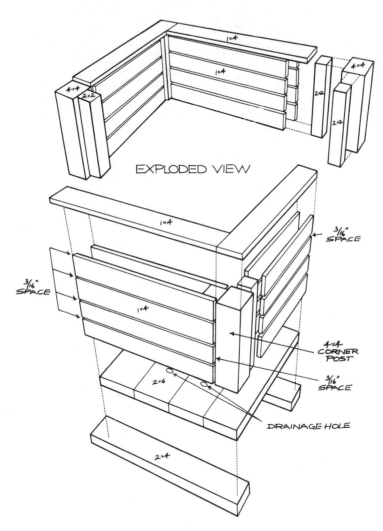

Figure 9-12   This large redwood planter left is a great project for your leftover pieces of heart 4 × 4s from the deck. If you have four pieces 15 inches long, they will serve as corner posts. You'll also need about 30 feet of heart 1 × 4 for the interior walls (cut to 22-½inches each), an eight-foot 2 × 6 for the bottom (cut into four pieces 22-½inches), and a little over four feet of heart 2 × 4 for the bottom cleat. The rest of the boards can be garden grade. For even longer durability, line the inside with sheet plastic before inserting dirt and plants.

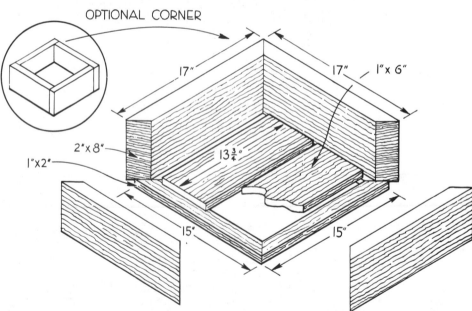

OPTIONAL CORNER

17"

17"   1" x 6"

2"x 8"

1"x2"

13 3/4"

15"   15"

Figure 9-13 This simple planter box can be made in no time, even without any carpentry skills. You can use the optional butted corners shown, if mitering makes you nervous. All you need is a six-foot piece of 2 × 8 for the sides, six feet of 1 × 2 for the bottom frame, and about 28 inches of 1 × 6 for the bottom. Use heart redwood throughout.

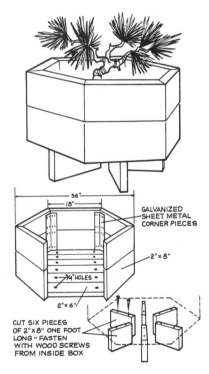

Figure 9-14 This hexagonal redwood planter box requires mitering all corners 30° to form 60° angles. Other than that, it's easy. You'll need 28 feet of 2 × 6 lumber for the sides and bottom. To elevate, make six feet, a foot long each, of 2 × 8s for the version shown in the drawing. For the feet in the photo, use six 2 × 4s, also a foot long each, and miter as above.

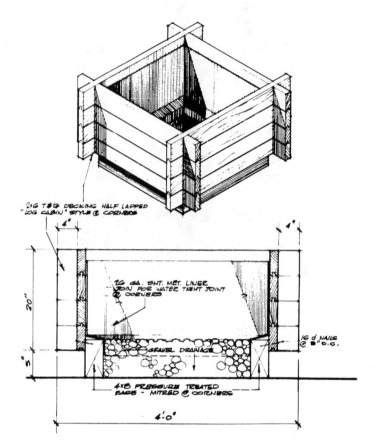

Figure 9-15 This is another large planter, made of 2 × 6 tongue-and-groove lumber, half-lapped at the corners as shown. You'll need 64 feet of this, plus 14 feet of 4 × 8 CCA for the feet. Douglas-fir, hemlock, spruce, ponderosa pine, or other western species are fine for the siding, since the galvanized liner will protect the wood. A coat of preservative wouldn't hurt, however.

MAKING UP YOUR OWN PLANS

Just like anything else, any of the plans shown can be altered to suit your tastes or purposes. It isn't even that difficult to design your own. Always use durable woods and fasteners, though, and prefer screws and bolts to nails for any furniture that gets banged around a lot.

If you want to use wheels for a chaise lounge or similar project, you can make your own easily out of wood, with large wood dowels for axles. Wooden wheels get a lot of rough wear, though, and may deteriorate rather quickly. You can buy regular wagon wheels at some hardware and hobby shops, which will last longer, even if they don't look as nice. You'll need store-bought axles for this type of wheel, however.

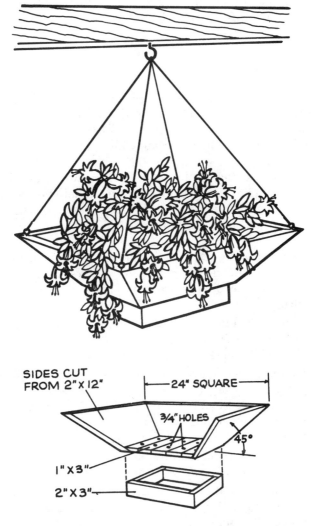

Figure 9-16 No planter smorgasbord would be complete without a hanging type. This one is relatively easy to make, with only the 45° angles to cause some difficulty. You'll need one eight-foot 2 × 12 for sides, six feet of 1 × 3 or 1 × 4 for the bottom, and another six feet of 2 × 3 or 2 × 4 for the base. (*Courtesy Georgia-Pacific Corp.*)

If you want cushioned furniture, you can use a wood frame for the cushions, with wood strips or molding on the sides to keep the cushions in place. This makes a pretty hard surface, however. It is better to make a suspension-type seat for the cushions. Use either ⅜-inch hemp rope or webbing, woven between sides of the frame.

Cotton webbing will be all right for awhile, but will deteriorate fairly quickly outdoors. For best results, cut three-inch wide strips out of eight-ounce canvas duck. Hem ½ inch on both sides to make two-inch webbing and weave between the frame. Attach with screws or cleats.

USING PVC

PVC furniture is usually made of 1-¼-inch Schedule 40 piping, with ¾-inch pipe for cushion supports and other subsidiary framing. Details on working with PVC are beyond the scope of this book, but we do recommend booklets on this from Syndication Associates, Inc., Dept. PHD, P.O. Box 1000, Bixby, OK 74008-1000.

Before starting, get together with a canvas shop if you want to use canvas for slings and cushions. They'll be able to help you plan, and get the canvas to fit. Don't attempt to work with canvas unless you've had some prior experience.

Some tips about working with PVC:

- Make sure to use piping made by the same manufacturer throughout. Although inside diameters are always the same, the outside diameters vary quite a bit among manufacturers. Using uniform pipe will avoid fitting problems.
- If possible, check out the different PVC colors and pick out one you like. While PVC can be painted, it will look better longer if you leave it unpainted. Paint should be oil-based or especially formulated for PVC.
- PVC is assembled with solvent cement for its usual purpose—plumbing. If you know what you're doing, you can use solvent for furniture, too. But it is better to assemble the parts with self-tapping sheet metal screws, which can be removed if necessary.
- Make sure that all cuts are square. Use a fine-toothed blade to cut PVC, preferably a band saw. If you use a hacksaw, tape a piece of paper along a marked line to ensure a 90° angle when you cut (Figure 9-17).
- No matter what assembly method you use, cut out all the parts and trial-fit them beforehand. Mark each piece with a code name before taking apart, for easy reassembly.
- PVC comes in standard lengths. Lay out your design carefully before cutting, doing the longer parts first. Use the excess for smaller parts.
- If you don't intend to paint, remove the company's imprint and other information stamped on the pipe with 240-280 wet-or-dry sandpaper, used wet. Acetone, nail-polish remover, automotive choke cleaner, or regular paint remover can also remove the printed information.
- Even if you use solvent cement as your main assembly method, some parts may need removal (such as frames for the fabric). For these sections, use #10 sheet-metal screws through predrilled holes, instead of solvent.
- Plan assembly carefully. Don't get caught with leftover parts that can't go into fittings, especially when using solvent cement (see Figure 9-18).

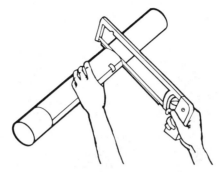

Figure 9-17 To cut PVC straight, wrap and tape some paper around the pipe as shown. Use a hacksaw.

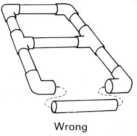

Wrong

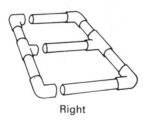

Right

Figure 9-18 Prepare assembly methods carefully to avoid the type of problem shown. Once the solvent hardens, forget about changing it. (*Courtesy Syndication Associates*)

MAINTAINING OUTDOOR FURNITURE

It is obviously difficult to give any hard and fast rules for taking care of outdoor furniture. There are so many different types and materials that generalities are somewhat meaningless. Nonetheless, we have an obligation to try. There are a few basic rules that apply not only to outdoor furniture, but to indoor furniture, too (and many other things).

- Keep it clean. (Your mother probably told you this, but in a different context.) Nonetheless, it's axiomatic that dirt and stains will only get worse if you don't keep after them. Wipe up spills promptly and give the

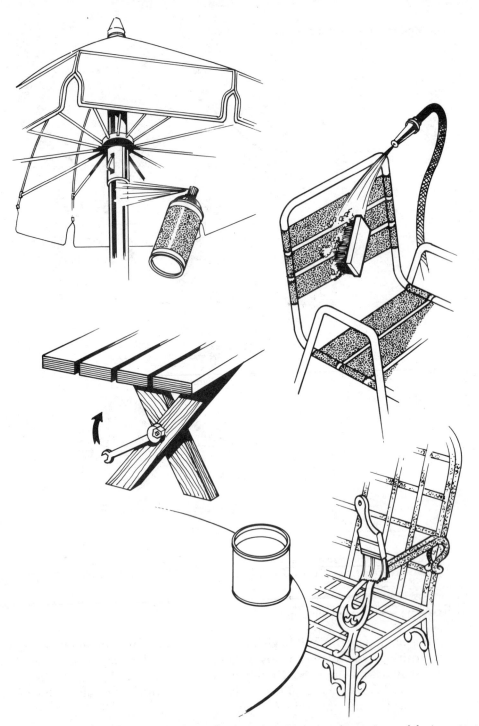

Figure 9-19 Routine furniture maintenance is easy, but also easy to forget. Some of the important jobs are shown: (A) lubricate moving parts frequently; (B) wash on regular basis with a garden hose; (C) check and tighten fasteners if necessary; (D) touch up and paint as necessary.

208

piece a good washing about once a week. Hose your furniture off at least once a month.

- Check all hardware at least in the spring and fall when you set the furniture out and take it in. Replace any rusted nuts and bolts, and tighten those that are loose. Regardless of what the original hardware was, use rust-free replacements.
- Any moving parts—wheels, folding umbrellas, swivels. etc.—should be lubricated frequently, using a moisture-displacing liquid such as WD-40 or silicone.
- Be sure to bring removable cushions, if nothing else, indoors or under shelter during the winter or other lengthy periods of nonuse. All fabric, including most plastic, becomes faded and lifeless by continuous exposure to the sun and rain.
- Touch up all painted furniture—wrought-iron, wood, or whatever—as soon as possible to prevent further rust or water damage. Remove rust before touching up, and apply a new coat of rust-inhibiting paint as soon as possible.
- Shine up tubular aluminum furniture with kerosene and fine steel wool. Wipe up all traces of kerosene with a dry cloth and apply a coat or two of automobile-type paste wax.

10

Deck Covers

Putting a roof on a deck may seem like wearing a raincoat in a shower, since most of us think of a deck as a place to take advantage of the sun. But there are lots of uses for a deck roof, even when sun-worship *is* the main purpose of having the deck to begin with.

If, for example, you live in the desert Southwest, you may well want to use the deck for sunning yourself—but not *all* the time. When Old Sol is beating down at 2:00 in the afternoon at 100° plus, you may prefer to sit outside with just a tad of shade.

A partially covered deck is a good solution for situations where you want sun sometimes, and sometimes not, but this is practical only when the deck is fairly large. Another possibility is a canvas cover, preferably retractable, as discussed on pp. 218–219.

And what about those days—even in the Southwest—when you've invited the gang over for a barbecue, and the heavens pour? You'll thank those very same heavens that you had the foresight to at least partially roof the deck. If you have an "outdoor kitchen," which is more than just a portable grill, it is usually a wise idea to put a roof over the cooking and dining areas in any case.

There are those, too, to whom the sun is more of an enemy than a friend, such as those pale-skinned people whose "tan" is mainly beet-red misery. The sun can be positively dangerous for these and many other people. Still, they want a place to sit and catch the breezes and enjoy the outside.

Figure 10-1 A deck cover comes in very handy when the rains come or the sun is just too hot. (*Courtesy Filon Division of SOHIO*)

Non-sun-worshippers may prefer to roof over the deck completely. As a matter of fact, one sensible option is a completely screened-in deck to keep the bugs away. When you want protection from rain and the worst of the sun, but want to retain the light and airy openness of the deck, consider tinted fiberglass panels. Construction is relatively easy, as shown later in this chapter.

Louvered or screen-type roofs are an effective compromise for those who want their sun, but don't want it, too. Proper angling and placement of the lumber allows more light and breeze than solid construction, but deflects the hottest sun rays.

Another consideration, when debating whether to roof in your deck, is the size and location. Large decks easily lend themselves to partial roofing, and we recommend doing so, especially over the dining and cooking areas. With smaller decks, orientation may be the deciding factor. When the deck faces North, for example, too much sun is rarely a factor. If it faces South, the primary consideration is probably just how much sun you want. South-facing decks and patios, if not at least partially covered, will be in sun most of the day.

Figure 10-2   Large decks are often partially covered, as in this award-winning design by Atlantic Nursery-Landscaping of Freeport, New York. (*Courtesy National Landscape Association*)

East-facing decks will be in sun during the cooler morning hours, when most people would prefer to feel the sun. The opposite is true when the deck is on the western side of the house. (See Chapter 2 for a full discussion of orientation.)

There may be other individual factors to consider, too. For example, your deck may be next to the pool. Usually, the sun feels good after a dip. Most of us would not want a roof there. Again, though, other factors come into play such as size. If the deck is large enough, you may well want to roof over a portion, and leave the poolside area uncovered.

There are other, more minor considerations, too, such as shape and esthetics. A rectangular deck is easy to cover. It is more difficult to roof over an oval or similar odd shape, since roofs are almost always rectangular in shape.

In some cases, too, a roof may detract from the looks of the house. A stately Georgian mansion, for example, may take on a rather bizarre appearance with a large, modern roof jutting out. Awnings, however, may be quite appropriate. If you have any doubts as to how a deck cover will affect the overall appearance of the house, it is wise to get the opinion of an architect.

MATERIALS

As discussed before, the type of deck cover—if any—that you choose will depend on the activities for which you will use it. By the same token, the materials also depend on use. Here, however, your choice can be more varied.

If, for example, your main purpose in building a roof is to keep the deck dry during rainstorms, you will *not* want a louvered or screen roof. But you still have a choice of using wood, plastic, canvas, or any other solid material that will shed the raindrops. If you want a roof that will let in the light but also keep out the rain, perhaps translucent plastic or fiberglass is best. Or maybe you want a roof that can be covered sometimes, but not always. In that case, a retractable canvas roof is probably your only choice. When you want a screen-type roof, wood *is* the only choice.

The size and shape of the roof may be another determinant, leaving you little choice of materials. A large roof will, almost of necessity, have to be flat—or almost so. You cannot build a solid roof with standard fiberglass or asphalt shingles when the pitch of the roof is less than "2 on 12" (two inches in height for every 12 inches in width, or a slope of ⅙).

When you have a slope of "1 on 12" or less, you have only two choices. Either build it of nonsolid materials, or go with an expensive and not-too-great-looking "built-up" roof of hot asphalt and gravel.

Theoretically, you can build a roof for your deck out of anything you want—garbage-can covers, for example—if that's your desire. People do use a

Figure 10-3   A fiberglass-reinforced plastic roof protects the deck from the weather, yet lets in some sunlight.

variety of materials for various reasons, such as price. People have been known to use plate glass, perforated aluminum panels, burlap, thin sheet plastic, regular window screening—you name it.

Practically speaking, however, most of these exotic materials are either too flimsy or too costly for the average homeowner. Many are just plain ugly. Unless you have a special reason for using another material, we recommend the following materials as being worthy of consideration:

Standard Roof

There are many different types of standard roofs, but all have the same basic wood deck construction. The difference here is in the finishing materials. Which type of finishing to use is a matter of choice and purpose. If you plan on a conventional-looking roof, like the one you have on the main part of the house, you should first install regular rafters on 16-inch centers, then lay a roof deck of at least ⅜-inch thick exterior plywood. After that comes building paper and shingles or other finishing materials of your choice. (On a clay-tile roofed house, for example, you may want to install clay tiles on your new roof.)

Figure 10-4   A standard-type roof protects this low deck made of western woods. Posts and part of the roof can be seen at left.

Wood Screens and Louvers

When weather-proofing is not the prime consideration, but you do want keep out the worst of the rain or sun, you may simply wish to install some 2 × 4s or other framing on their edges—or flat, if you prefer.

For other types of screens, louvers, or similar roofs that are intended mainly to fend off the hottest sunrays, use weather-resistant lumber, spacing them to deflect or let in the sun in accordance with your needs.

In some cases, where snowloads are not a factor, and you want an airy or casual look and feel, common lath, batten boards, bamboo strips, or other similar lightweight material can simply be laid over some framing. If the material rots out, it can be easily replaced.

Fiberglass and Plastic

Where strength is a factor—as it should be wherever there is a chance of substantial snowfall—fiberglass is stronger than acrylic or other plastic, and should be preferred. Fiberglass and plastic panels come in various colors, including clear. The choice of color is up to you, but remember that the darker colors let in a lot less light and sun.

Figure 10-5 Wood screen-roofs partially block out the sun, and can be angled to take best advantage as desired. (*Courtesy California Redwood Association*)

Figure 10-6 Fiberglass panels come in many styles and colors, and are suitable for full or partial roofing, like this large cover made of Filon.

Fiberglass and plastic come in sheets and panels, which are attached to a wood frame, with most manufacturers offering complete plans and kits. Fiberglass is something of a misnomer, since the panels are really fiberglass-*reinforced* polyester or vinyl plastics. In any case, the usual patio or deck cover in most climates is made of corrugated fiberglass, for extra strength. Flat panels are generally some type of acrylic plastic. Check local building codes or with other professionals as to what thickness is needed for your area.

One thing to remember is that translucent panels let light and heat in, but don't let much heat out. This is great for cold climates, but can be a disaster in hot regions. If your weather is primarily on the steamy side, prefer darker colors to keep out most of the solar heat.

Corrugated or Paneled Aluminum

Aluminum panels are not as popular as they used to be, but they are still available and a viable choice in some areas. The main reason for aluminum's fall from grace is the fact that this material tends to hold in the heat on a hot day. Those who live in Snowbelt regions may want to consider aluminum, but it is not a good option in more torrid climes.

Glass

While real glass has been recommended by some for deck roofs, there seems to be no advantage at all for glass in roofs. The only type of glass acceptable over head would have to be mesh-reinforced, for safety reasons. The cost quite easily outweighs any advantages of glass.

Canvas and Other Fabrics

It is possible to use fabrics other than canvas or modern plastics for patio roofs, but most have a very short life. Cotton canvas is most widely used, but is meeting stiff competition from vinyl-laminated polyester and solution-dyed acrylic. Dacron canvas is another good material for deck roofs, although it is expensive and rather hard to find. (It is widely used for top-notch sailcloth.)

Cotton-based canvas is relatively inexpensive, and holds up surprisingly well to the elements. Wind is probably its greatest enemy, but damage can be minimized by making sure it is laid firmly and tight. There are many types, colors, and thicknesses of canvas. Thickness is measured in weight, which may range from 7 to 15 ounces. The most common weight is 11 ounces per square yard. Vinyl-coated cotton runs about 15 ounces. There is also a wide range of colors, which are dyed by several different methods.

Without going into the relative merits of different weights, dyes, colors, etc., let us state that by far the most common type of canvas used for deck roofs (and awnings, for that matter) is painted Army duck. This doesn't mean it has to look like an Army tent, although that's where the name came from. Army duck refers to a specially woven, chemically treated material that is designed for outdoor use. It is (or should be) chemically treated to resist mildew and fungus. Polyester and acrylic, however, have an even better resistance to mildew.

In spite of the name, Army duck is available in a wide range of hues, including plain off-white and uncolored pearl gray. The gray is not very attractive, but the off-white is nice, because it lets a little sunlight through. Solids and stripes are available for nearly all these fabrics.

When choosing a color, painted canvas is best, since the modern acrylic paints used today adhere much better and longer than old-fashioned oil-based paints. Dyed fabrics may last a little longer, but may also fade and stretch, forming hollows for puddles. (Dyed fabrics are fine for vertical applications.)

Since canvas tends to hold water, make sure that any material that you buy has been treated to resist mildew and other fungus formation. Canvas without this chemical treatment will rot much faster than treated varieties.

Canvas has been used for many years as awning material, but was largely abandoned for many years because of fading and rot problems. It has rapidly been returning into favor in recent years, since ways have been discovered to ensure its durability. Properly designed and installed, a fabric deck cover can look quite elegant. If it is put up without much thought or care, it will look rough and sloppy. One outstanding advantage of canvas is its ability to be rolled

Figure 10-7 Awnings come in plain and multicolors, and these retractable-arm models can be easily put up when you need them, and pulled back in by hand or motor when you want to enjoy the sun. Options include sensors to extend and retract the arms automatically in case of rain or wind. (*Courtesy Pease Industries*)

up and stashed out of the way. A recent innovation is the retractable "lateral arm' awning, discussed later. When using canvas, flexibility can be built in, which is a boon to those with small decks, or where there is a multiuse area that will benefit from cover at times and openness at others.

COST COMPARISONS

Since the usual deck covers employ similar structural supports, the cost of one type versus another is not particularly significant. No matter what you use for the roof materials, a major part of the cost will be for framing and other structural members. These can be designed as part of the deck, using the same posts, for example, as you do for the deck, much as is done in railing design (Chapter 6).

There are exceptions, however, in the case of the standard type of roof like those used on homes. This type can be quite a bit more expensive. The opposite holds true of canvas and trellis-type roofs, which are lightweight and do not require extensive support.

Standard Shingled (Tiled, Etc.) Roof

In most communities, such roofs are governed by building codes, which will undoubtedly raise the cost. Even if not covered by codes, it is simply a wise idea to make any such roof strong and waterproof. This requires a wood deck of exterior plywood at least ⅜ inch thick, with 15-pound building felt, and shingles (or whatever) on top. In many cases, deck roofs must necessarily have a slope of less than 2 in 12. This requires special treatment too complex to be dealt with here.

All of the above construction means extra material and labor costs. The latter are, of course, minimized when doing it yourself. Any material other than standard shingles will raise the final cost significantly, even if you can do it yourself, which is unlikely in most cases.

Plastic (Including Fiberglass)

Plastic and fiberglass panels vary, of course, but their general price range is less than building a standard roof, although higher than the various types of wood roofs. A durable patio roof should be made of fiberglass-reinforced plastic or heavy-gage acrylic. These materials are relatively expensive.

Wood

Wood is generally an inexpensive building material. *How* expensive depends on the use and how durable or good-looking you want it to be. If you are designing an open, screen-type roof, the cost should be minimal, and could be less than canvas. Wood slats are quite cheap. If you want an elegant redwood roof that will keep at least most of the rain out, it could be quite expensive. Simple plywood and most other wood roofs are modest in cost. Any roof you'd like to keep for awhile should be made of weather-resistant materials. Any rot-resistant material, of course, will be higher in cost.

Canvas and Other Fabric

Good canvas is not exactly cheap, but it is relatively inexpensive if you plan well and don't waste it. If you like fabric, check the yellow pages for a local supplier and find out what sizes the material comes in before you even start to plan. Try to adjust your roof size to an area that will accommodate full pieces.

Remember that working with canvas and other fabric is not a typical skill of the do-it-yourselfer. To do a proper job, the material should be chosen with careful regard for flame resistance, durability, translucency, exact color, texture, sheen, and budget. The type and design for the framework must also be considered.

At the very least, the do-it-yourselfer must know how to cut and sew material, which can be very difficult for someone who doesn't know how to sew a button on a shirt. Those who are used to sewing and working with textiles will find it somewhat easier, but will still be unable to do a professional job, which may require such specialized skills as heat-sealing, silk-screening, spray painting, or air-brushing.

If your skills are limited to hammering and sawing, you have no choice but to have the canvas dealer make up the cover for you. Even those who have some basic skills may find the job beyond them. Again, this will raise the cost, perhaps prohibitively.

Although the homeowner can *install* a retractable lateral arm awning himself, it is virtually impossible to build one from scratch. This is therefore a pretty expensive item. By the same token, a regular canvas cover will need considerably less structural material.

STRUCTURAL DESIGN

Along with the other "musts" mentioned in this book, one of the things you "must" do before even thinking about constructing a patio roof is to check with your local building department. If you design the roof along with the deck itself, this will be automatic. Those building a cover after the deck has been built will have to start over.

In most communities, you cannot make any overhead structure that comes within a foot of your property line. In some communities, it is as much as five feet. Chances are that building inspectors will be less concerned with a deck roof than they are with the deck itself, but it is better to have approval before you build than later.

At the very least, determine what the "setback" is—and other requirements—for overhead structures. If you do get caught, you may get off with just a retroactive tax increase. You don't want to have to tear the whole thing down.

How deeply you must get into design characteristics depends on the type of patio roof you have in mind. Most screen-type and canvas covers are exempt from this kind of worry. The elements are not usually a problem. Wind, snow, and rain go right through screen covers. Canvas covers are not ordinarily considered as part of the house structure. If either of these covers is what you have in mind, there is no immediate worry.

Figure 10-8 A standard shingled roof was used for this deck with gazebo. (*Courtesy Southern Forest Products Association*)

REGULAR SHINGLED ROOFS

Standard solid roofs are usually designed for patios, especially those that may be later enclosed for a "Florida" room, or for other garden structures such as gazebos. They are most often used for decks that are to be screened in. If you think you want to build this type of roof, you need to know a lot more about roof construction, which is beyond the scope of this book. There are several books on this topic, including one by this author.

Briefly, here are some of the factors that must be considered when building a regular shingled (tiled, etc.) roof:

- Snow (and other) load. Your local building department can tell you the average snow load for your area. Even if there is no snow, the deck or patio roof should be designed so that it is strong enough so that someone will be able to climb up on top of it to paint, make repairs, etc.

- Wind pressure. No matter where you live, no matter how mild the usual breezes, there is always the occasional wind gust that can be surprisingly brutal in its force. Your roof must be designed to withstand any extraordinary lift force.

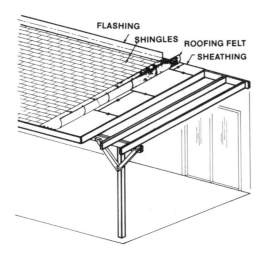

Figure 10-9 A conventional shingled roof should be built as shown. Sheathing is nailed across the rafters with staggered joints, as described in text. A layer of roofing felt goes next, then the shingles. Flashing is applied where roof meets house. (*Courtesy TECO*)

- Future enclosure. Enclosing a patio or deck to make a "Florida" or similar room may be the furthest thing from your mind when you're building your roof. But you never know when you or some future owner may want to make an enclosure, so it is wise and only a little more costly to design the roof so that it can be made a permanent part of the house, if need be. You may also find the insect population on your deck to be more than you can stand, and decide that it should be screened in, which may require a standard roof.

- Structural Strength. A solid deck roof must be built to the same structural specifications as the deck itself. Follow the same tables for post, beam, and joist construction as those given for decks in Chapter 4. The tricky part of roof design is in rafter size and construction, a topic discussed briefly below, but too intricate to go into at length. Again, hire a professional or get a good book on roofing.

STRUCTURAL GUIDELINES FOR FABRIC COVERS

Deck covers made of fabric are usually supported by some type of pipe—with the exception of the retractable type previously discussed. Most awning-type covers are removed in colder months, so that the usual design considerations such as snow load need not apply.

Still, anyone can get caught with his awnings up if snow arrives a little earlier than expected, so it makes sense for the homeowner to at least partially factor in snow and wind loads, water drainage, and similar elements when planning a fabric cover.

Sturdy structures for canvas or other fabric covers can be made of galvanized pipe (Schedule 40), Electric Metallic Tubing (EMT), .065 wall tubing, square tubing, or structural aluminum pipe. The key to any of these installations is a sturdy anchoring of the frame to the base of the deck.

Wrought iron columns are often used as posts for this and other types of covers, although it is easier to build the entire structure, including posts, of the same material used to hold the fabric. Since fabric covers are lightweight, the span between posts and "beams" can be much wider than for other materials. For specific spans and similar information, discuss the matter fully with your canvas dealer prior to installation.

TYPICAL DECK COVER CONSTRUCTION

Posts, beams, and other structural members should be designed according to the same standards as a deck. When planning a cover along with the deck, structural posts can be extended to also serve as roof supports. In most cases, 6 × 6 or larger posts will be required. For a new cover on an existing deck, 4 x 4s are often used, depending on the span. Post height should be at least 7 feet 6 inches above the deck floor.

If designing a new cover over an existing deck, the posts must be located either in line with the posts below, or over a double joist resting on the support

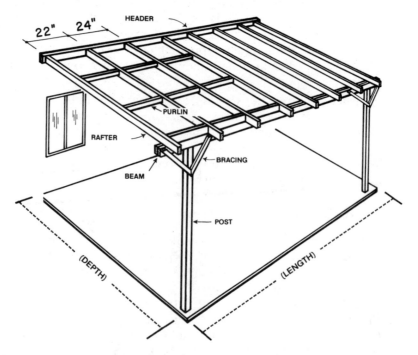

Figure 10-10   How to build a framework for fiberglass or plastic deck covers.

posts. When the deck has a small cantilever, do not place the new posts directly over the outside headers. If the posts are located near the edge, set them back so that they rest on the double joists, not on the outside headers or fascia (Figure 10-11). Attach posts solidly to the deck with post connectors as shown in Figure 10-12.

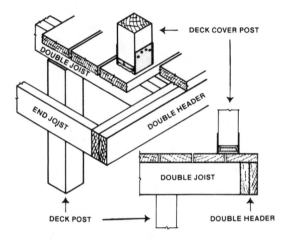

Figure 10-11   When setting posts on a deck, either place them directly over the decking posts, or on a beam or double joists, as shown. Make sure they rest on the joists, and not on the outside headers. Use Teco connectors to attach the posts for the cover.

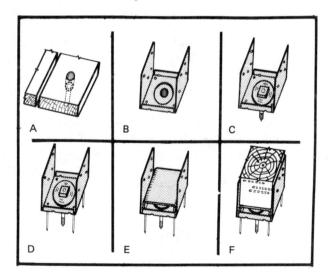

Figure 10-12   To use a Teco connector for your posts, drill a lead hole through the deck and into the post or joists below (A). The hole should be 5/16 inch into the framing, with a 9/16 inch "clearance" hole through the decking only. Place base over hole (B) and install 1/2 × 5-inch lag screw (with washer) into the deck (C). Also nail base into decking with 10d galvanized nails (D) and insert base support (E). Install post and nail into base support with special 10d nails supplied with kit (F).

Beams should be 4 × 10s for most roofs, usually 2 × 10s spiked together with 10d nails every 12 inches. Purlins, braces, and most other framing consists of 2 × 4 lumber. Headers are the same size as the rafters, as discussed later.

Rafter construction is something we haven't gotten into before. These structural members support the roof material and extend from the front beam to the header or house ledger in most construction. They are generally a little smaller than beams used for similar spans, since they are designed for lighter loads. But check local codes, especially in heavy snow areas.

Rafters can be as small as 2 × 4s for spans up to 6 feet, with 2 × 6s being used from 6 to 10 feet, and 2 × 8s for over 10 to 14 feet. Spans over 14 feet are generally not recommended. You'll probably have to go to "3-by" or "4-by" lumber for any greater lengths, which are tough to handle overhead. If at all possible, keep rafters 14 feet long or less.

In solid roof construction, rafters are generally placed on 16-inch centers. Fiberglass or plastic panels are usually 26 inches wide, with a two-inch overlap. If so, use 24-inch centers, with the outside rafters being 22 inches (Figure 10-10). This allows the edge panels to line up slightly over the outside rafters.

Experienced carpenters use a rafter square and a lot of math to calculate rafter construction. If you know how to work with a rafter square, by all means do so. While a rafter square is indispensable for some jobs, there is a simpler way to figure out the proper angles for rafting cutting—at least for this type of work.

After the ledger is in place, the next step is to determine the angle at which the end of the rafter is cut. Rest one end of the rafter on the front beam, and line up the inside edge with the header as shown in Figure 10-13. Hold a small piece of wood flush against the header, with the side against the rafter.

Draw a line down the edge of the board and cut carefully along this line. Transfer it to an adjustable level gage and mark the other rafters with the same angle. If you don't have a gage, lay each rafter exactly under or alongside the cut one, and draw a line using the first one as a template.

You must also cut a "bird's mouth" where the rafter rests on the beam. Nail the cut rafter temporarily to the house ledger, then use a square and ruler to measure the birdsmouth notch as shown in Figure 10-14. Make the cut on this rafter and check it for fit. Make any necessary adjustments, then transfer the notch to the other rafters as described above. If using Teco U-Grip hangers to

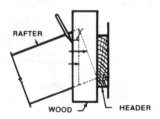

Figure 10-13 How to get proper rafter angle at header, as described in the text.

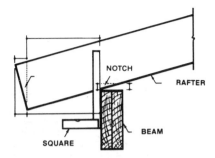

Figure 10-14   For proper seating at the outside beam, a "bird's mouth" notch must be cut as shown. (*Courtesy TECO*)

attach the rafters to the header, another notch must be cut on the underside or "seat" portion of the rafter to fit the slant of the rafter into the connector.

For the typical house-type roof, with a standard deck, ½-inch CDX plywood sheathing or 7/16-inch waferboard is nailed directly to the rafters, then the roofing materials themselves are laid.

Figure 10-15   It usually takes two people to install rafters. Note the bird's-mouth on rafter near bottom of photo.

Figure 10-16   Nail purlins between rafters as shown. (*Courtesy Filon*)

Other roofs, particularly fiberglass and plastic, ordinarily require some intermediate structural members called "purlins" (Figure 10-16). Standard plastic or fiberglass comes in lengths of 8, 10, and 12 feet. Purlins must be installed where the strips or panels meet. These are less technically part of the structure than nailing strips for the ends of the panels.

FIBERGLASS, PLASTIC, AND ALUMINUM COVERS

Manufacturers of aluminum and fiberglass-reinforced or other plastic panels usually supply detailed instructions for best installation of their products. Follow these instructions for best results.

Installation techniques are basically the same for all of these products, however, and are outlined below. Most covers of this type require nailing strips as described above.

If you want to paint or stain the framing, this should be done before attaching the panels. Corrugated fiberglass and plastic usually requires "configured closure strips," which match up with the figuration of the panels (Figure 10-17).

Figure 10-17 Nail through crown of corrugated fiberglass, not in the valleys.

Most paneling should overlap about two inches (or one corrugation) at the sides, and about four inches where they overlap from front to back. Allow at least a two-inch overhang at all edges. Apply waterproof sealant at overlaps. Most manufacturers offer their own special aluminum "twist" nails and neoprene washers. All panels should be predrilled with a ⅛-inch or 5/32-inch bit to avoid damage or "crazing" of the panels when nailing.

Nails should be driven every 12 inches along all framing members. For a waterproof roof, apply sealant all along the top of the frame before laying the panels, and use metal flashing between the roof and the house. With corrugated materials, always nail through the crowns (highest point), not in the valleys. If you have to cut a panel, use a fine-toothed hand saw or power saw, preferably with a carbide blade.

Figure 10-18   Apply sealant at joints of fiberglass.

Figure 10-19   Holes in Filon should be predrilled.

Figure 10-20 Apply flashing at juncture of roof and house. (*Courtesy Filon*)

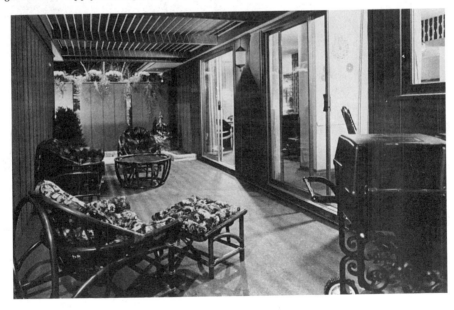

Figure 10-21 Flat-laid 2 × 4s make a good screen for keeping out most of the sun, but allowing breezes through.

Figure 10-22   Small poolside deck has open screen of 2 × 6s on edge. Note edge treatment of 2 × 6s for an Oriental charm. (*Courtesy Goldberg and Rodler*)

OTHER COVERS

Canvas and similar covers can be hand sewn with a #13 sailmaker's needle, but ordinary home sewing machines are too light. Unless you are familiar with canvas-working, it is almost always best to let the canvas shop custom-make your overhead. They are also better equipped to design and make the necessary grommets, ropes, cables, etc.

Louvered, wood screen, and other types of patio roofs are very individualized, and specific instructions are impossible. A few examples are illustrated in Figures 10-21, 10-22, and elsewhere in this book.

Figure 10-23 shows construction of a 12 × 16-foot deck with built-in trellis and privacy fence. Basic carpentry skills are all that are necessary for these types of roofs. Hardware is the same as that used for deck construction, using rust-proof nails or other fasteners for all areas that are exposed to the elements. Hot-dipped galvanized nails, screws, and bolts are essential for all wood framing members, and most other nailing.

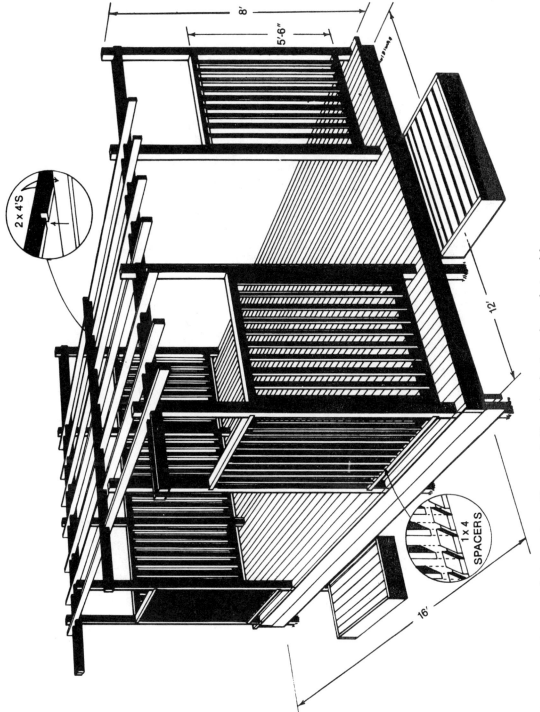

8'

5'-6"

2 x 4'S

12'

16'

1 x 4
SPACERS

Figure 10-23 A 12 × 16 deck, complete with screen-trellis roof and privacy fence, designed for Wolmanized wood. See text and materials list for details.

233

MATERIALS LIST—TRELLIS-COVERED DECK

Purpose	Number	Size	Length (feet)
Posts	10	4 × 4	10 (approximately, depending on terrain)
Joists	3	2 × 8	12
Deckboards	36	2 × 4	16
Trellis beams	5	2 × 4	14
Trellis joists	7	2 × 4	18
Privacy fence and step-decks—per requirements			

11

Lighting and Landscaping

Perhaps the most neglected part of any outdoor planning is lighting and other electrical facilities. This applies not only to decks, but to patios, pools, and other aspects of the exterior landscape. Builders and developers are woefully inadequate when it comes to this important part of home planning and hardly ever provide such items as a decent number of exterior outlets. Anyone contemplating outside improvements, regardless of type, should consider extra wiring and electrical accessories.

As far as decks are concerned, you will certainly get a lot more use out of yours if you can use it at night. Some sort of lighting is essential. You may also want to plug in a radio, TV, or other amenities such as a refrigerator. An overhead fan may be another nice addition—especially in hotter regions.

All of this means that you need outside outlets or fixtures, at the minimum. While you are at it, you may as well include other outdoor electrical facilities such as security, landscape, and general lighting for walks and driveways.

OUTDOOR ELECTRICAL EQUIPMENT

Outdoor electrical equipment is completely different from the type you are used to indoors. This is because it has to be protected from the hostile environ-

Figure 11-1

ment, mainly water. About the only equipment that is the same as that used inside are switches and receptacles. And these must be covered with waterproof covers and gaskets.

Every electrical device and cable used outdoors must be specifically designed to withstand the elements. Wiring must be either buried or otherwise protected from water, people, and dogs in search of bones. Cable, boxes, outlets, switches, lights, and all other devices must be approved by the Underwriters Laboratory (UL) for exterior use.

In addition, every exterior installation has to be protected with a special safety switch called a Ground Fault Circuit Interrupter, commonly called a GFCI or just GFI. (In all new homes, this same device is now also installed in the bathroom.)

A GFCI acts as a super-sensitive breaker or fuse that shuts down the entire circuit in 1/40th of the time of a standard fuse or circuit breaker. Only 0.005 of an amp over the regular amperage trips the device, ensuring that a shock caused by a defect will last only a small fraction of a second, thus preventing serious injury or death.

As discussed in previous chapters, many of us are inclined to try to avoid code requirements at one time or another. Don't ever do it with the National Electrical Code (NEC). And especially don't try to avoid installing a GFCI. This little gadget may well save your life—or your children's.

UNDERWRITERS
LABORATORIES
INC.

UND. LAB. INC.

Underwriters
Lab. Inc.

Underwriters Laboratories Inc.

UNDERWRITERS LABORATORIES INC.

UNDERWRITERS LABORATORIES INC.

Figure 11-2 Never use any electrical equipment that does not carry one of these seals of the Underwriters Laboratories.

Figure 11-3 Type UF exterior wiring has a very tough plastic cover that is difficult to cut through.

Even if you know how to do some wiring and other electrical work, think twice before venturing into the world of outdoor wiring. It is not only more dangerous, but more difficult. Exterior wiring is encased either in hard plastic cable, which is very hard to strip and cut, or in rigid conduit, which is costly and may be hard to find in handy sizes. All exterior boxes must be made of weatherproof aluminum or steel (known as T or PF boxes), and have waterproof connections, which can be difficult to make.

In addition, all lights must have waterproof sockets, and outlets must be protected by waterproof covers (Figure 11-4). Cable must be either the tough plastic mentioned (Type UF), or be protected by rigid conduit. (PVC can be used instead in most jurisdictions, but check locally.) Cable run underground must be buried at least two feet, perhaps deeper, depending on local requirements. Furthermore, any cable above ground, a certainty for decks, must be encased in conduit regardless of type.

If all this sounds like it may be too much for you, fine. That's the impression we're trying to convey. However, if you still want to install it yourself, we'll give you some pointers. But no guarantees, and don't call us if it doesn't work out. We're also assuming at least a rudimentary knowledge of electrical wiring, because you should never tackle exterior work if you haven't done any wiring before.

LOW-VOLTAGE WIRING

Those who don't want to get involved in all of this, and don't want the expense of a licensed electrician, should consider low-voltage lighting. Actually, low-voltage lighting is nice in a lot of outdoor applications, whether you know wiring or not.

One problem for decks, though, is that the lights—spiked fixtures in particular—are designed more for ground lighting. This may work fine for ground level decks, but not too well above that. Adapters are available, however, to convert the fixtures for use on walls, posts, etc.

Low-voltage wiring is excellent for those who don't want to mess at all with electricity. You can have an electrican install the transformer, which is

Figure 11-4 Some of the specialized units used in exterior wiring. At right is typical weatherproof box, with exterior outlet cover at left and switch cover in center.

Figure 11-5   Low-voltage systems like this one from Intermatic come with transformer, wiring, and four metal tier lights. This particular setup has a photo control and timer to switch lights on and off automatically. Adapters are available to convert spikes to wall units.

connected to the main wiring. Then you can handle the rest of the wiring and fixtures without fear of getting a bad electrical shock or worse. Systems, including transformers, can be bought for less than $150.

The transformer of a low-voltage system drops standard current from 110 to 12 volts, about the same as you have in a car's electrical system. With the lower voltage, you use a lot less energy, too, with six 12-volt lamps using about the same amount of power as one 120-volt spotlight.

Some of the newer models can be adapted to run the very efficient quartz-halogen bulbs. These can give off as much light from the same outlet as a similar incandescent light. A transformer that can handle six incandescents can take 12 units using quartz-halogen (the same type lights used for car headlights).

DOING YOUR OWN OUTDOOR WIRING

The basic techniques and overall circuitry of outdoor wiring are the same as inside wiring. The same general principles and methods are basically the same. We will spell out the differences between indoor and outdoor wiring. If you don't understand the terms and techniques, it is strongly suggested that you hire an electrician. It is suggested even if you do understand.

The theory of circuit planning is the same as for inside work. If the only thing you're installing is a little extra lighting, or a few outlets or fixtures, you should be able to tap into an underutilized circuit. If there will be any heat-

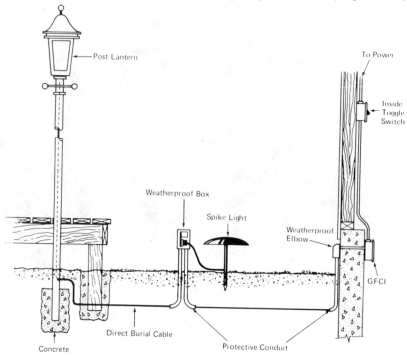

Figure 11-6 Outdoor wiring circuits often employ UF cable underground, and rigid metal conduit wherever the wiring goes above ground.

producing appliances, however, such as a barbecue starter or coffee-maker, you probably need a new circuit.

The only safe way to determine whether or not you need a new circuit is to find out what is on the circuit you plan on tapping, then add up the wattages of all existing and intended devices. Look for a 20-amp, #12-wire circuit to tap into. If you can't find a 20-amp circuit, you are better off installing a new circuit, using #12 wire—with ground, of course.

The first step is to determine where you will tap into the circuit, or the panel, then figure out how to get the cable from there to where you want it. Remember that a GFCI must be installed somewhere between the tap and the outside. You will probably want a switch to control all or part of the outside circuitry, and should find a place to do that. Inside switches are best, but there may be a spot on the outside wall that will do.

Depending on the routing, an exterior or interior GFCI may be used. For example, if you are running a new circuit from the panel to the deck, it is often a good idea to install a receptacle-type interior GFCI in the basement or garage. The basement or garage can probably use more outlets anyway.

Assuming no water or moisture in between, you can use Type NM cable (nonmetallic sheathed cable, popularly called "Romex") from the tap or panel to the incoming or feed side of the GFCI. Unless you are using conduit exclu-

Indicator Light

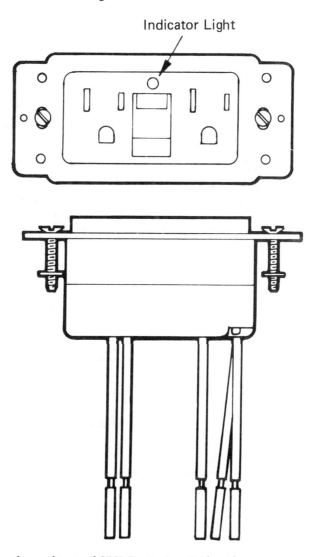

Figure 11-7   One of several types of GFCI. Don't wire outside without one.

sively outside, you will start on the outgoing (load) side of the GFCI with UF cable.

It is to be hoped that we don't have to tell you that any tapped circuit must be shut off at the panel before connecting to it. If you are installing a new circuit, you should also know that you shouldn't tap into the panel until all the rest of the work is done. You already know, also, that inside the GFCI, the black wires are connected to each other, the white wires with the white, and the bare or green ground wires are then attached to each other and the grounding screw. Solderless connectors (wire nuts) are used throughout.

The GFCI, you will note, contains a test button and a reset button. If there is only a temporary surge in current, which shuts off the circuit, the GFCI can be reset. If there is something seriously wrong, the reset button will not work. When that happens, shut off the circuit at the breaker, and test for a short or other defect. Better yet, call in a licensed electrician.

If you need to go underground to reach the deck, check local codes to see if they are more stringent than the NEC. If not, dig a trench about a foot wide and at least two feet deep, below the frost line. Install the UF cable as flat and as straight as possible. Where the cable extends above ground, lengths of rigid conduit must be installed.

Use rigid conduit throughout the above-ground wiring. If the entire project is above ground, you can skip the Type UF and use Type TW wires, which are pulled through the conduit between each device. You may also need "pull boxes" (Figure 11-9). Wherever there is an outlet or other device, install a T or PF box by screwing it onto the conduit.

Weatherproof boxes have "screw-outs" rather than the "knock-outs" found on interior boxes. They must be turned out with a screwdriver to allow for the conduit. If you unscrewed the wrong plug, be sure to screw it back in. Otherwise, you will destroy the waterproof integrity of the box.

If you are inserting Type UF wiring directly to the box with no conduit, special connectors with hard plastic bushings are used to ensure a waterproof connection. These are very difficult to squeeze into the box opening, and we

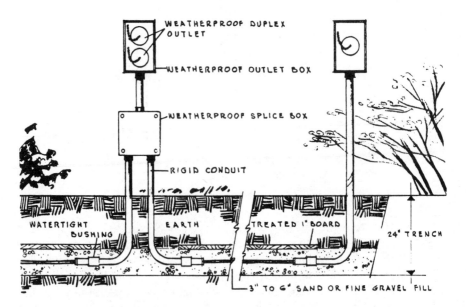

Figure 11-8 How to combine Type UF exterior wiring with conduit. Note how the conduit also serves as a post. Curved conduit is used at entrance of cable to prevent wear of cable on sharp metal (see also plastic bushings in Figure 11-10). (*Courtesy General Electric*)

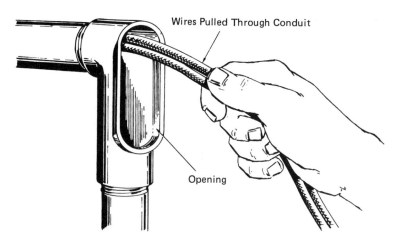

Figure 11-9   Pulling Type TW wires (for all-conduit work) through an elbow. Cover has been removed and is replaced after wires are pulled.

Figure 11-10   Use plastic bushings like these where Type UF cable enters a straight piece of conduit.

suggest using conduit at this point, even if not required by code. Use curved conduit or the plastic bushings shown in Figure 11-10 where the cable enters the conduit to prevent the rough conduit edges from tearing the cable.

Outside boxes can be attached to walls, fences, ties, or other solid objects through holes for this purpose in the back of the box. Boxes can stand on their own, as shown in Figure 11-8, by virtue of the rigid conduit. If the conduit does

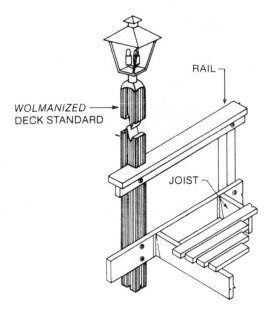

Figure 11-11   This type of fixture is excellent for decks: it is made of Wolmanized wood and also serves as structural post for deck and railings.

not hold it steady, install the other end into a concrete block and fill in with concrete. Boxes can also be recessed into walls, wood, or masonry.

A good way of providing handsome deck lighting is to use prebuilt CCA lighting posts, or Wolmanized "deck standards" (Figure 11-11). These are made of hollow laminated pressure-treated wood, and are also pictured on p. 109. The top is configured to accept a variety of lamp fixtures, and the hollow center makes it easy to run the cable up to it. Metal "patio" posts can also be used.

There are numerous outdoor lighting fixtures available, from simple and cheap to elaborate and expensive (Figure 11-12). Most can be adapted for decks, or placed nearby to provide the needed lighting. You can even make your own, as shown in Figure. 11-13.

Outlets, fixtures, and other devices are either attached inside the box, or with another piece of conduit, depending on the type of fixture or device. Be sure to use the special outdoor covers over receptacles and switches. If the fixture is attached by conduit, blank covers are used to cover the front of the box. Blank cover are also used on pull boxes.

Be sure to use proper gaskets with all box covers. To ensure a weathertight seal, caulk around box covers and at the edges of outlets recessed into walls. Inspect the entire circuit for loose wires, covers, or other defects. When you are satisfied that all is in order, tap into the line and reset the breaker. If the GFCI or breaker trips, check all connections over again. If it still happens, now is the time to call in the electrician. You tried.

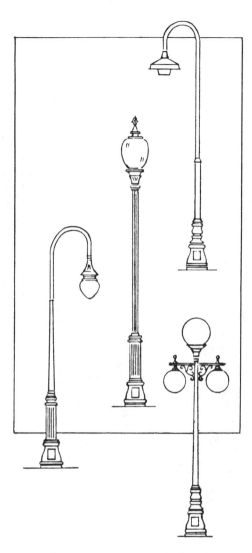

Figure 11-12   If you want to get fancy, you can use great-looking (but not cheap) fixtures like these from Sternberg Lanterns.

OTHER UTILITIES

Some other utilities that should be at least considered at the very beginning of your planning should be water, gas, phone, and other conveniences such as deck speakers for use with intercoms. The lines for these items may have to be installed before the deck itself is put up. This is especially true for ground-level and low-level decks.

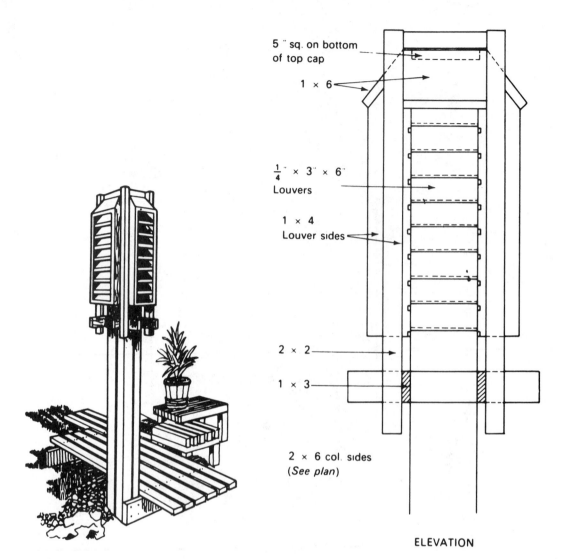

5 " sq. on bottom
of top cap

1 × 6

$\frac{1}{4}$" × 3" × 6"
Louvers

1 × 4
Louver sides

2 × 2

1 × 3

2 × 6 col. sides
(*See plan*)

ELEVATION

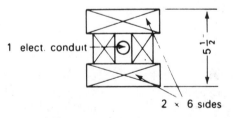

1 elect. conduit

$5\frac{1}{2}$

2 × 6 sides

Plan of post

246

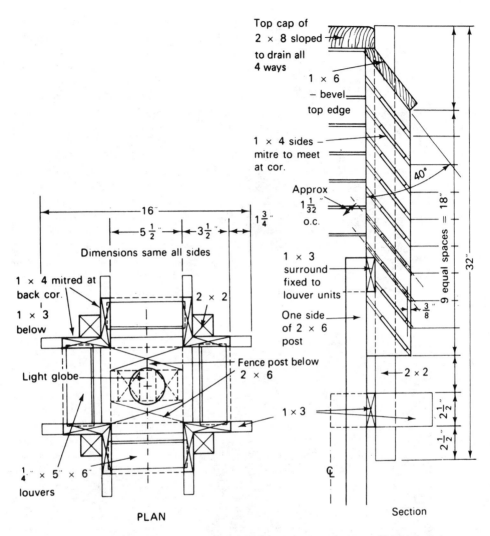

Figure 11-13 A handsome louvered garden light that you can make yourself. This unit is strong enough to serve as a post for benches and railings. It may serve as a structural post, too, but check codes. It may be better to use a 6 × 6, partially drilled through the center, with cable entering somewhere on the side. (*Courtesy Western Wood Products Association*)

A permanent outdoor barbecue should have its own gas line. Gas and water lines will both be needed if the deck includes an outdoor kitchen. A shower or wet bar requires a water line. These lines should be buried underground, so trenches must be dug and the connections made before the deckboards are laid. For very low-level decks, installing these utilities may be the first order of business.

And don't forget waste lines, if you have a sink, shower, or other water-using equipment. Although it's a lot cleaner to hook up waste lines to the main

Figure 11-14 Always use the gaskets that come with outdoor outlets and switch covers. (A) shows the gasket in place, with the cover installed in (B).

waste system, this is usually very difficult or impossible because of the length of pipe needed and the necessary slope needed to carry the water away.

The most practical method to carry away waste water from a sink or shower is to run the waste lines to an innocuous place or to a dry well (if codes permit one). It is a rare deck that would include a toilet, but if you are thinking

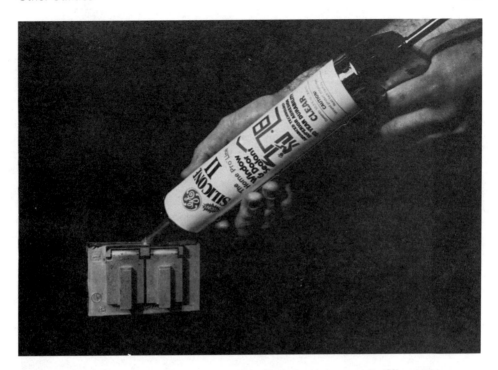

Figure 11-15 Water can seep around the edges of this type of exterior outlet. Caulk around the edges with silicone such as GE Silicone II, which claims to have "50-year durability."

of one, you'll have to figure out a way to install the waste lines to the main drain. Unless you live in the *real* country, you don't want waste lines draining anywhere else but to the sewers or septic system.

Many people forget all about the telephone until it rings one day as they are enjoying a dip in the pool or a restful snooze on the sundeck. After the first mad dash into the house (whereupon the phone invariably stops ringing), they wonder why they didn't install a phone to begin with.

Fortunately, phone lines can easily be installed at a later date. Usually, though, these will be more easily and less visibly put in as construction progresses. When the deck is very large or multilevel, it is a good idea to install jacks in various places on the deck. (Portable phones may be used, however, instead of all these jacks.)

Installing a deck doesn't create a need for an intercommunications system, but it may be the final straw that makes you decide you need one. Modern intercom systems come combined with stereo or security equipment that may prove indispensable for a sprawling family on a sprawling property.

Intercoms are available with exterior speakers and receivers that are weatherproof and can be a big boon when you're far away from sleeping babies or sick grandmothers—or just for listening to music. They can be hooked up before or after construction, but it's best to plan the lines ahead of time.

LIGHTING

Deck lighting should always be low-key, at least in the areas intended for quiet tasks such as relaxing, reading, and conversation. Wall- or post-mounted fixtures or table lamps should be provided in several places for maximum convenience.

Make sure that whatever you purchase for your deck is certified for outdoor use. Since you will be installing brand new fixtures, be sure to check out the newer type of fluorescent units called PL lamps. These are long, thin units that provide a lot of light much more efficiently than incandescent or older fluorescents. Fluorescents, in general, use much less energy, and many new types are available for outdoor use.

If your deck is large or you are installing a new flood or security light in conjunction with the deck, look into the possibility of using mercury vapor or high-pressure sodium floods. These produce a great deal of light at much lower cost than standard floodlights. High-pressure sodium bulbs last about 24,000 hours, as opposed to 800 hours for PAR floodlights. The sodium lights are particularly good for high or awkward places, where changing the bulb can be difficult.

But try to avoid the "shopping center" syndrome when planning outdoor lighting. Bright lights are fine for basketball courts, security, and other intensive activities, but not for decks or patios. When the deck is small, and must be used

Figure 11-16 Flood lights can be mounted on the deck or cover to provide garden or security lighting. (*Courtesy General Electric*)

both for relaxing and occasional parties, you may want to opt for stronger lighting with a dimmer switch. Then you can have as much or as little light as you desire.

LANDSCAPING

In the broader sense of the term, your deck itself is (or should be) an improvement of the landscape. If it's designed and built decently, it should make the setting of your home more pleasing in and of itself.

The view of the landscape from the surface of the deck should already be soothing to the eye, but sometimes the view from below or elsewhere might not be that great. To some, the structure of the deck is in itself an architectural statement. Heavy posts and beams by themselves should give a feeling of beauty and strength.

Not everyone feels that way, though, and sometimes the structural part of a deck does look rather ugly. Lattice and other woodwork can often disguise or diminish the harshness of the structure. Often, however, this type of treatment gives the deck too much of a "fortress" look.

Nothing works better to blend in your deck (and your home) than landscaping in its narrower sense. Whether used in conjunction with wood "disguisers" or by itself, intelligently planted shrubbery does the best job of transform-

Figure 11-17 Landscaping for this poolside deck won an award in residential lighting for Contemporary Landscapes of Fair Lawn, New Jersey. (*Courtesy National Landscape Association*)

Figure 11-18 The view from the deck, large or small, should be soothing to the eye, such as this winner of a certificate of merit for Landesign of Minneapolis. (*Courtesy National Landscape Association*)

Figure 11-19 Evergreen shrubs, flowering shrubs, ivy and vines on textured plywood blend in this high deck and stairway nicely with the lower deck and rest of the landscape. Redwood was used for decks and stairways.

ing the obtrusive into a coordinated, eye-pleasing scene. On low decks and high, plantings are the ideal method of smoothing out rough spots in the setting.

Just as foundation plantings ease the impact of a house suddenly plopped into a building lot, so do shrubs erase the harsh lines between any new structure—including decks. They can set off a low-level deck or cause a high one to recede more gradually into the backyard.

Those who have no experience in landscaping or little knowledge of plantings available in their area will have to look elsewhere for detailed information on landscaping. Ideally, if expensively, a landscape architect should be consulted. In addition to reading up on the subject, many garden centers and local nurseries have a great deal of knowledge about which plants are available and suitable for your area.

Local climatic and soil condition are so varied, even in local areas, that any generalities must necessarily be brief. One good idea is to use the same sort of plantings used for foundations to serve around the deck. In the North, there are yews; in the Southeast, wax myrtle; and cactus in the Southwest—to name just a few of the most popular.

High decks are, of course, a problem, since ordinary foundation plantings are too small. Vines might be helpful here, or ornamental trees such as crab, cherry, peach, or dogwood. Shade trees such as oak and maple will grow too high, with their trunks and branches crowding the deck and the roots possibly harming the footings and posts.

Figure 11-20 Foundation plantings work well with a semihigh deck such as this. Keely's Landscaping used junipers, rhododendrons, and other broad-leaf evergreens, with pine-bark mulch, to help ease this handsome deck into its setting.

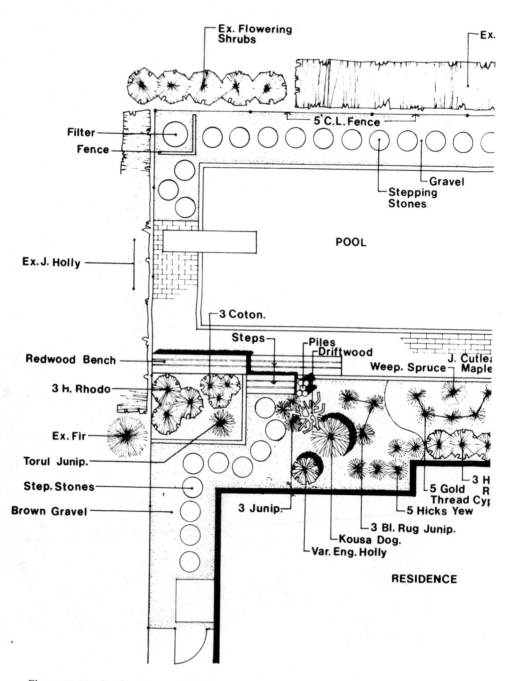

Ex. Flowering Shrubs

Ex.

5' C.L. Fence

Filter

Fence

Gravel

Stepping Stones

POOL

Ex. J. Holly

3 Coton.

Steps

Piles
Driftwood

Redwood Bench

Weep. Spruce

J. Cutle
Maple

3 h. Rhodo

Ex. Fir

Torul Junip.

Step. Stones

Brown Gravel

3 Junip.

3 H
5 Gold   R
Thread Cyp

5 Hicks Yew

3 Bl. Rug Junip.

Kousa Dog.

Var. Eng. Holly

RESIDENCE

Figure 11-21 Good professional landscapers will draw up a complete landscaping plan for the entire property, including the deck. This is from Keely's Landscaping of Hauppauge, New York.

254

N

Scale: 1"= 10'- 0"

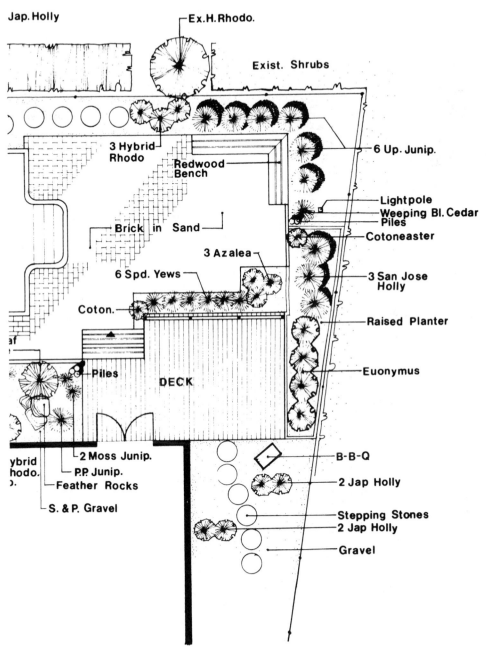

Jap. Holly

Ex. H. Rhodo.

Exist. Shrubs

3 Hybrid Rhodo

6 Up. Junip.

Redwood Bench

Brick in Sand

Lightpole
Weeping Bl. Cedar
Piles
Cotoneaster

3 Azalea

6 Spd. Yews

3 San Jose Holly

Coton.

Raised Planter

af

Euonymus

Piles

DECK

ybrid
hodo.
).

2 Moss Junip.

B-B-Q

P.P. Junip.

2 Jap Holly

Feather Rocks

S. & P. Gravel

Stepping Stones
2 Jap Holly

Gravel

255

Figure 11-22 Here is another gem from Keely's, an entrance deck surrounded by junipers, yews, and mugho pines.

Figure 11-23 Another example of why it pays to hire a professional landscaper. Goldberg and Rodler of Long Island not only designed the attractive entrance deck, but the entire landscape surrounding it.

As discussed early in the book, shade from a high deck will make it difficult to grow most plants beneath it. If you want grass, find out from local extension agents or nursery workers what type of grasses do well in shade for your region. You can always use gravel, but get some marble chips or other more interesting stones. The same kind of gravel used underneath your footings may not look so good on the ground. Pine-bark chips are another possibility.

As far as other plantings go, most evergreens usually are shade-tolerant (but check before you buy). Certain flowers and groundcovers grow nicely in shade, too. Impatiens are wonderful in the summer and early fall, with numerous, bright blooms. Hosta, periwinkle (vinca), and ivy do well in shade, too.

Almost any shade-loving plant will suffice under a deck. The important thing is to tell yourself that you won't tolerate an ugly, brown-parched spot under your beautiful deck. Talk to people, look through catalogs, read a few books. You'll come up with something to perk up that potentially ugly spot.

12

Finishing and Upkeep

If you've followed our advice so far, there is really nothing further you *have* to do to finish your deck. You should have either used rot-resistant wood, or soaked regular wood in preservative, before assembly. Having done this, the wood will last a long time. The wood will now mellow into a silvery-gray surface that looks pretty nice.

This author happens to think that weathered wood is quite good-looking, but I also know that I'm in the minority. Or maybe I'm kidding myself, because I hate maintenance chores in general. I built a redwood fence, for example, and just let it weather. I like it that way. But I also built a spruce fence years ago and painted it. And regretted it. Did you ever paint a fence? Horrible. And even more horrible when you have to do it again.

I love my silver-gray redwood fence because I won't have to do anything with it again, the same way I love the red cedar shingles on my house. After 15 years, some of the shingles look gray, some almost black, and some are still somewhat reddish-looking. That's because the sun and water don't hit them evenly. One of these decades, long after I'm gone, my cedar shakes will turn very dark, like a lot of the older houses on Long Island. And that's fine with me and most Long Islanders.

But I know that a lot of people like to put preservative on redwood fences and cedar shakes. It keeps them nice and cinnamon red for as long as they can keep putting preservative on. My guess is that after the first application or two, many of these people will say "the heck with it" and let their fence and shingles get naturally gray (like their hair).

It's a lot of work to put preservatives on a fence or a house. A deck may not be so bad—low-level ones anyway. High decks are different. I don't know many people who'd like swinging on a scaffold or whatever, brushing perservatives on the bottoms of deckboards. And hardly anyone puts preservatives between deckboards, which really should be done if you're trying to do a uniform job. The only time I'd personally consider preservatives is on redwood furniture. And I said "consider," because I have enough to do without giving myself extra work. Lazy? You might say so.

But all of this, obviously, is personal. There is no denying that redwood and red cedar are awfully good-looking woods when they're freshly cut. Many people love the color, and want to keep it that way. I can't blame them. If I lived at a beach house, I would also want to use preservatives to ward off corrosive salt air.

Figure 12-1 The author would (maybe) use preservative on the handsome red cedar table, but would let nature weather the good-looking western-wood fence.

As a matter of fact, I personally love the color, texture, feel, and grain of most woods. Being somewhat of a wood freak, I would even leave fir, pine, hemlock, and other softwoods alone if they would stay that way. But they wouldn't last long outdoors.

So, for those of you out there, we'll use this chapter to explain how to preserve and keep your deck looking as if you just built it—or almost so. (It isn't really all that difficult, just lots of work.)

At the other end of the spectrum are those people who love the silvery-gray look so much that they want to make it look that way from the start. The way to do this is to apply a bleaching oil or stain, which turns the deck a uniform driftwood color.

For those who like a little color in their life, there are a wide variety of stains. Stains will cut down on grain visibility to some extent. Transparent and semitransparent stains do this from a slight to moderate degree, depending on type and brand. Opaque stains act like paint, which they are, more or less, and hide the grain completely or almost so. This may be desirable in some woods and not others. As mentioned earlier, finishing is a highly personal thing.

The primary reason for applying any type of preservative is to repel water and insects, but many of the water-repellent types are applied after a deck is built not only to keep the color, but to give an extra measure of protection against water damage. These water-repellent types also help keep the wood from warping and bending.

We haven't said much about pressure-treated woods, because we don't think of them so much in the nice-when-new category. As a matter of fact, CCA is not really very pretty when new, all green and raw-looking. Pressure-treated lumber will weather silvery gray, too, but it may take a year or two.

Still, there are people who like the look of new CCA, and are anxious to keep it that way. They do apply preservatives. This doesn't seem to make much sense, but there are some legitimate reasons, as discussed later.

We still say, just leave pressure-treated wood as is for a year or so, and it will look a lot like weathered redwood or cedar. If you want to bring the wood to that state sooner, use the bleaching finish mentioned above.

You can paint or stain pressure-treated wood if you like, and cover the stain with preservative just to keep the stain color looking the same. But you'd be much better off getting a combination stain and water-repellent type—and it makes no sense to paint over pressure-treated wood, then apply preservative afterwards.

As far as applying preservative to CCA lumber is concerned, the idea is to provide more protection where there is extra exposure to fresh water or at ground level. Sometimes called "water repellents" or "sealers," these products also help prevent warping, cupping, and splitting.

It would seem that a better solution for such problems would be to use wood with a higher retention. If there is a lot of water or ground contact, why not just use .60 treatment instead of .40? Water-repellent products are beneficial, however, around pools, hot tubs, showers, or other places where there are extra-heavy doses of water.

Figure 12-2 Two preservatives and their effect on the wood. Note how water stays on surface.

Preservative solutions are not just recommended, they are essential, for woods that are not rot-resistant. Those woods should be soaked in preservative before assembly. The same solutions can also be brushed or sprayed on after the deck is built, but it is not as effective. The ideal method of preserving non-rot-resistant wood is to do both—soak before assembly, then brush the preservative on again after the deck is built.

BANNED PRESERVATIVES

You may be familiar from experience or word-of-mouth with some wood preservatives that are no longer on the market. Creosote, for example, is an old preservative that you no longer see at paint or hardware stores. "Penta" (pentachlorophenol) and its sister brands such as older "Woodlife" have also been banned by the Environmental Protection Agency (EPA).

If you have used creosote, you may have guessed why it was banned. This author has used it—in a short-sleeved shirt yet—and gotten some pretty red arms because of it. There were no warnings in the old days. Penta never seemed so bad, but tests have shown apparently toxic effects on some people, and long-term exposure has produced cancer and birth defects in animals. As a preventive measure, creosote, penta, and inorganic arsenic (not often seen anyway) have been banned from retail sale by the EPA.

If you have any of these older wood preservatives laying around the garage, they should really be thrown out. And don't dump them near any vegetation you like, because it is likely to kill or severely damage it. Take it to the town dump or leave it for the sanitation department—in the can, since it may injure the workers if it spills on them.

Creosote and penta are still available, but not at the retail level. They will no doubt continue to be used for railroad ties, telephone poles, and similar applications, but the preserving is done by professionals. A few local retail outlets may still have some of this bad stuff around, but they shouldn't. If you see it around, remind the proprietor.

Inorganic arsenic is the main ingredient in the CCA solution used to make pressure-treated lumber, as discussed on p. 58. Oddly enough, inorganic arsenic is less of a threat to humans than creosote or penta, according to EPA, even though it sounds a lot worse. (See p. 62 for precautions in using CCA lumber.)

ACCEPTABLE PRESERVATIVES

There are still a lot of acceptable wood preservatives around, much of them new since the EPA was announced a few years back. You will still see Woodlife, for example, but it's called "Woodlife II" and contains "polyphase" instead of penta. What's polyphase? Sure you want to know? Okay. It's 3-iodo-2-propynyl butyl carbonate. Any further questions?

There is actually quite a wide variety of wood preservative brands to choose from now. The chemicals that are used in them are complicated tongue-twisters, and—like the polyphase example—listing them doesn't help any (unless you're a chemist). Some of these preservatives—most in the napthenate family—have been around almost as long as penta types. Most, however, have been tested mainly in laboratories, and it is difficult to vouch for their efficacy. On the other hand, there is no reason to doubt their effectiveness.

The new chemical formulations are considerably safer than the banned ones, but anything that repels bugs, rot, and mildew has got to be a little bit worrisome. Wood preservative isn't exactly something you'd put in baby bottles. Be sure to follow the manufacturer's recommendations as to safe handling.

Preservatives come in clear and colors, and many of them are part stain, part preservative. Most are water-repellent. We won't attempt to distinguish the different characteristics, because it is truly mind-boggling. Read labels thoroughly and get advice from a knowledgeable dealer before you use anything.

Many of these products are clear, some green, and some come either way. Some manufacturers, such as Olympic and Koppers (Wolman), have a combination stain and wood preservative in a variety of colors.

Other large manufacturers (ZAR, Minwax, Red Devil, Woodguard, and Sherwin-Williams) put out clear water-repellents only—as of this writing. More and more coatings manufacturers are putting out various stains and combinations for outdoor applications, and the trend will no doubt continue.

There are numerous chemical formulations in this wide array of products, some of which are paintable (and pronouncable)—and some not. Several brands have a water base, rather than mineral spirits, which makes them a little safer to use. Prices of all wood preservatives, with or without stains, range from a little over $12/gallon to over $20. "Sales' are fairly common.

All of these products are formulated so that they can be applied with a brush, roller, or pump sprayer. Many wood manufacturers, however, believe that brushing is most effective, and some do not recommend spraying at all for their products (redwood, for example).

DO-IT-YOURSELF IMMERSION

We have stated several times in this book that it is better to buy rot-resistant wood to begin with, rather than trying to build a deck of untreated pine, spruce, fir, hemlock, or other softwood. Untreated wood is less expensive and often stronger, however, and some of it looks and performs a lot better than pretreated woods. For those on a tight budget, self-treatment may be the only game in town. It may not be the best way, but it may be the difference between having and not having a deck.

The best way to immerse wood in preservative is to make your own dip tank. There are several ways of doing this. If you are using only short boards, as

Figure 12-3 If you apply preservative to redwood, brush it on before and after construction.

for a parquet deck, a large garbage pail or bucket can be filled with preservative, and the boards can be dunked in that. This takes several gallons of preservative and isn't much good for long boards. For boards of medium length, you can dip one end first, then turn them around and immerse the other ends.

When there are only a few long boards to be treated, a piece of rain gutter is an ideal pit dip. (It won't replace sour cream and onion soup, but it will do the job.) Gutters usually come in 10-foot lengths, which should be more than enough for this purpose.

Gutter lengths are open at the ends, so you will have to close them up to keep the preservative inside. There are many ways of doing this, but the best way is to simply buy gutter end pieces at the same time you purchase the gutters. You can also improvise with pieces of wood, metal, or plastic covering the ends. Wrap some duct tape around any end pieces to keep the preservative from leaking out.

When there is a great deal of wood to be preserved, the only realistic way to accomplish the job is to dig a dip pit. Find an innocuous corner of the yard, and dig down at least two inches deeper than the thickest piece of lumber. If the thickest lumber is 4 × 4, for example, dig the pit at least six inches deep.

Line the pit with sheet plastic, to keep the preservative from running out into the ground, and put the cut pieces into the pit. If you have a lot of lumber to preserve, you can save the fluid by digging another hole next to a corner of the pit. Put a pail or bucket large enough to hold the preservative in that hole, and make some sort of dam between the pit and the bucket. (Plain earth will do, as illustrated in Figure 12-4.) When you are finished for the day, break down the dam and save the preservative for the next immersion. Twist the plastic to form a spout as shown at right.

No matter what method is used, we remind you that the wood should be cut to size before immersion. Any untreated ends are an open invitation to water damage and termites. If you cut the piece incorrectly, redip it, or—if impossible—brush a heavy coat of the preservative onto the ends after assembly.

Since wood will float in almost any fluid, including preservative, lay some rocks or bricks on top of the boards to keep them immersed in the solution. See the manufacturer's directions for how much preservative should be used, and for the length of time it should be dipped. It takes a few hours at least, and sometimes 24 hours, to allow the preservative to work right.

OTHER OUTDOOR WOOD FINISHES

There are lots of other ways to finish wood, if you so desire. When used outdoors, it can still be stained, painted, or bleached, much like indoor wood. The only stipulation is that the finish should be formulated for exterior use. You can't (or shouldn't) use varnishes, lacquers, "shake or shingle paints," or any other finish that is susceptible to mildew or prone to attracting dirt.

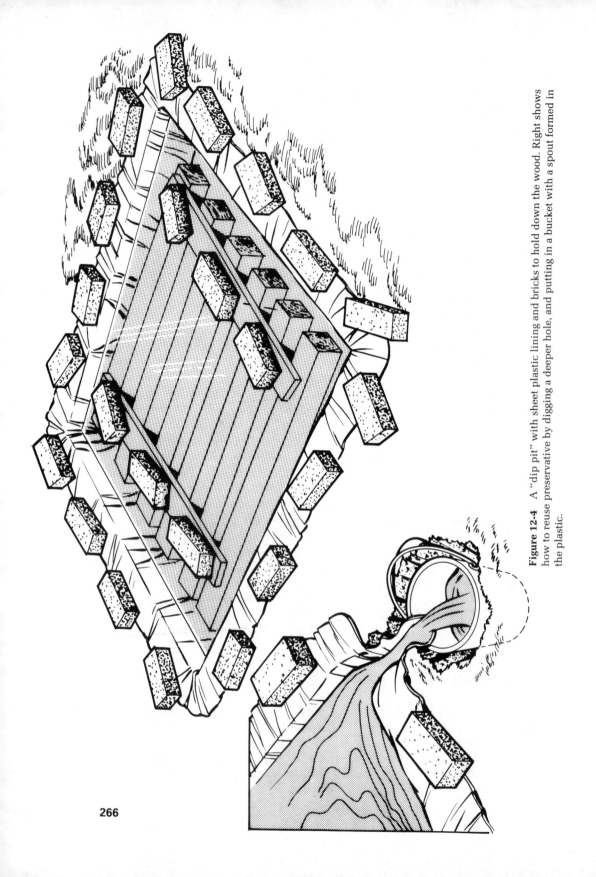

Figure 12-4 A "dip pit" with sheet plastic lining and bricks to hold down the wood. Right shows how to reuse preservative by digging a deeper hole, and putting in a bucket with a spout formed in the plastic.

FINISHING RECOMMENDATIONS OF THE CALIFORNIA REDWOOD ASSOCIATION

Description	Effect	Application	Maintenance
Clear water repellents with mildewcide Clear finishes that modify weathering characteristics and let color and grain show through	Minimize weather and mildew attack. Stabilize redwood's color at buckskin tan. Help eliminate redwood's natural darkening period. Areas exposed to direct sun and rain may eventually bleach to gray.	Apply with brush or roller. Lap marks and brushstrokes will not show through. Two coats recommended for new wood. For best results, coat sawn ends, backs, and edges before nailing in place. *Read Labels: Mildewcides may be toxic*	Reapplication may be required after old finish has lost it effectiveness. In humid or harsher climates, reapplication may be required every 18–24 months. Before applying, wood may be restored to its natural color.
Bleaching oils Low maintenance, natural appearance with a gray-toned finish.	Provide for low maintenance and give redwood a uniformly gray or naturally weathered look.	Apply with brush or roller. Lap marks and brushstrokes may show through as many bleaches include gray pigment. Use one or two coats according to manufacturer's directions. Bleaching is aided by sunlight and moisture, so it may speed the process to periodically dampen surfaces with a fine spray from a garden hose.	Bleaching oils and stains provide nearly maintenance-free performance. Reapply finish only if wood begins to darken or bleaching is uneven. One refinish coat should be enough.
Semitransparent, or lightly pigmented stains "Breathing" finishes available in a variety of semitransparent colors including several redwood hues. Oil-based stains are recommended.	Provide color in a finish that lets wood breathe naturally. Semitransparent stains let the grain show through but present a uniform single color. The amount of pigment contained in stains will vary according to brand.	Apply with brush for best results; next best is a roller. Avoid drips and lap marks. Two coats usually required for new wood—follow manufacturer's directions.	Refinishing may be necessary every 3–5 years. Color in pigmented stains may wear away gradually after weathering. Light brushing with a bristle brush will help remove old finish in some spots. One refinish coat is usually enough.

FINISHING RECOMMENDATIONS OF THE CALIFORNIA REDWOOD
ASSOCIATION (*continued*)

Description	Effect	Application	Maintenance
Opaque stains "Breathing" finishes available in a variety of opaque colors. Oil-based stains are recommended.	Provide color in a finish that lets wood breathe naturally. Opaque stains will obscure the grain but highlight the texture and have an appearance more like paint.	For best results use a brush. The next best applicator is a roller. Avoid drips and lap marks. Two coats usually required for new wood—follow manufacturer's directions.	Refinishing may be necessary every 3–5 years. Color in pigmented stains may wear away gradually after weathering. Light brushing with a bristle brush will help remove old finish in some spots. One refinish coat is usually enough.
Paints Durable, attractive "nonbreathing" finishes for traditional exteriors. Quality paints are generally worth the extra cost. Not recommended for deck boards or seating surfaces	Provide attractive colorful finishes which obscure grain and texture of the wood.	Apply with brush for best results, roller is next best applicator. Do not spray. One prime and two finish coats are recommended for new wood. Backpriming is advised. Use oil or alkyd resin base prime regardless of type of top coat. Latex top coat recommended.	Repaint one coat after most of old coat has weathered. Paint films that are too thick tend to peel and crack. Sand or scrub with stiff bristle brush. Paint and varnish removers may also be used. If sanding, countersink galvanized nail heads to protect their coating.

If you insist on using paint, try to confine it to tables, benches, and other accessories, and keep it off those surfaces that are walked on. There are deck and porch enamels on the market, but they look pretty bad when they start to wear. Constant exposure to the elements makes these products more usable for basements and porches, or under some sort of cover.

When you are looking for a finish, be sure to purchase the type that is compatible for the intended purpose. This may require some intensive reading of labels and literature. For the deck itself, the finish should be capable of bearing heavy traffic. This is not a problem with formulas that are primarily water repellents, or bleaching oils and stains. If you intend to use a semitransparent or opaque stain, however, check the label to see if it says something like "traffic-bearing formulation."

When you intend to use the finish on tables, chairs, or benches, check all finishes for words such as "nontoxic formulation." Be especially careful about mildewcides, which can be dangerous. Those parts of the deck or accessories that are not walked on, eaten on, or seated on, can be finished in whatever type of formulation you desire. There are no extra cautions, for example, concerning planters, fences, or the structural elements.

If you are using two separate finishes, such as separate stain and water-repellent, make sure that they are compatible with each other. It is wise in such instances to purchase the finishes from the same manufacturer, if possible. Water-repellents, stains, and bleaching oils should also contain mildewcides.

As for application, generalities are impossible, and the label or accompanying literature is the only sure guide. Practically all manufacturers suggest two coats, and there are no primers required for anything but latex paint (where an oil or alkyd primer is usually recommended).

Most finishes can be brushed or rolled on, and many can be applied with a sprayer. Check instructions carefully, however, especially as regards spraying. The California Redwood Association does not recommend that any finish be applied with a spray system.

Figure 12-5 Most preservatives and finishes can be rolled on, in addition to brushing.

Figure 12-6 You can spray finishes or preservatives on some decks, like this one of Wolmanized wood, but don't do it on redwood.

MAINTENANCE

Here comes the bad part. Except for bleaching oils and stain, all of the finishes for decks and other outdoor applications are not very long-lasting. (See the accompanying box.) That is why lazy people like this author eschew them. According to the California Redwood Association, as stated, water-repellent finishes should be reapplied every 1½ to two years. That's pretty often.

As far as semitransparent stains are concerned, they last 3-5 years at best, and the same applies to opaque stains. Fortunately, bleaching oils and stains do not need any reapplication, and latex paints will last up to 10 years.

There's a hitch in the longevity for latex paints, however. They are recommended only for seating, tables, and garden shelters. As discussed above, you really shouldn't use any type of paint on deckboards. It just doesn't look good for long.

If you have used the recommended materials in this book, and haven't applied any finish over rot-free wood, there is very little maintenance involved. You might, each year, preferably in spring, check the joints to make sure that none of them is pulling apart. As the deck gets older, this is more important.

With aging lag and carriage bolts, take a wrench every year or two and give them a turn to make sure that they are tight. Look for nails that may be popping out of joist hangers and similar connectors. If they are loose, pull them out and replace them with a bigger nail, not set into the same hole, if possible.

Go over the deckboards once a year or two, checking for popped nails, warping, or other defects. Drive extra nails wherever there is a defect, or replace the boards if renailing doesn't help. Watch for splinters in the deckboards, and sand or plane them down.

Those people who don't get much rain should rinse the deck occasionally with water from a garden hose. Any built-in dirt should be removed by scrubbing. For mildew, apply household bleach after washing, then rinse. If, in a few years, the deckboards start to deteriorate, any rotted or badly damaged boards should be replaced. When the deck starts just to plain look bad, you might then consider applying a semitransparent or opaque stain. But this shouldn't be necessary if you've used decent wood to begin with.

Which brings us to the final paragraph. Buy the best rot-resistant materials you can, use only corrosion-free nails and fasteners, put it together as strongly as you can, leave the wood unfinished, and there shouldn't be any upkeep.

Enjoy.

Index

The Book Club offers a wood identification kit that includes 30 samples of cabinet woods. For details on ordering, please write: Book Club, Member Services, P.O. Box 2033, Latham, N.Y. 12111.